LOVE YOU, MEAN IT

✦

Love You, Mean It

A True Story of Love,
Loss, and Friendship

BY

Patricia Carrington,
Julia Collins,
Claudia Gerbasi,
and Ann Haynes

✦

WITH EVE CHARLES

HYPERION NEW YORK

Note to Reader: Some of the names and identifying characteristics of persons written about in this book have been changed to protect their identities.

"Let Us Have Faith" poem by Helen Keller. Copyright © 1940, The American Foundation for the Blind. Used by permission of The American Foundation for the Blind.

Lines from the poem by Nicholas Evans included in his novel *The Smoke Jumper*. Copyright © 2001 Nicholas Evans. Used by permission of Dell Publishing, a division of Random House and A.P. Watt Ltd. on behalf of Nicholas Evans.

Excerpt from the article by Anne Lamott. Copyright © 2003, Anne Lamott. Used by permission of the author.

Library of Congress Cataloging-in-Publication Data

Love you, mean it : a true story of love, loss, and friendship / by Patricia Carrington . . . [et al.]. —1st ed.
p. cm.
ISBN 1-4013-0229-7
1. September 11 Terrorist Attacks, 2001—Biography.
2. September 11 Terrorist Attacks, 2001—Psychological aspects.
3. Widows—New York (State)—New York—Biography.
I. Carrington, Patricia, 1966-
HV6432.7.L69 2006
974.7'10440922—dc22
[B]   2006017514

Hyperion books are available for special promotions and premiums. For details contact Michael Rentas, Assistant Director, Inventory Operations, Hyperion, 77 West 66th Street, 12th floor, New York, New York 10023, or call 212-456-0133.

Design by Victoria Hartman

FIRST EDITION

1   3   5   7   9   10   8   6   4   2

"To The Boys . . ."

Jeremy "Caz" Carrington
Thomas J. Collins
W. Ward Haynes
and Bart J. Ruggiere

CONTENTS

✦

Prologue   I

THE WIDOWS CLUB   3

Part I

1. CLAUDIA AND BART   17

2. THE FIRST ANNIVERSARY   38

3. IT WOULD BE WRONG NOT TO . . .   47

4. LOVE YOU, MEAN IT   57

5. ANN AND WARD   65

6. TESTING THE WATERS   90

7. THE PERFECT WIDOW   94

8. NOT THE WORST THING   103

9. JULIA AND TOMMY   108

10. YOU'RE AS YOUNG AS YOU FEEL   133

11. PATTIE AND CAZ   140

12. LOLA TO THE RESCUE   167

13. A TRULY PERFECT MOMENT   173

14. TURNING POINTS   178

15. I LOVE HIM, I LOVE HIM NOT   187

16. THE SECOND ANNIVERSARY   192

Part II

17. GOOD TO GO   197

18. IT'S A DATE?   208

19. TRANSFORMATIONS   211

20. THE MANTRA   216

21. THE GIFT   221

22. A DIFFERENT LIGHT   228

23. WHAT IF?   244

24. HEAVEN SENT   249

25. LADY LIBERTY   256

Part III

26. THE THIRD ANNIVERSARY   261

27. THE LIST   264

28. THE NEW YEAR   271

29. THE MISFITS   276

30. REALITY   289

31. THE CROSSROADS   301

Epilogue   315

TO THE BOYS   317

ACKNOWLEDGMENTS

✦

Above all, the authors would like to thank our loved ones. This book wouldn't be possible without all those people who stuck by us—not just through the writing process—but also throughout the experiences this book describes. Thanks are also due to our agent Emma Parry, our writer Eve Charles, our publisher Ellen Archer, our editor Leslie Wells, and our publicist Katie Wainwright.

A percentage of the authors' royalties will go to charitable causes.

For information on the Thomas J. Collins Memorial Fund go to www.thomasjosephcollins.com. For information on the Bart J. Ruggiere Foundation go to www.bartjruggiere.com.

For updates and information on the Widows Club members go to www.loveyoumeanit.com.

LOVE YOU, MEAN IT

✦

Prologue

✦

Security is mostly a superstition.

It does not exist in nature,

nor do the children of men as a whole experience it.

Avoiding danger is no safer in the long run than

    outright exposure.

Life is either a daring adventure, or nothing.

To keep our faces toward change and

behave like free spirits

in the presence of fate is strength undefeatable.

—HELEN KELLER

The Widows Club July 2002

Claudia, Julia, Pattie, and Ann

It was a Tuesday in July, the second Tuesday that would change our lives forever. We'd decided to meet in a bar on Park Avenue South, not far from where we all work in midtown Manhattan. "Let's do early drinks," we said, like we were going on a date and wanted to see how things worked out before committing to dinner.

Clear blue skies over the city were deepening before sunset as we left our offices. Not too hot, no signs of storms. The kind of perfect summer evening that makes New Yorkers want to go out and *do* something. And everyone was going somewhere with someone that night, or so it seemed. Just because our lives had come to a standstill, it didn't mean the world stopped turning for everyone else. Happy couples were strolling arm in arm to dinner. Husbands and wives chatted over drinks in sidewalk cafés. Everywhere we turned we were faced with the reminders.

On the way to the bar, we tried our best to focus on the evening ahead and not to look back. Ten months later we were still too defeated for anything like excitement—we knew that whether we were in some Park Avenue bar or on top of Mount Everest, this constant ache would be right there with us. But what we can say is that we were thankful we had plans that evening and that we were going to meet one another. We were all friends with Claudia by now and we'd met everyone else in the group at least once. We'd all been attracted to Claudia's determination, her refusal to let the unthinkable destroy her life forever. We sensed that we had much more in common than the obvious. And let's face it, at the end of every working day, there were so many hours left over in the evening that if we didn't arrange to meet someone—anyone—it would be yet another evening of go-home-and-get-under-the-covers-again and pray for the time to pass. Time seemed like an eternity.

Ann:

I was the first one to arrive. I sat at the downstairs bar and ordered a drink to steady my nerves. My main worry, as I watched the door, was that I was going to be the odd one out in the group, the fish out of water. I'd met Julia and Pattie, so I knew that they were city girls, just like Claudia. And here I was, fresh from the suburbs, a mom with three kids. I hadn't lived in the city for years. My life right now revolved around juggling a full-time job and raising my children by myself, keeping my broken family together, not trawling the bars of Manhattan. I was wondering if I was going to fit in. Why was I worrying? This wasn't like me. Or was it? It was hard to remember anymore. To my relief I looked up and recognized Pattie coming toward me, glasses on and hair pulled back, dressed all in black.

Pattie:

I was the next one to arrive. At that time, I was barely going through the motions, staying functional; I wasn't allowing myself to operate beyond the immediate demands of get up, get dressed, go to work, come home.

I recognized the pretty woman with the blond hair at the bar right away. Claudia had introduced us briefly a few weeks ago. I'd been at a bar with work colleagues and Claudia and Ann happened to be sitting next to us having drinks.

"Hi, remember me?" I said to Ann.

She pulled me in, kissed me on my cheek. "Of course!"

Over the past ten months it had been so difficult for me to connect with new people. But with Ann, right away we had an easy rapport and I sensed a willingness in myself to be honest and vulnerable.

Apart from anything else, I felt relieved not to have to answer the question "How are you doing?" I never knew how to answer it and Ann didn't ask.

That night, I was wearing black, as usual, not because I was following any traditional guidelines for mourning but because for me, the lights had gone out.

Julia:

I know I was nervous about coming to meet everyone. I was so unhappy at the time that I often worried about how I would react in social situations. This had never been a problem for me before. In fact, not so long ago, I had a reputation for being the karaoke-party-throwing girl, a big personality wrapped up in a small frame, always ready to have fun. Although I was anxious on my way to the bar, at the same time there was also this underlying numbness about me, because by this stage, I'd pretty much given up trying to feel better. It was like I was waving the white flag. I'd surrendered. I was in a "nothing to lose" state of mind.

I saw Ann and Pattie at the bar, took a deep breath, and made my way over.

Claudia:

I was the last to get there.

"I'm so happy we finally managed to get together," I said, and I meant it.

All three of these women had given me so much already. They'd been there for me and let me be there for them. Any small hurdle they'd managed to overcome—driving a familiar route alone without bursting into tears, sleeping without pills, managing to make it a day without melting down—if they could do it, I could do it. It gave me hope. So I was pleased that they were going to get a chance to spend time together, because my instincts told me they were going to get along.

I saw that the other three had ordered their cocktails of choice. A good start. "Vodka martini up, with olives," I told the bartender.

This evening, like Pattie, I was wearing black, but not because I was grieving. This is New York. Everyone wears black in New York. Even if it's the height of summer. Even if you're not in mourning for your husband, killed in the World Trade Center ten months ago and still not coming home.

IF YOU PASSED us on the way to the restaurant that night, or rubbed shoulders with us at the bar, you probably wouldn't have guessed that we were widows. To the bartender, we must have looked like yet another crew of girlfriends meeting for drinks after work, probably commiserating the latest terrible date, the Mr. Big who didn't call, the guy who stood us up again. We were all in our thirties. We're all successful, independent businesswomen. We looked the part. Even under the circumstances, we pulled off the charade.

But if you'd stopped and looked for another moment, you might have also seen us for what we were beyond the outfits we wore and the faces we put on each morning. We were changed. We'd almost forgotten the women we used to be before September 11. When we looked in the mirror, we tried to recall what our faces had looked like without the harshness in them. The anguish we were experiencing infiltrated every part of our beings. We were thinner than we'd been, physically thinner—but we were also less substantial in the psychological sense. We no longer felt like we were fully ourselves. It was a dark, depressing feeling. We missed our husbands more than seemed bearable.

And although it was only the middle of July, the anxiety about the first anniversary was building. The one-year mark was coming around too soon, and none of us wanted it to arrive. We would have done anything to make time stand still. The idea that we could live through a whole year without our husbands seemed impossible. There was no way all these months could have passed, every day taking us further away from his actual existence. More than anything, we didn't want to leave him behind in the past, like a memory. We wanted to hold on and never let go. In our minds we would trace his fingers, his toes, imagining a hug or his touch. Even thinking about the eleventh stirred up such an array of deep and difficult emotions, big giant waves pounding us, throwing us under the water, forcing us down so we couldn't breathe.

RIGHT FROM THE start, we always skipped the trivial stuff—the weather, the movies—and cut to the chase.

"Does anyone have any news?" Claudia was asking.

It was always her first question to the other widows. Claudia was paralyzed with fear that the police would show up to give her the news that her husband Bart's body had been identified. She had heard the stories about families being woken up in the middle of the night by a knock on the door, the policeman on the doorstep. Every morning her first thought was "I wonder if today's the day."

"I promise, you would be the first to know . . . ," exhaled Ann.

"Same here," said Pattie. Both Pattie and Ann were waiting as well. Julia's husband Tommy's body had been recovered right away.

Claudia went on: "Last winter, I came home from work one night and there was a police officer in the lobby of my apartment building. I assumed he was there for me. He wasn't, but that didn't matter. By the time he'd explained to me that he'd just come in to warm up from the cold, I was inconsolable."

Bart's work ID and his credit cards had been recovered from Ground Zero, but not Bart. Claudia would hold her husband's Amex in the palm of her hand and wonder how the hell a sliver of plastic had managed to survive but Bart hadn't. She'd show the cards to people and they'd look like they were afraid to touch them, like they could catch being murdered.

"Either way, hearing or not hearing, it terrifies me," Claudia was saying to the others.

We all lived with these thoughts each moment, replaying them over and over again. They were paralyzing, keeping us from sleeping at night and from getting out of our beds in the mornings.

"I'm obsessed with the images of what happened inside that building," Claudia continued. "Did Bart try to go down the stairwell and the stairs were gone? Or instead of being stairs was there a wall of flames? Did he try to climb the stairs to the roof and it was locked? I know he would never jump, but I'm so afraid he was trapped."

She told the others about a conversation she'd had with Larry, her brother-in-law, one of Bart's best friends and married to his sister, Kathleen. One day over lunch they'd been talking about Claudia's obsession with what had happened. Larry knew she needed to find some relief from these images.

"He told me: 'Claudia, we have to come up with a story you can live with and stick to it.'

"So that's what we did," Claudia explained. "We imagined Bart's thought process. We decided that Bart would have said to himself: 'Well, I can be rescued here on the one hundred and fifth floor—or I can go up to the bar at Windows on the World, pour a Macallan Scotch, and the firemen can rescue me there.' Now whenever the thoughts come back to me, I say to myself, Windows on the World, Macallan, Bart . . ."

JULIA REMINDED HERSELF that, after all, she'd been one of the "lucky ones." She'd had a wake and a proper funeral for her husband a week after September 11, one of the first of the thousands of funerals and memorials that would take place over the course of the coming year. As she listened to the rest of us talking that night, she knew she wanted to share her own experience with us. That a funeral hadn't brought her any closure or acceptance. That she was just like us in so many ways.

"You know, when I went to the funeral home to pick out a coffin for Tommy . . ." Julia stopped mid-sentence. "What am I even saying? Ten months later and I still can't believe I'm talking about a coffin for my husband. How is that possible? A funeral for Tommy? At the funeral home I started begging the—what do you call him, the funeral director?—to let me see the body, to let me hold his hand or something. I told him I needed to see him because I had to make sure it was Tommy. The funeral director wouldn't let me. He assured me that I needed to remember him as he was."

Julia explained that, at that time, she was still convinced that Tommy was alive. She'd figured it out. The CIA must have been so impressed with Tommy's cleverness in getting out of the building, that they'd hired him on the spot. They'd told him he had to go away for a while, but he would be back in a year or two when his mission had been completed. Tommy couldn't be dead.

Julia had a body, a wake, a funeral, a tombstone, and a gravesite. She even got his wallet, cell phone, computer, and Day-Timer, all the things he had with him that day.

"But you know what?" she told the rest of us. "All these months later, it hasn't stopped me thinking he's coming back. It hasn't taken away the pain. It doesn't make it any better."

MAYBE WE'D RECOGNIZED it from our previous meetings, but at the bar, it was becoming clearer. One of the reasons we were drawn together had to do with the license we gave one another just to talk and talk without worrying about bringing others down or saying the wrong thing or making anyone uncomfortable with the degree of our unhappiness.

That night, we traded stories, going back and forth. We were getting to know one another, tracing the invisible threads pulling us together, figuring out the links. We talked about our husbands, how special our time with them had been. It uplifted us to talk about our marriages. Our husbands were our best friends, our soul mates, the men we'd taken it for granted we'd grow old with. We'd had these men in our lives and now they were gone. What were we supposed to do? How were we supposed to move forward? How is it possible to be planning your future one day and the next thing you know, all that planning doesn't mean a thing? We were all asking the same questions.

Had nostalgia set in? Maybe every widow thinks her husband is perfect in retrospect. It's much easier to idolize someone who's no longer around, when he's not here to make you roll your eyes when he leaves his dirty underwear on the bathroom floor, or he drives too fast, or hogs the remote control. It wasn't that we thought our husbands were perfect. We'd known they'd had their faults. It was just that we'd tried not to let the petty annoyances come between us. We'd shared a bond that made the inconsequential seem just that.

Now we would give anything to walk into the bathroom and find the seat up again.

There wasn't a single day that we didn't momentarily forget and feel that he was still alive. Any accomplishment, any success, any failure, any concern—our first instinct was to call him to let him know. We'd think, "I've got to tell him about this" and actually reach for the telephone. We would dream about running into him in the street, working ourselves up to a point where we actually believed that we were going to see him again. We'd wake up in the morning and roll over to hold him, and for that split second, we would forget that our lives were shattered. And then, the ugly reality hit us one more time. In those moments, it was like he died all over again.

Now there was no one to share life with. Even the small things, deciding what we were going to have for dinner, or what to do for the weekend—these were the daily pleasures that had been ripped away from us. Instead, here we were, in some godforsaken bar on Park Avenue, drinking and talking and talking, still in so much pain, so far from the women we used to be. This was a club that none of us wanted to be members of. But the cocktails were doing their work, softening edges, blurring the spaces between us, drawing us closer and closer. It wasn't just that we were widows, or that our husbands had been killed in the World Trade Center. It had to do with the kind of men our husbands were and the similarities between our relationships, this chemistry that existed between us.

As we spoke about our marriages, someone pointed out—"It's gone, but at least it was *there*."

At least we'd had it.

Someone else raised a glass. "A toast!"

No one remembers who was the first to say it. It just happened, the only natural thing to say. Ever since that first meeting it's always been our toast and it always will be. Our first drink—and believe us, there have been plenty of drinks—is always to them.

"To The Boys," we said.

"To The Boys."

BY NOW, ANN had forgotten any worries she might've had about being the odd one out. She looked around at the rest of us and could sense that we were getting swept away in this as much as she was. Ann recognized that part of the comfort of being here was that she didn't have to worry about protecting anyone's feelings.

"You know, I was taking my oldest son to camp last week," she told the women at the bar, "and all I could think about was that this was the first sleep-away camp, the first summer without his father, and I was trying so hard not to cry because I'm the one who has to be strong. But soon the tears are streaming and my son's patting my arm and saying, 'Mom, it's okay, it's going to be all right.' And I'm saying to him, 'No, no, I'm the one who's supposed to be comforting you!'"

She'd had to remain so strong, not break down completely, for the sake of her family. But in this huddle of widows at the bar, there was no one watching her, not her parents, or her in-laws, her kids, her community. Ann's feelings of missing Ward were sharper, more intense and more overwhelming than she could ever begin to describe. But right now, she didn't need to find the words. We all understood, viscerally. Ann could be exactly how she felt.

WE WERE AT the bar for two hours before we realized we'd better eat something. As we sat down in a booth, the conversation switched to the subject we were all dreading. The anniversary of the eleventh.

"So what's everyone going to do?" asked Julia.

There was such overwhelming anxiety surrounding this question. Every eleventh of every month was a date to be reckoned with. We counted every day, week, and month that slipped away from us. How could it have been three months since my husband and I talked? How could it be seven months since I last saw him smile? How could it be six weeks until the one-year anniversary?

"I don't want the time to go," said Ann. "It's too soon for it to be a year."

"I know," said Claudia. "It's only July and I'm already sick to my stomach."

We all knew there was going to be a ceremony downtown, and we all felt the push and the pull to go.

"I want to go," Pattie told the others. "After everything our husbands went through that day—I couldn't imagine being anywhere else."

We knew that Pattie was right. And if we went together, maybe somehow we could make it through the day.

Pattie picked up the wineglass in front of her, but as her hand brought the glass to her mouth for the much-needed gulp, her elbow slipped from the table edge. The full glass of wine emptied itself across the tablecloth, and all over Pattie. Ann, Claudia, and Julia were reaching for napkins. The four of us were suddenly laughing and calling to the waitress for more napkins. This, like so many other things, came under the category of "not a problem." In our former lives, we might have said "disaster." Not surprisingly, that word had a whole new connotation these days.

CLAUDIA STARTED DIGGING around in her bag. She'd remembered the gifts she had brought for Ann and Julia, two small books in colored calfskin leather made by the company she worked for, Cole Haan. Pattie always carried around a little black photo album filled with pictures of her husband, Caz; Claudia had been inspired and done the same with photos of her own husband.

"Here, ladies, pick a color," Claudia explained. "They're called brag books. They are supposed to be for new parents to show off pictures of their children, but Pattie and I use ours for pictures of The Boys."

When we were with one another we could actually laugh about such things. Putting pictures of dead husbands instead of new babies in brag books. Saying good night to the empty urn on the bedside stand. Wondering if a person can "roll over in a grave" if they don't have one. In the moments of black humor there was connection and hope. Because if we could make one another smile that meant that we could inch ourselves up from the bottom. We'd paid for these laughs with a million tears.

Someone made a toast to being able to laugh again.

"I'll drink to that," we said, before remembering that Pattie had emptied the last of the wine.

Perfectly on cue, the waitress appeared carrying another bottle of red.

"It's on the house," she said.

THAT EVENING, A bond was forged. There were no awkward pauses between us. No one felt sorry for anyone. No one said, "It's going to be okay. . . ."

We were four women who could look into one another's eyes and recognize what we found there.

And by the end of the night we'd agreed to the following: We would go to Ground Zero for the anniversary. We knew it would be incredibly hard and painful, but knowing we'd have one another to lean on made it seem possible for the first time. We wanted to go to honor our husbands, but also to honor the thousands of others who'd perished that day.

Then, the following weekend, we would go away together. When Claudia suggested the trip, the rest of us agreed. We sensed that the simple fact of having something to look forward to would help give us the strength to get through the weeks ahead. Someone suggested Scottsdale, Arizona. Why not? It was as good a place as any.

In the last toast of the evening, we drank again to "The Boys." And to us.

"To the Widows Club."

Julia:

In the cab heading home that night, I remember having a feeling of actual hopefulness, like that feeling you get after a first date when you know you want to see that person again. I knew I wanted to spend time with these women; I wanted to confide in them. They understood what I was going through and I felt safe in their company. That night, for me, was like coming up from the deep end of the swimming pool and I'd just reached the surface and could breathe again.

Pattie:

Ten months later, I was barely functioning, not able to truly connect with anyone. It was as if I was always floating outside of situations. But these women gave me the sense that I didn't have to pull back into isolation; I *could* become involved with the people around me. It wasn't the amount of time that we'd known one another that counted—I'd only just met Ann and Julia—it was the experiences we'd shared already. Now I was curious to see what we might share in the future.

Ann:

At the time of that first meeting, I was still reeling from grief and fear and loneliness of life without Ward. He was the one person who would give me the confidence to move forward and the self-esteem to believe that I could manage on my own. I needed his comforting and his reassurance that it would be okay. I needed him to help me, hold me, and make me feel better. But he wasn't there. Now there were these three women in my life and we were going to help one another. It was an understanding that existed between us from that first meeting. They were my new friends and we were going to try to make life a bit more bearable, somehow. It was amazing how quickly it came about, that commitment. It was like something was being sparked in all of us— signs of life after a winter that had lasted into July.

Claudia:

I could tell that everyone had more than gotten along. I knew that we were going to see one another again. I was hopeful that we would really take this trip to Scottsdale together. But even so, when each of us stepped through the front door to pitch darkness again, it hit us just the same. Our husbands were gone, murdered. And in that instant, anything good is lost.

Still, every one of us can relate to the words Julia wrote in her journal that night: "This evening has been the happiest I've had since Tommy died. In a journal of bad days, this has been a good day."

Part I

———————

◆

September 2002 to September 2003

What we were, we are.

What we had, we have.

A conjoined past imperishably present.

— Nicholas Evans

1 · Claudia and Bart

Claudia:

On Tuesday, August 6, a few weeks after the Widows Club's first meeting, I was working late and got home around 10 pm. I was exhausted, pushing my way through the revolving door of my apartment building. As I walked into the lobby, I said hi to my doorman.

He came out from behind the desk, with his hands deep in his pockets, his eyes on the floor. He told me that a New York City detective had been by earlier and was asking for me.

"He wanted me to call him when you got home," my doorman explained. "But I'm not supposed to tell you that."

My thoughts couldn't move fast enough to process the information. I took the elevator up to my apartment, needing to know but not being able to face what I feared was coming. I called the detective.

"Hello, this is Claudia Ruggiere. You were at my apartment earlier."

He asked if he could come over.

"Was Bart identified?"

The detective replied: "I'm not allowed to talk about this over the phone."

I pleaded: "Don't do this to me, it's not fair."

"Yes, your husband was identified."

I called my sister Marcella and Bart's sister Kathleen. Then I called Julia, who lives ten blocks away. She was by my side within minutes. The detective arrived. He explained to me that Bart's remains had been identified using DNA testing. He couldn't tell me what they had found. I was going to have to go to the Medical Examiner's Office at 8 am when it opened in the morning. My sister would come with me.

If there could be a day as painful as September 11, this came close. That night, as it was on the night of the eleventh, my apartment was filled with family and friends, everyone offering me their unconditional love and support. It was like reliving the day Bart was killed without any of the hope that he had survived.

WE DECIDED TO have the burial on September 11—this day was going to be so incredibly painful that nothing could make it worse. I was thirty-three years old, looking at cemetery plots for my husband. Where should the plot be? Should we cremate the remains? What should be put on the headstone?

I met my father-in-law, Frank Sr., for lunch and I took a photo of the marker I'd selected. I showed him where the cross would go, the family name, Bart's birth date and death date, the space for my name.

"Claudia, it will break my heart if you end up here," Frank said. "You have to make another life for yourself."

I had been married a little over a year and a half. I was adamant that I wanted that space left open. I couldn't imagine anything different.

I'd chosen the epitaph: "Life is not measured by the number of breaths you take, but by the moments that take your breath away." A friend had sent me a copy of this quote because it reminded her of Bart. I agreed. My husband would have hated the traditional "beloved husband, son, brother, friend." At least this epitaph sounded like Bart.

I WAS TWENTY-SEVEN the summer we met. At the time, my sister Marcella was dating her future husband John Crewe (JC), who was

Bart's roommate. That summer, the four of us and twenty friends decided to rent a beach house in Westhampton—we were young and overextended on our credit cards so we figured, the more the merrier.

This was how I first got to know Bart, out at the beach, in the sunshine, by the pool.

Things I learned about Bart that summer: He'd grown up in the neighboring town to mine on Long Island and had moved to the city around the same time as me. Out at the beach house, Bart was the instigator—always the one planning the parties, writing the grocery lists, and manning the grill. His nickname that summer was "Leisure Boy" because, at that time, he owned his own seafood packaging company and could work from the beach during the week. While the rest of us arrived exhausted from the office, there was Bart, already in weekend mode, tan and radiating ease, cocktail in hand. Even when he did have to return to the city, he would find some excuse to stay late on Sunday, persuading one of us to remain sober to be his chauffeur.

Bart and I were both dating other people that summer, so it wasn't like I ever thought of him as a romantic prospect. Instead, we became friends. Bart would often call me during the week to ask for suggestions on where to take his latest date. I can remember looking over at him at some point that summer and thinking that he was handsome in a dashing Cary Grant sort of way. He was tall and slim, with dark brown eyes, wire-rimmed glasses, and a Roman nose. At the age of twenty-eight, he already had a full head of salt and pepper hair, which gave him a definite air of sophistication. He was always impeccably pulled together, even at the beach—his polo shirts and flat-front khakis were perfectly pressed. He had a certain charisma and an incredibly witty sense of humor. But he was my sister's boyfriend's roommate; it was just too close to home to think about him as anything more than a friend.

The summer ended and we stayed in touch, mainly through Marcella and JC. I was always genuinely pleased to see Bart when I ran into him.

LATER THAT YEAR, on November 20 to be exact, Marcella called to tell me she had an extra ticket for a Scotch tasting in SoHo. Great. I was looking forward to spending some quality time with my sister. I'd just found out that the guy I'd been seeing—someone I'd thought was special and who'd looked good on paper—had turned out to be a major disappointment. Bruised from the breakup, I was in a pretty miserable state of mind. I'd assumed that it would be just me and Marcella and I would be able spend the evening pouring out my woes to my sister.

When I showed up at the Puck Building, Marcella was there with JC and Bart. At that point, Marcella and JC were in that annoying mushy in-love stage and I knew I wasn't in the mood to spend the evening with the happy couple. Luckily, I *was* in the mood to sample Scotch.

And at least Bart was there, looking as cute as ever. Navy blazer, charcoal trousers, and a checkered shirt—a dapper combination for a casual evening out with friends.

The last time I'd seen Bart, he'd just broken up with his girlfriend and I'd been consoling him. Now the tables were turned. Bart was sympathetic, but in typical male fashion, his main words of advice were: "Hey, Claude, get over it, the guy's obviously a loser."

We made our way around the room, catching up with one another as we went. By the end of the night we must have polished off more than our share of Scotch. Even so, Bart decided we needed a nightcap. He suggested we all go across the street to Temple Bar, a dark, sexy downtown lounge.

Marcella and JC didn't stay for long. After barely a few sips, they snuck out to be alone. Once my sister and her boyfriend had left, I remember feeling giddy and not just from the whiskey. Bart and I were clicking; the one-liners were going back and forth between us.

At one point Bart turned to me and said: "Claudia, I think you're flirting with me."

"You're out of your mind," I told him, laughing.

The next thing I knew, Bart kissed me, full on the lips. I laughed again and told him not to get the wrong idea.

But he kept kissing me. Bart, it turned out, was an excellent kisser.

We stayed until last call. When it was time to go, we shared a cab and kissed the whole way home. But for some reason, when I got to my apartment building I didn't invite Bart inside. As much fun as it was, it never occurred to me that we would ever be more than friends. Before I got out of the cab, I swore Bart to secrecy, making him promise not to tell Marcella and JC what had happened between us. He agreed.

Sure enough Bart called me the next day, but I had plans all week. The following Friday, I knew I would see him at a surprise party I was going to with Marcella and JC.

AT THE PARTY, Bart came and stood next to me, slipping his hand into mine.

"What are you doing?" I wanted to know. "Everyone's going to see us."

"Don't worry about it," Bart informed me. "I told your sister about us the next day."

Great, now I had to confess to my sister that I'd been withholding the truth from her all week.

I went to find her.

"Don't worry about it," Marcella said. "Bart called me the next day and told me he kissed you. Oh, and then he told me he was going to marry you."

I still couldn't believe that Bart had let the cat out of the bag. I went back to find him and to give him a piece of my mind.

The following morning, a huge bouquet of all-white Casablanca lilies appeared at my door. Attached was a handwritten note card from Bart saying he was sorry but that he didn't want to play games. Intrigued and, I'll admit, flattered, I called him to say thank you. We talked and I agreed to go on an actual date with him the following week.

It was the night before Thanksgiving and we were both home in Long Island visiting our respective families. He picked me up at my mother's house and we drove to a local restaurant. Because we were already friends, there was such a natural flow to the conversation. This was the first time it was just the two of us having dinner. At some point during the meal I admitted to myself that there was something incredibly special about Bart. He had this spark. He made me laugh. He was going to London and Prague the next day—he loved to travel, as do I. The date ended with us kissing again, this time on my mother's couch, like a couple of teenagers.

· · ·

AFTER THAT EVENING, we gave up trying to keep our affair under wraps and became a couple. I looked up one day and realized that I was going out with my best friend, my soul mate, and someone who made me feel completely loved. There were no secrets between us, no crazy ex-girlfriend in the closet that I didn't know about. Falling in love with Bart was effortless. Our already busy social lives quickly merged. We loved being out every night. Our calendars were booked up months in advance. We were a "yes" couple. We were always on the go.

Life was good. I loved my boyfriend's energy, his spirit. Bart was a man whose name was an adjective among his friends. Things were "so Bart." In between jobs and leasing a black Mercedes? "So Bart." Eighty friends for a holiday party in a six-hundred-square-foot apartment? "So Bart." Seersucker suits and saddle shoes at a barbecue? You get the picture. It's no coincidence that Bart chose to make his home in New York City. New York was his kind of town, with its fabulous restaurants and bars, its energy and panache, its glamour.

Bart had a talent for savoring good times and not worrying too much about the consequences. Take, for example, his dietary habits. My husband had a dyslexic approach to the food pyramid. Steaks, veal chops, Scotch, and good wine were his staples. He refused to eat fruits or vegetables. To this day, his friends continue to meet at the famous New York steakhouse The Grill at Smith and Wollensky's on the first Thursday of every month to celebrate his life, starting with his favorite meal. Despite his lack of interest in eating anything green, Bart was a fabulous cook, whipping up gourmet meals in record time. If we weren't eating out, I came home to a delicious dinner he'd cooked for me. Under continual duress, he would agree to prepare some vegetables for my benefit.

Although Bart was committed to his business, after we met he was offered an opportunity to take a job on Wall Street. He knew he would miss owning his own company, but he went for it regardless. Bart wasn't fixated on work, not by a long shot. He always reserved his passion for people, placing his family and friendships at the very center of his life. He had friends from every elementary school, high school, college he'd attended, every job he'd ever had. He was the kind of guy who stayed in contact with all his ex-girlfriends. He organized beach houses and ski houses, always including people, always drawing others into his circle. Bart was always the one throwing the party.

His life philosophy was infectious. When I first met him, I was working for a small Italian fashion company, with a team that felt like family to me. I wasn't paid much but I was devoted to the work, staying late, working weekends. When an American fashion brand recruited me with a substantial salary increase, I didn't want to take the job. I told Bart I was happy where I was and wouldn't enjoy working for a bigger company. What's more, I would miss going to Italy on business several times a year.

Bart took a different stance.

"Claudia," he told me. "We're not the kind of people who live to work. We're the kind of people who work to *live*."

Bart reminded me of all the extra trips we'd be able to take with my new salary—we could go to Italy on vacation instead. Despite my initial resistance, I decided to take the job, surprised at how confidently I negotiated the terms and navigated a new set of responsibilities. I'd always considered myself a confident person, but like many young people, my bravado was often a mask for my insecurity. Bart helped legitimize my confidence. He gave me the love, support, and encouragement that made me believe anything was possible.

When Bart proposed in March of 1999, it was a crisp and cool spring day in Central Park. We had walked to a secluded spot on a grassy slope by a flagpole when Bart got down on one knee and reached into the pocket of his coat. I didn't have to pause to answer.

We started planning the wedding, and for our future together. I knew I wanted to be with this man for the rest of my life. What drew me to Bart was his innate determination to live without regrets. It's almost always easier to take the path of least resistance, to exist instead of to live, but Bart knew how to *live*. With an uncanny prescience, he realized that all of us have an allotted time on this earth and that it's up to each one of us to make every day count.

IT'S ALSO IMPORTANT to me not to let life slip away without experiencing as much as I can. I think that's an attitude that people who have lost a parent at an early age often tend to take on. I was nineteen, and ending my sophomore year at Maryland, when I got the news that my father had died unexpectedly of an aneurysm while my parents were on vacation in Italy. He was only fifty-two. We buried him on my mother's fiftieth birthday. I remember looking at my uncle Nick, my father's only brother, and realizing that his hair had turned gray overnight. This was my first indication that grief can change people completely, without warning, in an instant.

I'd always thought of my parents as equals and my mother as a strong and outgoing person. But when my father died, everything changed. Without her husband, my mother lost her will to live. It took two years before she could even begin to comprehend that he was gone. I would come downstairs in the morning and find her at the kitchen table already crying, or, worse, she wouldn't get out of bed at all. She refused to go out, to drive her car. She wouldn't have the television or radio on. She couldn't sleep. She lost weight, became less like herself in every sense. In those days, my mother would either be crying or she would just zone out. Every so often you could hear the sound of moaning. We would say to her, "Mom, stop moaning." She would say, "Was I?"

Distraught, my mother would tell us she had nothing left to live for, that her life was worthless without her husband. I remember how angry it made me to hear her say that—as if my father's life was worth more than hers.

My father, Salvatore Gerbasi, had filled our house with his presence, and now he dominated it with his absence. My sister and I missed him beyond belief. Dad was the quintessential family man, always making plans, throwing parties, having people over. He was an incredibly dynamic, popular, outgoing man, one of those types who are often described as "larger than life." He was six foot one, with a full head of wavy gray hair, hazel eyes, and black-rimmed glasses. He had broad shoulders, massive hands, and size 13 EEE feet. His impressive stature often gave people who didn't know him the impression that he was imposing, but the opposite was true. Small children might be timid around him for a second, and then realize he was really just a big marshmallow—and soon they would be putty in his oversized hands.

When I was growing up, my father and I were partners in crime; I was his little sidekick. If my father said, "Let's go on vacation," I would pick up the phone and call the airlines to find the lowest fares. If my father said, "Let's have lobster for dinner," I'd be first in the car to drive with him forty-five minutes to the harbor where they were pulling them fresh out of the ocean. Growing up, he taught me to play backgammon and gin rummy. On a family vacation in Puerto Rico, I ended up winning the hotel backgammon championship against a sixty-year-old man. My prize was two bottles of rum. I was twelve. I was definitely my father's daughter. The summer of my freshman year in college, he gave me a job working for him. When he wouldn't give me a raise, I quit, telling him I would get some other work that paid better. I landed a job selling steak knives door to door and made three times as much money. My father couldn't have been more proud.

My mother is an amazing person. After having children, she gave up her teaching career to be a full-time mom—a decision she never regretted. But this meant that my dad was the sole provider. Like many women of her generation, my mother wasn't financially independent. My father had always paid the bills, taken care of everything. He thought he was invincible. After his death, my sister and I spent hours with our mother poring over the family finances, trying to sort through the expenses, creating a family budget.

My mother always said that bad luck came in threes. She was the third young widow in our family. Both her mother and her mother's mother before her had lost their husbands. My great-grandmother was twenty-nine when her husband died of influenza, leaving her with four young children. Next there was my grandmother—my grandfather had fallen ill with cancer the year after they got married. She was thirty-five when he died and her daughter, my mother, was five at the time. I'd grown up hearing so many stories about the grandmothers. They'd become exemplary figures for me and my sister—strong, independent, hard-working women who were stoic in their acceptance of the hand they'd been dealt.

Now, by some unimaginable twist of fate, it was my turn.

· · ·

THERE'S NOTHING THAT can prepare you for the things that happen to you in life. No matter how much you try, something will always be beyond comprehension, even after it's over and you can contemplate it with hindsight.

The morning of September 11 at 8:46 the phone rang and it was Bart. I was still in bed in our apartment in midtown, drowsy and half-awake. "Listen to this," Bart said and he held up the phone. I just heard a lot of noise but thought it was some kind of prank on the trading floor. After waiting for what seemed like minutes, I hung up. He called right back. "Did you just hang up on me? Don't you know what's going on? Claudia, turn on the TV. A plane hit my building." Bart thought it was a small private plane and sounded more annoyed than anything else. "I'm okay, I just wanted to let you know that I'm okay. Tell everyone I'm okay. This place is crazy, I'm getting out of here." Then I heard an announcement of some kind in the background. Bart said "I've gotta go" and hung up. Ever since the first time Bart told me he loved me, we never ended a conversation without saying, "Love you." All of a sudden, I got a bad feeling, but pushed it to the back of my mind. Bart sounded somewhat exasperated, but most importantly calm and in control. He sounded exactly like himself.

I rolled over and turned on the news. I was confronted by images of One World Trade Center on fire. Since Bart said he was okay, I turned on the shower and was about to get in, when my brother-in-law Larry called. I told him not to worry, I spoke to Bart and he was fine. Larry's office is in New Jersey and faces the Twin Towers, and he knew I wasn't absorbing the enormity of what was going on. He kept saying, "Claudia, this looks really bad." I kept my eyes on the TV. All of a sudden I saw a burst of flames erupting from the South Tower and I heard Larry saying, "What the hell was that?" I kept trying to reassure him: I spoke to Bart, and he was getting out of there.

I hung up the phone and went to turn off the shower—I could be late to work today. I started calling our family to let them know I had spoken to Bart and he was okay. My mother didn't know either, and I told her to turn on the TV. I heard the *Today* show mention the word "terrorism" and thought, This can't be happening. Our friend Paulette called and I told her Bart was okay, but she volunteered to come over and wait with me until he got home.

I VAGUELY REMEMBER Paulette arriving. I must have blocked out the exact sequence of events from that day. Paulette tells me she'd gone into the kitchen to get me a glass of water when Bart's building fell. I was on the phone with Kathleen, Bart's sister, and Paulette heard me screaming at the top of my lungs. "It just went down. Oh my God, it just went down. Bart's building went down."

At some point, my brother-in-law JC arrived, the sleeve of his shirt ripped off—he had used the cloth to cover his face from the smoke. Our friend Chrissy stumbled in as well. They had both walked to midtown from Wall Street. The look in their eyes was of barely concealed horror.

Eventually, someone told me to get dressed. Friends started showing up one after the next, carrying alcohol, food, paper plates, flowers.

Someone asked me if I knew anyone else we could call to get any kind of information. Bart had only been at Cantor Fitzgerald for six months and I didn't really know anyone who worked with him. Then I remembered Ward Haynes. I had met him twice because he used to work with Bart at his previous job. Ward had just started at Cantor the month before. I remember Bart referring to Ward as the "Mayor of Rye" because he knew everyone in that small suburban New York town.

I called information and got the number for Ward Haynes. A woman answered the phone. I asked for Ward's wife and explained that my husband sat next to Ward. The woman told me to wait and she'd get Ann right away.

Ann said she hadn't heard from Ward, but she was so grateful to hear from me and hear that I'd spoken to Bart. We both felt that since our husbands sat next to each other, Ward must be okay as well. We agreed to maintain constant contact, never imagining how instrumental we were going to be in one another's lives.

That night I remember sending someone to sleep in my bed around 3 am. I was going to stay on the couch—facing the door—for when Bart walked in. It had not entered my mind that he might not be coming home.

. . .

BART AND I have friends in the Secret Service, and the following day I called them in case there was news the press wasn't reporting. Rumor had it there were people in the shopping area under the towers. I decided that Bart had made it to the Duane Reade and he could survive a week on Oreos and Diet Coke.

Over the next seven days there was a constant flow of people in our six-hundred-square-foot apartment. We had our own little triage unit. We were calling every hospital in the city. People went out to get extra chargers for cell phones, to Kinko's to make copies of flyers—anything to help. I watched the image of the towers falling incessantly, scouring the crowd for Bart's face to see if he had gotten out.

I had one rule: you weren't allowed in our apartment if you didn't believe Bart was still alive. I didn't want anyone there who was hysterical. Marcella and JC were with me nonstop, and Marcella would tell me to take a shower mid-morning. I would turn on the water and sit on the floor of the shower and cry until there was nothing left. Of course everyone outside heard me, but I felt like it was the only place I could be alone. This was the one time during the day I would let the weight of what was happening hit me with its full force and break down completely.

That week, I went to meet Ann at the Pierre Hotel, where Cantor had set up a meeting room to help provide support and information for the families. I found her quickly and we embraced. Although we'd come to the hotel with family and friends, we only wanted to be with each other. We continued to give each other hope. Later that evening, Larry pulled me into the bedroom and said: "Claudia, at some point you may have to start to think about the *possibility* that Bart may not be coming home." I told him that as long as Mayor Giuliani said there was hope, I was not going to give up.

Exactly one week after the eleventh, on Tuesday the eighteenth, around noon, the mayor came on television and said there was "no meaningful hope of survivors." The words were like a ton of bricks hitting me in the chest. I was sitting on the floor Indian-style and I collapsed with my head in my knees. No one could say anything. Kathleen put her arms around me, picked me up, and took me out of the apartment.

We walked over to a small alcove alongside the East River. It was another beautiful Tuesday in September with bright blue skies and a breeze coming in from the water. We started talking about what kind of service Bart would want. It would be in Manhasset, where I grew up and one town over from Port Washington, where Bart had grown up. I would ask Larry, our best man, to give the eulogy. When Bart's stepfather had died the year before, I remembered Bart turning to me and saying, "Claude, there's no way I'm having a wake. When I die, I want a party and make sure you play Sinatra's 'My Way.'" I'd laughed and told him he was crazy. Who was crazy now?

THE CHURCH IN Manhasset was overwhelmed with memorial services—almost fifty people from my hometown had been killed in the attacks. We would have to wait another week before Bart's service. In the meantime, no one wanted to leave me alone. We came up with projects for the service and reception—a booklet to give out in church with some of Bart's favorite quotes, pictures, a slide show, music.

My biggest breakdown came when I went to see Bart's father. For that entire first week I kept insisting that his son was alive. I would call Frank Sr. and tell him that I knew in my heart that Bart had to be okay, that we couldn't give up hope. Now when I saw Bart's father, I couldn't stop sobbing. Somehow I felt like I'd let him down.

The day of the service, I remember walking down the aisle with Bart's mother, Pat, both of us leaning on each other, needing the support to stay upright. There were so many people in that church, too many to count. Who knows? Over one thousand people?

Ann was at the memorial. I was desperate to be with her. Despite all the family and friends who had gathered to memorialize Bart and offer me their support, I remember only wanting to talk to Ann, needing to. She was truly the only person who understood how I felt. We had said that whatever happened, we would share the same fate. And now here we were.

THE NIGHT AFTER Bart's memorial service, I decided to call one of the twenty-four-hour hot lines that had been set up for victims' families. I snuck upstairs to my sister's guest room to make the call. A woman answered the phone. I tried to get the words out, to explain why I was calling. The woman on the other end of the line kept saying, "What? I can't hear you. . . ."

"My husband . . . was . . . killed . . . on September 11." It was the first time I actually used the word "killed." I almost fell off the bed, jolted by the magnitude of that word coming out of my mouth.

The woman gave me the number of a therapist in the city and I made an appointment to see him the next day.

The day of my appointment, barely registering what I was doing, I took a cab to the therapist's office. I had never been to therapy before.

The therapist came out and greeted me in the waiting room, a short man with glasses and dark curly hair. I sat down in his office and let the words come tumbling out. I sobbed. I told him about Bart and how much I loved him. I told the therapist that I thought I was losing my mind. That I was never going to be happy again, that I had lost any chance of having a family. It was like someone had highlighted my entire future and then hit the delete button.

The therapist nodded his head and offered the occasional "um-hmmm."

I kept talking, pouring out my pain.

Halfway through the session, the therapist told me the following: "Claudia, at some point in the future, you are going to have to move on. You don't want to end up like some old Italian widow wearing black and sitting out on the stoop all day."

After that, I tuned him out and waited for the balance of the hour to be up.

I went home to the apartment where Bart should be and where Bart was not. Bastard, bastard, bastard. My rage was like a knife stabbing through my insides. I was mad at the therapist, I was mad at the terrorists, I was mad at the world. I took my clothes off and got into the shower, letting myself sink to the bottom of the bathtub where I could put my head between my knees with the water beating down on me and only cry.

Eventually, I managed to get out of the shower and I called Marcella. She wanted to know how it went with the therapist. I told her the guy was a jackass and I was never going back. No wonder he was giving out free sessions. Who would pay him?

. . .

WHEN MY MEMORIES of that first year return to me, they are confused and out of sync. They tumble out in no order because there was no sense of what came next, only a series of moments to be endured. I remember the skin on my face feeling ragged and tender from tears. My insides ached from weeping; I was hoarse from crying. Everything about my body and person felt different—head different, face different, hair different. From the bones in my jaw to the ends of my fingernails, I hurt. I would look in the mirror and feel no connection to the strange horrified woman staring back at me.

I needed to hear from my husband. I needed for him to call me, to tell me that he was okay, that we were going to be okay. Bart called ten times a day, a real phone junkie. He was constantly in contact. At the end of the day, my phone would be ringing off the hook—it was always Bart, telling me I had eight minutes to walk home, he had just thrown the water on to boil the pasta, or he had just put the steak on the grill, and he wanted to know when I was leaving work so we could have dinner together. Now, although the phone had gone silent, I kept up my dialogue with Bart, from love and from habit. "Hi, honey, how are you? I'm getting up now; I'm going to wash my hair. I know you would want me to wash my hair. Okay, here I go. . . ."

Nights were harrowing. I would lie awake, locked in my thoughts, or, just before dawn, when sleep finally came, there were dreams of buildings burning, of being trapped, where I could physically feel the heat of the flames. I would take sleeping pills to obliterate consciousness for a few hours, but nothing else. I refused to take any other drugs to hold back this avalanche of pain.

"My husband was killed," I told people who urged me to seek relief. "I'm supposed to feel sad."

The relief that I craved was impossible for anyone to bring me. The days were brutal, endless, and agonizing. I went back to work, just to have something to fill up time, mindlessly following the routine of getting up, going to the office, attempting to function, coming home.

In the evenings, I kept my calendar full. Monday through Thursday I was always out, surrounded by people, keeping busy. I was juggling balls in the air, knowing that when I dropped one, I would fall to pieces. Weekends, I let myself go there. I crawled under the covers. I would watch bad TV for hours on end, never shower, never eat, and never answer the phone from Friday night to Monday morning. Weekends are for spending time with your husband and family, and I didn't have the strength to be around people who had what Bart and I were supposed to have. My refrigerator was home to Kraft singles and cottage cheese. Bart had always done the food shopping, and even the thought of going to D'Agostino on First Avenue made me hyperventilate. I stopped brushing my teeth before climbing into a bed that had suddenly doubled in size.

I focused all of my remaining energies into memorializing Bart and doing the best job possible to honor his memory. I was determined to find a matchbook from every restaurant my husband and I had ever eaten at. I'd be in a cab and suddenly shout to the driver to stop because I had seen another place we'd been together. Cabs all over New York City were screeching to a halt while I ran out to get another matchbook. My friend and I stayed up until 3 am one Saturday night filling a leather-bound album with all the photos and letters that people had sent after Bart's death. I have no artistic ability, but I knew I wanted this to be perfect. My friend understood that it had to be the most beautiful scrapbook in history, with every photo positioned perfectly in the center of the page. She had the patience of a saint that night.

Despite the fact that I work in fashion, I made a point of wearing a piece of Bart's clothing every day. On my worst days, this meant showing up in a pair of his jeans and his favorite gray cashmere V-neck hanging from my thinning body like a sack. I remembered my mother waiting years to go through my father's clothes and then the tearful Sunday afternoon when she finally did it—the experience brought her to the brink of a breakdown. In the months after Bart's death I thought to myself, Clean out his closet now while you're still numb. I saved the clothes that were important to me and gave the rest away to his two brothers, Mark and Frank Jr., and his closest friends. I had a quilt made from Bart's dress shirts that I would wrap myself in for hours regardless of the temperature. The same seamstress turned the remaining shirts and ties into seven teddy bears for our nephews and nieces so they would have something of their uncle's to hold.

. . .

IN DECEMBER, I went to Miami, my first trip since Bart was killed. Bart's sister had organized the trip, and asked the Fontanas to come along. The Fontanas had grown up in the house next door to Bart's family. They thought of Bart as a brother. These were the perfect people for me to go away with because I found it too painful to be around people who didn't know and love Bart. I knew I didn't want to go somewhere Bart had never been. It made me so angry to have experiences that he would never have. So we went to a hotel where I had been twice with my husband, and it comforted me to know that I was in a place that he'd loved. I could picture him in my room, at the bar, down by the pool. I could convince myself that he was there, somehow watching over me.

I tried to stay focused on Bart, on his legacy, on doing the right thing. In the new year, I purchased the apartment we'd rented from his mother. I had no intentions of moving. I made plans to renovate. This had been a dream of ours, so I turned to Bart's sister, an interior designer, for help. This was the only way I would be able to change the apartment—making decisions with Kathleen was as close as I could get to making decisions with Bart. My husband had an amazing eye for even the smallest detail. Kathleen and I both knew him so well that when we looked at a swatch or a sample, we would just know if Bart would love it. "So Bart," we'd say. The plan was to knock down a wall, gut the kitchen, build a bar, and put in a brand-new bathroom. This would be a place that Bart would have been proud to call home.

I tried to find solace in doing things I never would have done with Bart. I took a film class because he never liked to go to the movies—his legs were too long for the seats. I went out for sushi because I loved sushi and Bart didn't. This was my form of rebellion. It didn't work. Then I tried taking classes that I knew Bart *would* like, so that I could feel closer to him. I took a wine tasting class because Bart loved wine. I got a theater subscription because Bart liked going to see off-Broadway shows. I took a writing class because I thought it would be therapeutic to get my feelings out and onto paper. Every week, regardless of the subject, I would end up writing about my dead husband. Finally the teacher suggested I write about something else. I wrote about my dead father instead. I showed her!

At a certain point, I recognized that I was losing my mind. Evidently another life, one that used to be mine, was happening elsewhere. This life, the one I had been forced into, was some kind of bad dream that at some point I would wake up from. Until then, I'd been banished from heaven to hell, trapped in Dante's inferno. Just when I thought I'd reached the lowest circle, another circle would open up below. There were many times when I believed I couldn't physically withstand another minute.

I could sense how hard it was for my mother to see me, knowing everything that lay ahead for her daughter. She never tried to tell me what to do. She only advised me never to do something if I didn't feel that I could, never to force myself into situations I didn't have the strength for, and to be kind to myself. More than anyone, she was aware of my need to grieve in my own way.

My mother would ask me: "Do you feel like you've lost your identity now?"

"No," I said. "I lost my soul mate, my partner, my best friend. But I'm still me."

I was still "me" but a completely diminished version of myself. It was everything that we had planned for that was lost. We were going to go to France that September. Canceled. We were going to have children. Canceled. We were going to buy a home together. Canceled. We were going to grow old together. Canceled. The myth of happy endings was canceled. I had been denied my happy ending because my husband had gotten out of bed one morning and gone to work. If anyone could explain to me how I was supposed to wrap my head around that, I wanted to know.

IT WAS A while before I tried individual therapy again. Instead, I joined a support group of families from Cantor Fitzgerald and a second group for September 11 widows. I was cognizant enough to know I needed whatever help I could get. A good friend persuaded me that despite my bad experience with the therapist the first time, I should give individual therapy another try. She recommended a sensitive and intelligent therapist, named Cheryl Cornelius, whom I credit with helping me begin to navigate my way through the morass.

As much as I hated that first therapist for putting the image in my mind, that "old Italian widow on the stoop" had hit a nerve. She was everything I refused to become. Bart would never want me turn into some bitter old woman who had given in. I knew if I didn't force myself, if I didn't keep going, I would be admitting defeat. Every day was a struggle, but I wasn't going to stay home and be scared. I wasn't going to let the terrorists take anything more from me than they already had. I had been broadsided and I was furious, but determined to survive. Survival became a form of protest for me—survival was the opposite of murder, the opposite of destruction, the opposite of obliteration. I was not going to have my life taken from me along with Bart's. I knew from the hard experience of watching my mother that I would have to be the architect of my future. My life would be what I made of it.

My new friend Ann was part of this. We were going to help each other. We would have strength in numbers. I have never met anyone with such incredible strength, grace, and courage. Here was a woman who'd been divorced before the age of thirty, had a handicapped child at thirty-five, and become a widow before she was forty. Through all of this unimaginable pain and heartache she could already see there was hope for us. It was Ann who kept encouraging me to stay strong, to be kind to myself, to do whatever I could to help endure this, something that's very hard for a new widow to do.

She understood how furious it made me when people didn't mention what had happened. Often, people who didn't know me very well would clam up and not be able to bring up the subject. Or they would say something that reflected their discomfort. I would have people telling me: "Don't worry, everything's going to be okay." They would say that they knew "how I felt." People wanted to do what they could; they wanted to offer condolences and to help. But I hated it when the person offering the advice had no idea how things would turn out, or how I felt, or tried to minimize my loss. The worst was my doctor of eight years, who had the audacity to tell me, "It could be worse—you could be thirty-nine and fat with shingles." Needless to say, I got a new doctor.

Even when I was with my family and close friends, the people I depended on, I could always sense how hard this was for them. It was terrible for them to see me in so much pain. I was becoming wary of continuing to expose them to my ever-widening sadness. If I called my sister, retching with sobs, saying, "I don't want to do this anymore," Marcella would say, "What do you mean? I'll be there in half an hour."

But when I made the same call to Ann, she knew that this meant "My life sucks. I want today to be over. I just want to stay in bed and pretend I don't exist."

With Ann I was safe. She always knew what to say. When I was with Ann, I didn't need to mask the extremity of my suffering.

At the end of October, I met Julia and in the new year, Pattie. These three women would eventually become the Widows Club, my safe harbor. I consoled myself in the knowledge that Bart had been the thread connecting all of us. At work, he sat next to Ward, Ann's husband. He knew Caz, Pattie's husband, through a mutual friend. He had met Tommy through a family friend. This was my solace—Bart had brought the Widows Club together.

I wanted to do everything I could to continue to live in Bart's spirit. Bart and I had a saying: "Never say you can't afford a vacation, because memories are priceless." The year before he died we had been to Switzerland, Italy, Puerto Rico, Florida, and Colorado, and had plans to go to France in September 2001. Going away with the widows to Scottsdale was a means of continuing his legacy.

Thank God for the girls and for the trip we'd planned after the anniversary. The girls' support, and knowing we were going away gave me something positive to focus on in the weeks leading up to that day.

THE NIGHT BEFORE the first anniversary, I went to Il Mulino with my sister, Bart's sister, and Peggy Fontana, one of his oldest friends, who was giving the eulogy at the burial we were having the following day. I was adamant that I was going to Il Mulino every year to toast Bart on September 10. This marked a different anniversary, an anniversary that commemorated Bart's life, not the circumstances surrounding his death.

Il Mulino was the restaurant I had been to with Bart on his last night alive.

You can only get a reservation at Il Mulino a month in advance unless you know the "secret number." Even though Bart didn't have the number, he'd always wanted to go to this old world Italian restaurant, with its amazing food and genuine service. So on August 10, 2001, he made the reservation for September 10. I looked on my calendar.

"Bart, that's a Monday. Can't we go on a weekend?"

Bart's response was: "Why wait?"

Thanks to my husband's insistence, we had gone to dinner that Monday night and had a phenomenal meal. By the end of the night Bart had procured the secret number for future use, much to his delight. Afterward, giddy from champagne, we came home and made love. We fell asleep in each other's arms.

The following morning, I'd woken up with a slight champagne headache from the night before. The shower was running. Bart always got up first. I snuggled in the covers warm and naked and happy to be stealing the extra sleep. Bart came back into the bedroom and began to get dressed. He came over to my side of the bed and asked if there was something in his eye. I was barely awake, and without even opening my eyes I said, "No." He insisted that I look, and I told him it was probably a sty, again making my diagnosis with my eyes closed. Before he left for work I was already drifting back to sleep. Bart came and sat beside me on the bed, put his hands on my shoulders, and said, "Claudia, wake up and look at me." Immediately, I woke up and looked right in his eyes and he said, "I love you." I smiled, eyes wide open, and said, "I love you too, honey." As he was walking out the bedroom door, he turned over his left shoulder and said, "Love you, call you later!"

A year later, no matter how hard I tried to listen, there was no sound of running water, no sound of Bart taking a shower. A year later, I looked at the door like I did every morning. I pictured Bart walking out on that last morning, saying, "Love you, call you later!", our last moment together. Bart had shaken me awake so I could look in his eyes one last time and tell him I loved him, but I couldn't help wishing I'd been more awake. Why couldn't I have opened my eyes right away? We could have talked more. I would be able to remember what he was wearing. One year later, that Bart wasn't taking his shower and kissing me good-bye and saying "Love you, call you later!" made absolutely no sense. It was a travesty of reality.

Bart

Caz

Tommy

Ward

We all made our individual journeys to Ground Zero that morning, carrying our heavy unease and sadness under bright blue skies overhead. Another uncannily perfect, cloudless day in September.

We knew that so many had been affected, but it wasn't until we joined the crowd of mourners that we realized the true extent of the ripple effect. Three thousand victims multiplied by mother, father, spouse, lover, daughter, son, friend, brothers, sisters, cousins, confidants, mentors. We'd been worried there would be chaos, but instead the atmosphere was incredibly calm. Everyone was making his or her way slowly, somberly toward the site.

The Widows Club managed to meet up within minutes, finding one another easily, a sign that we were meant to be together, a sign we needed one another to get through this difficult day. Each one of us came with a group of friends and family members. We exchanged embraces; no one was talking.

We walked in silence toward the site. As we entered, grief counselors and Red Cross volunteers approached us, handing us water, snacks, and tissues, acknowledging, with the compassion in their eyes, that no one could give us what we truly needed.

We went with the flow of the crowd and came to a slow and natural stopping point facing where the buildings had been, not far from the platform where the ceremony would take place.

At 8:46 am bells rang at Ground Zero and there was a moment of silence. At exactly that moment one year ago, our lives had changed forever. Part of us wanted to run away, to make believe none of this had happened.

Mayor Giuliani gave the introduction, invoking Winston Churchill, reminding us to stay firm and of previous generations that have suffered through war and strife. In a powerful and commanding voice, he began the reading of the names of the victims. Behind him, Yo-Yo Ma started to play, the sound of the cello drifting across the crowds, a low, sighing plea. As the names were read, the mild breeze that had been gathering all morning began to swell. Soon a gusting wind was lifting the dirt from the ground up into the air, swirling about us. The dust got into our mouths, our eyes, our hair, our clothes; it became part of us. The force of the wind gathered, a continuous howl that thundered through the microphones, blowing flags from buildings and signs off the fences. Three thousand souls wanting to be heard, telling us they were still here. The wind was a living presence.

People were holding up pictures of their loved ones and crying, and as we watched them, it was like looking into a mirror where we saw our anguish reflected. As we waited, we listened to each name, wondering who that person was. Was he married? Did she have a family? How were his loved ones coping? We wanted the people who read The Boys' names to do them justice. It was important that they weren't mispronounced and that they were read with strength and conviction. The first name we were listening for was Caz (Jeremy Mark Carrington).

Another moment of silence at 9:02 am, and bells ringing to mark the time the second tower was hit.

Pattie remembered thinking that if they didn't read Caz's name, maybe none of this was real. As we neared the C's, she felt her heart pounding, her breath shortening, knees weakening, blood rushing in her ears. She braced herself as if waiting for a physical blow. We all gathered around Pattie. She was inconsolable.

Thomas Joseph Collins was next. The span between CA for Carrington and CO for Collins stretched to infinity. As the names were read, we would recognize others we knew through work, through friends, through support groups, and through the "Portraits of Grief," profiles of the victims that the *New York Times* had run. As we watched the people around us crumple at the sound of a name, we knew whose family members belonged to whom.

At 9:59 am the second tower fell. Another moment of silence. This was Tommy's building. Was this the exact time of his death? Was he still alive when the tower began to fall? For an entire year Julia had been running the events of that day on a loop in her mind. Although she would never know for certain, she felt in her heart that this was the moment. As the bells rang, the loss was coursing through her, swamping her tiny frame with its force.

Ann's son TJ was sitting on the ground, head between his bent knees, looking at a picture of his father, his baseball hat pulled down low over his eyes, trying to hide his tears. You could tell he was sobbing by the shaking of his body. He was fourteen years old. Ann's parents gathered around her. Their helplessness at not being able to protect their daughter and grandson was visible in their every movement. Ann's father went over to comfort TJ. Ann was so grateful that her dad was consoling him; she knew that if she attempted to go over to him, it would be more than she could bear.

At 10:28 am Tower One fell. Another moment of silence.

We waited for the R's. We waited and waited. It had been almost three hours, and we were only halfway through the alphabet.

People started to sit from the heat and exhaustion. Claudia wouldn't sit. She didn't speak. She wanted to stand and listen to every name out of respect. Larry was holding her up and the girls each had a hand on her shoulder. When they read Bart Joseph Ruggiere, her body shuddered with sobs. Once those names were said, there was no turning back; the loss was etched in our hearts forever.

As we reached the end of the alphabet, families began filing down a long ramp into the footprints of the towers. The bowl of the site was like a desert, still swirling with dirt and wind, empty sky above. People had brought pictures and letters and flowers. Pattie brought beautiful white lilies, Caz's favorite flowers. A volunteer gave us each a single long-stemmed rose. There were thousands of roses. We placed our flowers on a makeshift memorial made from cardboard arranged in the shape of a ring. We wrote notes to each of our husbands then stood together and said a final prayer.

As we were leaving, Claudia picked up a small rock and put it in her bag. This afternoon she was going to bury her husband's remains. For the rest of the day, she would hold onto that rock like she was holding onto a piece of Bart.

Claudia:

After the ceremony at Ground Zero, Larry and I left to go to the funeral. In the car on the way out to Manhasset, Larry played me the new Bruce Springsteen album, *The Rising*, for the first time. I read the words as we drove. Every single line spoke to me. I would play that CD over and over in the coming months.

We got to the church, and this time I just walked quietly in the side door and sat in the front pew. We had wanted to keep it small and private, but the people who mattered most were there. Pattie and Julia had come out from the city, as well as our closest friends and family. Ann couldn't be there as she had returned to Rye for a gathering honoring Ward.

After the service, the wind was howling harder than before. I got back into my car, put my sunglasses on, and stared into space, unable to speak. After what seemed like a long time I realized that I was in traffic that wasn't moving. The windstorm had blown out power lines, and all of the streetlights were out. When we finally got to the cemetery, the car with the urn still hadn't arrived. When we were at last ready to begin, someone said, "Where's the priest?" Apparently, we'd forgotten to arrange for a priest at the gravesite.

If Bart had to go, then it would have to be kicking and screaming. I could practically hear him saying, "You're not putting me in the ground just yet."

We held hands and said a prayer. Someone instructed me to walk up to the grave and place my flower first. I tried to be stoic; I wanted to make Bart proud. I was talking to Bart, telling him how much I loved him, how much I needed his strength to get through this. I placed the flower on the grave, and at that moment, it was all just too much. I ran to the car. I wanted to be alone and to cry until the pain killed me or I became numb enough to stop feeling. There was nothing anyone could say to comfort me. We went to Bart's mom's home afterward. I spent the rest of the day with our family and friends, all of us telling Bart stories, doing what we could to comfort one another.

Pattie:

Claudia was so courageous at the burial. I remember wondering how she was going to make it. How was she going to live through being at Ground Zero and burying her husband on the same day? At the church, when the names of The Boys were read again, the feeling of finality, that this was truly happening, registered with a new impact I could barely countenance.

Afterwards, I met members of Claudia's extended group of family and friends. Over drinks, I found myself drawn to Claudia's mother, Annette, and Annette's widow friend Phyllis. Phyllis was one of the four women whom Annette bonded with after the death of her husband. Both women had this feisty energy about them—even on this harrowing day—an energy I've since come to associate with people who have the will to survive.

Together, we commiserated about the challenges of running a household alone. Phyllis and Annette told me about the time they'd gone to a hardware store together. Annette needed a mirror; Phyllis needed a screen door. When the salesman offered to deliver the items the following day, Phyllis told him she wouldn't be home because she was working. The day after that, Annette would be at work, so that was no good either.

"Working?" the salesman asked. "I can't get my wife to do anything but play mah-jong. How did your husbands persuade you to *work*?"

Annette and Phyllis looked at each other before turning to the salesman and saying in unison: "They died."

The release of laughter after such an arduous day.

I told Annette and Phyllis about the time an underground sewer pipe broke at the beach house and I had a massive water spill in my backyard. When the plumber arrived, he reviewed the situation and then wanted to know if he could discuss the matter with my husband. I told him my husband wasn't here right now. But the plumber insisted he speak to the man of the house. I told him my husband was out of the country. The plumber wanted to know when my husband would be back.

My back was against the wall. I'd tried to spare him. But he'd asked for it.

"My husband is in heaven. He won't be back. Ever. Now could you please explain the situation to me and get the show on the road?"

More laughter, more tears.

We talked about how much widows need the support of other widows, just to have someone to tell our stories to and affirm that we aren't alone in trying to figure it all out.

At one point, Annette turned to me and said, "Believe you me, I'm so glad you girls have each other. This Widows Club is going to save you."

And so when it came time to get myself ready for the trip to Scottsdale, I thought about Annette's widows and how much they had helped her. I was leaving my home to spend four days with women I didn't really know so well—I had only met Ann and Julia a handful of times. I was skeptical about the role the group would play in my life. Traveling meant being separated from my dog Lola at a time when I was especially hurt, confused, and needed my familiar comforts more than ever. Even so, I knew that if I stayed behind, it would mean a failure of imagination on my part. Maybe I could gain something from going—what did I have to lose?

On a whim, I threw a light blue shirt into my bag, uncertain if I would wear it. I was still refusing to wear anything but black. Everything else in the bag was black—black swimsuit, black t-shirts, black pants. At least the shirt had the virtue of having been bought the summer before, when Caz was alive to see it.

Ann:

The buildup to the first anniversary was more exhausting than I could have predicted. There were family members coming from out of town for a memorial in Rye, and our local friends wanted very much to be involved too. Who would be invited? Who should speak? There was so much coordination going on, accompanied by my constant concern that I was doing the right thing. I wanted Ward to be proud of me; I wanted his friends and family to be happy. I just kept thinking: What would Ward want? What would he have done?

I remembered how proud Ward had been of his decision to have a golf outing as a tribute after his dad died. Ward often spoke about that day, and his friends remembered it as a pivotal afternoon. And so for me, the decision was made easier by knowing Ward's thoughts. Of course I needed to have a golf tournament for him. Over fifty people were going to play and there would be a party afterward. The perfect celebration honoring Ward's life.

After the ceremony at Ground Zero, I headed back to Rye with my family. Although the tournament and party were a great success, my part in organizing such an emotional event only added to my feelings of complete fatigue. And now I had to get the household ready so that I could go away with the Widows Club. Leaving my children to go to Scottsdale was heartbreaking for me, but also, I knew, entirely necessary. In order to look after them, I knew I had to keep a grip on my sanity; I had to look after myself so I could continue being strong for them. TJ and Billy were being incredibly brave, but it was such a tough time of year. For the children of September 11 victims, this month also meant the beginning of a new school year. They had the additional upheaval of new teachers, new classes, new routines. I felt powerless to protect them from the endless reports on TV and in the newspapers. Although I worried as usual about leaving them, I knew I was doing the right thing. When Ward was alive, we made sure to take an occasional vacation alone, to reconnect, to have time together. Every Sunday we took a couple of hours to play golf together, just the two of us. Time alone brought a healthy balance to family life. That's what the Widows Club could give me now—a break from the daily realities of being a mom.

Leaving the family, even for four days, was like planning a small military operation. The children would be with their regular babysitter. Their pickups from afterschool, tutoring, and sports were all arranged. As I prepared everything for my departure, at every turn I kept coming up against the same brick wall—Ward wasn't here to help, this situation wasn't temporary; our family would never be complete again.

Julia:

This trip with the Widows Club marked a big step for me. When Tommy was alive, our lives seemed to revolve around traveling. I was either meeting him on a business trip or we were taking a vacation. Every weekend, Tommy and I had something planned. Both of us traveled independently for business, so we knew how important it was to spend the weekends together—whether it was going to Florida to entertain clients or driving out to Long Island to play golf or visit friends and family. That was how Tommy lived, always on the go. After he was killed, that stopped. My life stopped. In the first year, I didn't leave town to go anywhere for more than a few days, much less to go on a vacation.

I knew I needed this getaway. It had been a year without Tommy, and now there was another year stretching out ahead of me with no end in sight. Over the past six months I'd taken on the additional pressure of planning a memorial golf outing to raise money in Tommy's name. Planning the event, which took place two weeks before the anniversary, had been a labor of love with all our family and friends rallying around. It was a great opportunity for all of us to remember and honor Tommy, to do something positive, after such a sad year.

During the ceremony held after the golf outing, I had the job of introducing a video of my husband's life. By the time it was my turn to step up to the microphone, I was ready to back out. There were over three hundred people in the room. I didn't know what to say to them, how to tell them what this meant to me.

"I can't do this," I told my friend who was sitting next to me.

My friend told me: "Think of Tommy, he would want you to do this, do it for him."

I had no idea what I was going to say. Walking up to the podium, all I could think about was that everyone's eyes were on me. Be the dignified widow, I told myself. Say the right thing. I was so nervous I nearly turned on my heels and went back to my seat.

I got up to the podium. The room was silent. You could have heard a pin drop. I opened my mouth and the words came out.

"Wow, I haven't talked into a microphone since I got fired from Burger King."

Everyone in that room burst into laughter, and I sensed their relief that I hadn't just collapsed in front of the podium. The funny thing is, I'd had no intention of telling the joke; it came out of nowhere. I truly believe that it was Tommy who put the idea in my head.

But now that the event was over, I felt bereft. The tournament had given me a purpose, something to focus on, a reason to get out of bed in the morning. What was I going to do now? I didn't know how I was going to get through my days.

By going on this trip with the Widows Club, I was forcing myself to go beyond survival mode. I was breaking the routine of getting up, going to work, making it to the end of the day, repeat and repeat and repeat. By leaving town with the widows, I was making time for some of the things Tommy and I had prioritized in our marriage—travel and friends. It wasn't that I didn't feel guilty for doing something good for myself, because I did. It was almost as if I wasn't keeping faith with Tommy's death by going away. But even so, I knew I was stumbling into something positive, and what's more, I was doing it in good company.

3 · It Would Be Wrong Not To . . .

Julia, Ann, Pattie, Claudia

Two days after the anniversary, we found ourselves standing in line at the check-in for our flight to Scottsdale. Despite all our carefully made plans to go away together, none of us had taken it for granted that we'd actually make it to this point. For so many months, our lives had been dominated by apprehension about the anniversary. And now what? What happened next?

We can remember how surreal it felt. The intense planning and dread leading up to the anniversary and funeral had made it seem impossible that there would be a day after the eleventh. How could it be possible to live through this and come out the other side? But now here we were. It was a feeling almost of guilt for being here—because how could anyone continue to exist after such experiences? We watched as everyone around us went on his or her way, shuttling around the airport. The world had returned to a normality we had no connection to. All we wanted to do was to lie down and go to sleep, to shut everything out. We were exhausted, hauling our bags behind us.

It was Claudia's suggestion to upgrade. "Why don't we see if they'll bump us up? I've definitely got enough miles to cover it." More than anything right now, Claudia needed to sleep.

We protested. Those were her miles. It was too generous.

But Claudia insisted, because when else was she going to use them? Like the rest of us, Claudia only operated in terms of today—we could no longer plan or save for a future we couldn't envision. And anyway, Claudia argued, upgrading would be "so Bart."

And then Claudia said the magical words: "Ladies, it would be wrong not to."

It would be wrong not to. In all the self-help books on grief, we'd never found words that offered the solace of those six words.

SOON AFTER TAKEOFF, Claudia fell asleep. As she slept, she began to dream. She saw images of the Manhattan skyline flashing outside the window, and felt the plane plummet, nose-diving toward the city. Soon, the plane's wings were slicing through the buildings of Fifth Avenue, heading for her office and St. Patrick's Cathedral, where she and Bart had gotten married. Claudia was terrified, unable to breathe or scream. She knew she was going to die. But in that moment of realization, her fear vanished and she felt only serenity. It would be okay. She was going to see Bart.

At the moment of impact Claudia woke up.

She turned to the others and told them about the dream, and how real it had been. Her moment of calm and resignation was familiar, not just from our dreams, but from our waking lives too. We carried around with us an ever-present awareness of mortality. Sometimes we felt completely overwhelmed by the fragility of life, but mostly this awareness created a kind of fearlessness. There was so much that would never be within our powers to influence. In the past, we'd made so many plans for the future—we'd saved, prepared, plotted—but now we recognized that none of it mattered. It didn't make any difference. There were some outcomes that would always be beyond our control.

Did it really matter that we were flying on Friday the thirteenth? We even joked about it when we booked our flights. It didn't make a difference. We didn't feel as if flying on another day would keep us from harm. What did we have to be scared about? Our husbands had been killed because they went to work one morning. Safety was an illusion.

"Oh God," said Julia. "What a headline that would be! 'Four September 11 Widows Killed in a Plane Crash on Friday the Thirteenth.'"

Nothing like a little gallows humor to lift a widow's mood.

WE TALKED ABOUT how much we needed to hear from The Boys. One year ago, overnight, communication had ended. No e-mails, no calls, no response. The silence was audible.

"I have these dreams that Bart's ignoring me," Claudia said. "I can see him in the next room, and I'm banging on the glass window and he won't turn around. Or sometimes I'm calling his cell phone, and I can see him look at his caller ID, and he won't answer."

We'd all had dreams where we could see him, and where we called out and he wouldn't turn around.

"Did you ever have the dream where he visits you and you're so surprised to see him? And he can't understand why you're so excited. You tell him, 'I'm excited because you're alive! I thought you were dead, but you're alive!' And then he acts as if nothing's happened, brushing you off when you try to reach for him?"

Pattie had a dream where Caz was alive but he was with someone else. When she asked him about the other woman, he couldn't understand why she was so upset.

There were the dreams where we just felt his presence so strongly.

When Julia first slept in her bed alone again, over a month after Tommy's death, she dreamt he was with her.

"We were on vacation, and I asked him, 'Tommy, how the hell are you here?' He told me, 'I got a pass to get out!' We spent the day together and in the evening we went to bed and it was in our bed. Tommy was behind me, spooning me, and I remember lying there and the feeling of relief. He was back. I was safe again. I said to him, 'I wish you could stay with me; I need you to come back.' Then he whispered into my ear, 'Julia, I'm not with you physically but I'm with you every single day,' and then he kissed me. The kiss was so real that I woke up. I felt that kiss. Tommy was there; he came to visit me."

Ann told us about her dream where she was skiing with Ward and the children, even Elizabeth, her daughter, who is unable to walk. It was a perfect crystal-clear blue day, not too cold, no wind.

"As we were skiing downhill side by side, Ward started picking up speed and moving farther and farther away from us. I called out to him, 'Ward, slow down, the kids can't keep up with you.' Ward said: 'I'm just going to go on ahead; you guys are going to be fine.'"

By this time all four of us were crying. We agreed that whether the dream was bad or good, when we woke up, more than anything else we wanted to go back to sleep again, just to spend more time with him.

OUTSIDE THE SCOTTSDALE terminal, while we were waiting in line for a cab, an old beaten up white limo pulled up alongside the curb. The driver stuck his head out, asked if we wanted a ride to our hotel.

"Well, it *would* be wrong not to . . . ," we said, smiling at one another.

AT THE HOTEL we were sharing two rooms, but there had been no discussion about who would room with whom. Claudia and Pattie went in together. Ann and Julia took the other room. The ease with which this fell into place is worth noting. A widow mostly spends her days moving against the current. It's hard work, and it tires her, but makes her so thankful for any small opportunity to go with the flow. When we were together, this would often happen and we would notice it.

A bottle of champagne was waiting for us from Kathleen, Bart's sister, so we took it out onto Claudia and Pattie's terrace, commenting on how generous the gesture was. Claudia explained how supportive Bart's family had been. This thoughtful gift reinforced how blessed she was to have the Ruggieres.

The views from the terrace were breathtaking, the landscape of the desert immediately affecting us—its massiveness and purity, the dryness of the air and the magic of the light. The quality of the place struck even Pattie—who grew up by the water and preferred to be near the ocean. But the mysterious desert had a quiet power of its own, not the same as the ocean, but just as majestic. It settled us, grounded us. Pattie, who was once hesitant to leave her home, found herself trying to figure out if she could stay a few more days. Four days wasn't going to be long enough to appreciate the spiritual nature of this environment.

. . .

THAT EVENING, WE had dinner in the hotel's restaurant. Our Boys would have loved this place. We talked about how hard it was to be here without them. We were immersed in talking about our husbands, about the anniversary, the guilt of survival. What would it be like when we got back and there wasn't the focus on commemorating the eleventh?

Claudia reminded us of one of her favorite quotes, given to her by her aunt Barbara's mother, who had also been widowed at a young age: "Living well is the best revenge."

We toasted to that.

Then we called it an early night and sank into comfortable cool hotel sheets where his side of the bed didn't exist.

THE NEXT MORNING, we made our way down to the gym—our first experience with the Widows Club's personal trainer, Julia Collins. After a thirty-minute warm-up, she had us sprinting on the treadmill, the speed cranked up to 8.5.

"Just for two minutes," she promised. Two minutes later, the speed went down but the incline went up to 12. Then the incline went down and the speed went up. Julia called it interval training. We called it torture. Claudia reminded Julia that she'd barely worked out for an entire year—she had lost so much weight already, what was the point?—all the while racing to stay on without being thrown off.

But Julia kept us in line. Maybe if we could keep up we would get to look as good as Julia did, with her toned abs and defined upper arms. So despite the screaming pains in our chests and the burning sensation in our legs, we kept on running.

Although the rest of us found it hard to believe, Julia had only recently started working out again. After Tommy was killed, she'd given up going to the gym altogether. Working out was something that she and Tommy often did together, and she didn't want to face it alone. As much as she knew that working out would be good for her, it was hard to imagine anything could make her feel better. Julia kept saying she wanted to go back to the gym, but she kept failing—never doing something today when she could put it off until tomorrow.

This wasn't like the old Julia, not at all. Before Tommy was killed, she actually prided herself on her energy and efficiency. She usually worked out every day. She was a hard worker and a good multitasker, always with her files, her desk, and her apartment in order. But this too had changed. Every day, Julia's "to do" list got a little longer, with nothing checked off it. It was too exhausting to work up the necessary enthusiasm. The practical details of her life began to trickle through her fingers. Simple tasks that she'd taken for granted before—paying bills, balancing a checkbook, doing laundry, keeping the apartment clean—things that should come naturally, took so much energy and concentration that it was always easier to sit on the couch and watch TV.

"If it wasn't for friends and family coming by to help," Julia pointed out, "I would have needed to have the couch surgically removed from my backside."

Along with her luggage for the Scottsdale trip, Julia brought her big tote bag of outstanding paperwork. Inside were forms from the Federal Emergency Management Agency, the Red Cross, and the Victims Compensation Fund. There were forms from insurance companies; letters from attorneys, from the IRS, Workers' Compensation, and the list went on and on. Julia would rather do anything than face those forms, so she kept sympathy cards in the bag as well. That way, she could write thank-you notes to the people who had remembered Tommy on the first anniversary, instead of confronting the reams of forms with all the questions she didn't ever want to answer.

"Every time I try to do one of the tasks on my checklist, it's like I'm having to face the reality that Tommy's gone all over again," Julia explained, and we told her we knew how that felt.

A year later, it wasn't just Julia who was burdened with a stack of paperwork as long as her arm. There was so much left on all our "to do" lists—the ugly reality of having a husband who was murdered. With or without a body, we were still filling out endless forms sent by attorneys, insurance companies, and charities. Here we were making the most important decisions of our lives and the hardest part was that our husbands weren't around to discuss these decisions with us.

"In a marriage, if you make the right decision, then that's great," Ann pointed out, "but if you make the wrong decision, then, hey, at least you know you're in it together and you'll figure it out. Now I'm doing this alone, and if I mess this up, I could mess up the entire future for my family. The stakes are as high as they'll ever be. And I'm putting even more pressure on myself because I want to honor Ward and do right by him."

Julia's bag made its first appearance on the plane out of New York, where it was left at her feet while she slept and talked to the rest of us. Now when we went down to the hotel pool in the afternoon, the bag came with us. That bag became the joke of the vacation; it was half the size of Julia. Maybe that was how she got her upper arms so defined.

WE WERE LEARNING a lot about one another on this trip. We were identifying all the similarities in our suffering—the complete despondency, the moments when you wondered if you were losing your mind, the anger at being forced into this life we hated. We talked about all the sleepless nights, and about all the days when we couldn't get out of bed.

Then there were the memories that came back to us, all the crazy things he used to do, that we never stopped to think about when he was alive, and that now seemed the most meaningful things in the world.

In the heat of the mid-afternoon, waiters appeared, passing around ice-cream bars.

"I probably shouldn't be eating this in my bathing suit," someone said.

"As Caz would say, 'If you can't tone it, tan it,'" said Pattie.

We ate our ice creams with relish while watching the local iguanas basking in the sun, each wizened creature slowly roaming around in the desert heat before coming to a perfect halt again.

LATER THAT AFTERNOON, we checked in at the spa. Claudia, taking on the role of ringleader, had booked massages for all of us. She explained that deep tissue massages allowed her to feel a physical pain, something her mind could comprehend and control. She was living with such emotional pain, but it wasn't tangible to her. She needed to feel a physical hurt, to match the internal anguish.

At the spa we were asked if we preferred a male or female therapist. We all said in unison, "Male, please."

If we were going to have a choice, then yes, definitely, we might as well have a male therapist. We didn't mind admitting we wanted to know what it would feel like to be touched by a man again. We had gone from being in loving, intimate relationships to being alone in the blink of an eye. To have no one touch you for a year, when you were used to being physically affectionate with someone daily, was completely unnatural. Although it was a poor substitute, the choice between a male and a female therapist was an easy one to make.

ON OUR WAY to the gym the next morning, the hotel's friendly doorman introduced himself. We introduced ourselves and for the rest of the trip he remembered our names. Of course, he had no way of knowing how much we dreaded questions like "So where are you from, what are you doing here?"

More and more, we found we had to hesitate before telling the truth about our situation to strangers—not because we didn't want others to know that our husbands had been killed, but because we knew that our story, our losses, would shock them and bring them unhappiness. It was impossible to tell people in an offhanded way, so we had to be sure we could follow through, because it wasn't like we could drop the bomb and just walk away. It generally meant tears; it meant opening up your life to someone.

And sure enough . . .

"So where are you ladies from?"

We told him we were from New York City, assuming he'd put two and two together. It seemed so obvious to us that we were four widows recovering after the anniversary.

"You mean, like the *Sex and the City* girls?" said the doorman. Okay, maybe we wouldn't have to tell him, at least not yet.

"No, more like the NO Sex and the City girls," we replied and shot him four big smiles before we went on our way.

But it wasn't always easy to withhold the truth. The day before, Ann was getting a manicure and pedicure and the technician doing her nails asked her, "So where are you from?"

Ann hesitated. "New York."

"Oh, did you know anyone who was killed in the attacks?"

Sitting face to face with the woman a foot and a half away, Ann knew she couldn't lie, and all of a sudden she found herself crying in front of a complete stranger. The woman opened up and started crying too. She told Ann that she knew how hard it was, that she was a single mother raising two children on her own. Most people have a cross to bear. By sharing their stories, when asked, Ann and this woman quickly formed a bond of empathy.

And then there were other times when it was kinder to hold back. On Sunday, we gathered in the hotel's restaurant for brunch. As we sat, reading the *New York Times,* Claudia was looking through the Sunday Styles section and noticed that sitting across the room from us were a beautiful African-American couple featured in the wedding announcement section. It was Pattie's idea to send over a bottle of champagne by way of congratulations. When the waiter took it over, the couple raised their glasses in our direction in acknowledgment. Soon afterward, they came over to say hello and to thank us. They were from New York; in fact, they lived on the East Side, on the same street as Claudia. A nice coincidence. Then the groom asked: "So what brings you ladies here this weekend?"

There was a pause. Finally Claudia answered.

"Girls' trip!" she said, and no one added any further information. There was no need to tell the couple. They radiated happiness. We knew that if we told them, they would only be sad for us. We could all remember how happy we'd been the morning after our weddings, and why would we want to ruin that for them? It's a very strange thing to have to announce that you're a September 11 widow, as if in doing so you could pass on your bad luck.

THAT EVENING WE decided to stay in. It was Sunday, usually the worst day of the week for us. This was the day we would always spend with our husbands—going to mass, to the beach, playing a round of golf, watching football, reading the *Times,* preparing a big dinner, or commiserating about the Sunday night blues. Now Sunday was the day we felt most alone, when we missed our husbands more than ever.

So we ordered in junk food, pizza and grilled cheese, and watched *The Sopranos*, just the four of us.

. . .

ON OUR LAST evening in Scottsdale, Pattie's cousin, who lives in the area, arranged for us to take a helicopter ride over the city. We were all excited—Julia had been in a helicopter once, but for the rest of us, this was a new experience.

Julia climbed in confidently beside the pilot. The rest of us got in the back. The blades started to spin and we lifted off into a high wind that rocked us back and forth as we floated over the buildings below, the roar of the blades in our ears. The pilot began pointing out landmarks—Camelback Mountain, with its giant hump to give it the name. He tipped the helicopter to one side to give us a better view of the Scottsdale stadium, the rows of seats no bigger than squares of chewing gum. The pilot told us we were about fifty stories up. At that moment, we were forced to confront what it meant to be 105 stories in the air, more than twice as high as we were now. As far as we traveled from New York, we could return to that place in an instant.

Throughout the flight, Julia kept up her conversation with the pilot, asking questions, pretending to play with the controls, making him laugh. By the time we turned back to the heliport, the sun had gone down, and the lights of the city in the middle of the desert were like an oasis pool reflecting stars.

We said our good-byes and got into the car. Julia still felt exhilarated from the flight, such a contrast to so many weeks of misery. As we pulled away, she rolled down the window, stuck her head out, and shouted to the pilot: "Love you, mean it!"

Julia, Claudia, Ann, and Pattie

We began finding our way into this new year, the second year without him. After returning from Scottsdale in September, we started e-mailing and calling one another every day.

Every time we got together, we were already planning for the next meeting, greedy to spend more time together. Our calendars began to fill up with reasons to be in one another's company. The Widows Club had become a priority. We would smile just to see another widow's name on the caller ID, looking forward to meeting that evening, to saying all the things we wanted and needed to say.

Being in one another's company in Scottsdale had brought us glimpses of how pain and hope could commingle. The relief of having survived would bubble to the surface when we were together, and for the moments it lasted, it was miraculous—we were four women who traveled quickly from tears to laughter and back again. Maybe if we spent more time together, this sense of connectedness to joy as well as to sadness would begin to seep into our everyday lives.

We began to realize that by helping one another we gave ourselves a respite from always being the one who needed to be helped. Helping one another felt healing. We could take turns being strong and being weak.

Ann e-mailed everyone the quote that she kept posted above her desk: "Some take life experiences and build out of them something constructive and lasting. Others collapse under the weight of that burden and walk away, bitter and miserable, having learned or accomplished nothing. It is up to us to build from the wreckage of loss or walk away broken and hopeless."

We knew that fate had dealt us this terrible blow, but we all wanted to believe that our reaction to this was within our control. We shared a commitment to positively influence what had happened to us. We had to keep tipping the scales. Even if we couldn't overcome this, we needed to believe we could learn to tolerate it better, to cope better. This was our pact. Not to pull back into despair. Life was too precious for that. Our husbands' lives had already been senselessly cut short. If our lives were destroyed because of what happened, then we would know that the terrorists had truly won.

We were always talking to our friends and family members about the Widows Club: "I'm doing this with the widows, I'm doing that with the widows . . ." "All you ever talk about is the Widows Club! Do you have to call it that?"

The word "widow" not only didn't bother us, it was the most direct description we had. It linked us to our husbands; it linked us to one another. But the word seemed to bother other people. So we shortened the Widows Club to the WC. As in: "I'm doing this with the WC, I'm doing that with the WC."

We did sense people's relief that we had found this new source of support. Friends and family were willing to do anything for us, but there were some things they simply couldn't provide—they couldn't walk in our shoes, they couldn't truly know. Pattie's brother put it best when he said: "It's like your family was one leg of the stool trying to support you. Your friends were the second leg, but the stool was still wobbling. The WC provides that third leg, and it's bringing you some degree of stability."

. . .

THAT FALL, PATTIE was spending most of the weekday working hours in the office. The bank that she worked for was launching a real estate fund. This was a new venture for the company and people were energized and focused on the product. Up to this point, Pattie had been using work as a crutch to get herself through the day. Now she wanted to become excited by this new challenge, to use the project as a way to get engaged with her work again.

But there was a major drawback. During the long due diligence process, Pattie was part of the group that reviewed each sector along with the status of the economy for that sector—and almost every aspect under review involved making some reference to September 11.

Pattie found herself in meetings where her colleagues would be discussing the square footage of office space lost in the Towers, the number of companies involved, the demand deficit, the price depreciation. Pattie would have to sit, silently raging and biting her tongue. Were these people for real? Didn't they know we lost more than just square footage that day? Pattie had crossed over into a place of total sanity, seeing through the bullshit facts and figures to the true meanings and values of things, and she couldn't come back again. She couldn't relate to such trivial discussions. Are the people you love safe? she wanted to ask the team gathered around the table. If the answer is yes, then that's all that's important.

But she would have to listen to everyone talk about the sprinkler systems, the safety guidelines, the building structure. Now all she could think about was Caz, how much he must have suffered. The questions flooded back. How? Why?

Finally, when asked her opinion, she'd ask, "Could you repeat the question?," her eyes glazing over.

As soon as the meeting was over, she'd escape to call Ann or Claudia or Julia.

"NO, YOU'RE NOT going crazy," we could reassure one another when the call came through. Those were the days that our office doors would shut intermittently for a breakdown over the telephone. There were so many reasons to call.

"Am I losing my mind? Every time I look at the clock it's eleven minutes after the hour." "Oh my God. I do that too."

When Claudia's boss told her he just got a new Porsche 911, all she could think was "Can't they give that car a new name?"

"I almost tackled this guy on the street the other day," Julia told us, "because he looked like Tommy from behind. So I ran up to him to see him from the front. What was I expecting?"

There was someone to call after we'd just come back from a meeting with yet another advisor, yet another attorney. There was the relief of calling one another afterward with the words "Done, done, and done!" because we'd checked another task off the endless "to do" list. There was someone to share how surreal it felt to get over these hurdles we'd dreaded for so long. And to understand how sad it made us feel. Because no matter how hard we worked, no matter how bravely we did the best that we could, none of it made any difference. He still wasn't there when we came home at the end of the day. He wasn't coming back.

WE ROLLED OUR eyes as we went over the things people said to try to console us—as if we would ever be consoled.

"Maybe it was meant to be," they told us. As if the murder of thousands of men and women, just because they went to work that morning or got on a plane, was part of God's great design for the universe.

"Don't worry, you're young and beautiful, you'll meet someone else. . . ." As if a husband was someone you could just leave behind or replace, when the shadow of his absence was walking alongside you every second of every day.

And the one Julia, Pattie, and Claudia hated the most: "Well, at least you didn't have kids. . . ." There was no good reply to that.

Most comments were forgivable, some very hard to forgive. One of Claudia's customers told her: "You think it's tough being a thirty-two-year-old widow? Try being thirty-five and single in this town!"

In any other circumstance Claudia would have given this woman a piece of her mind, but the woman was a customer, so Claudia suffered in silence.

Julia told us about how Tommy always used to tell her, "Zip it! Zip it!" when he wanted her to stop talking before she put her foot in her mouth. Now when people gave her crazy advice, she'd say silently to herself, "Zip it! Zip it!" Before long, all four of us found ourselves muttering the words under our breath.

IN OCTOBER, WE were all attending the benefit that Claudia was helping to organize—the event was to raise money for the Bart J. Ruggiere Memorial Foundation. So many friends and family were attending the dinner and silent auction.

Bart, we knew by now, loved any opportunity to get dressed up and put on his tux and in his honor the evening was going to be a black tie event—this was a man who knew that life was special and worth dressing well for. Up to this point, it had been very hard for the four of us to imagine making an effort to look glamorous. Why? What would be the point? Who was going to see us? But this was different. Claudia was going to wear a stunning beaded gown for the occassion. The rest of us wanted to make an extra effort for Claudia and to pay tribute to Bart. Pattie decided to go the extra mile and booked an appointment to get her hair done at a Madison Avenue salon, followed by a complimentary makeover. Afterward, she ran over to Julia's, where Ann had already arrived to finish getting ready.

Julia and Ann opened the door to a vision of Pattie as they'd never seen her before—glasses off, hair down, and makeup on.

"Oh my God, Pattie, you look like a movie star." We knew Caz would have loved to see Pattie like this. He would have bragged about how gorgeous she looked. Now we were the ones doing the bragging on his behalf.

Without discussing it, Ann, Julia, and Pattie had all picked out black dresses to wear. Ann was going back and forth between two dresses, her hair blown out, heels on. In many ways, it could have been any other evening in New York City, three friends getting dressed to go out to a swanky event together and asking the usual girly questions— "Does my underwear show in this?" "Which shoes shall I wear with this dress?" "Can I borrow your lip-liner?"—but as always, there was the contrast to the carefree moments. When we were with the WC, we quickly seesawed, veering from excitement to reality in seconds.

This was the first time Ann and Pattie had been to Julia's apartment, and Julia wanted to share with them Tommy's items that had been re-covered from Ground Zero. She pulled out the precious cardboard box that contained the plastic bag filled with his belongings. When she opened the bag, the smell was all too familiar to Pattie—that powerful combination of toxins and metals that had lingered in her Brooklyn home just across the river from the attacks for weeks afterward. Inside was Tommy's briefcase, his Day-Timer, computer, calculator, check-book, credit cards, even the cash from his pocket—all the things he had packed up before leaving his desk. Julia felt almost guilty showing Ann and Pattie these things. She had so much. The other two had received nothing—no body, no possessions.

The only consolation Julia could offer was that having these things hadn't brought her any closer to understanding what happened to Tommy. She was still confused, just as sad, equally bewildered.

"How could these things come back and Tommy couldn't? How could he be gone but his belongings remain?" So many months later, none of this even began to make sense.

THAT NIGHT AT the fund-raiser, Claudia wanted to give a speech to thank people for coming and for their generosity. It was a daunting prospect. She had been so busy planning and preparing for the event that she didn't write the speech until the night before.

Just before Claudia went up to the podium, she realized she couldn't be sure how she was going to make it through to the end of the speech. The room was at capacity, over three hundred people, and she was con-vinced that when she looked up and saw everyone she would lose what-ever composure she had. But as she walked toward the stage, Claudia found herself buoyed up by an unexpected strength, a self-confidence that arrived like a gift. She'd been through unimaginably tough experi-ences; she could do this. Bart was with her, telling her what to say.

She'd written her speech as if it were a letter from Bart. Everyone in the room knew that Bart was famous for staying in touch, and after thirteen months, everyone needed to hear from him.

"Sorry you haven't heard from me in a while, but I'm having an amazing time up here." The words came loud and clear. "My days are split between the slopes of St. Moritz in the morning and taking out my old wooden speedboat in the afternoon. Sal, Pop Pop, Joe Pop, Julius, and I have big Sunday pasta dinners. There's an incredible selection of Super Tuscan wine, and Sinatra drops by to sing us a few tunes. . . . Also, in case you're wondering, there's an unlimited supply of closet space. . . . Please tell the WC not to worry, that Caz, Tommy, and Ward send their love. . . . Tell everyone that even though they may not know it, I'm watching them and appreciate the donations—proceeds go toward high school scholarships for inner city children and an adaptive sports center for people with physical and mental disabilities. It will help others to live life to the fullest, something I was able to do because of all of you. Well, I've got to run. I'm late for a gin rummy lesson with Sal. Tell your mother he sends his love. I love and miss you all. God bless."

Claudia nailed the speech. When she looked up from her notes, there wasn't a dry eye in the house. It was her first and only standing ovation. She knew Bart was up there looking down, saying to himself, "Not too shabby . . ."

THAT FALL, THE WC started signing off our calls, conversations, and e-mails with Julia's words to the helicopter pilot: "Love you, mean it." In e-mails, this quickly became abbreviated to LUMI. What had started as a lighthearted good-bye to a stranger became something with much more meaning. The more we said the words, the more we realized how much we *did* love one another and how grateful we each were to have the other women in our lives.

We'd been so wounded that we'd had to protect ourselves. To survive, we'd sucked in all our resources, isolated ourselves, and inevitably shut down our hearts in the process. But feeling this love for one another meant our hearts were beginning to open again. It was a risk—love brought with it the ever-present possibility of loss. But this was a risk worth taking. Our husbands knew how much we loved them, and knowing this had helped in our healing process. More than ever, we understood how important it was to put love at the center of our lives.

"Love you, mean it" started to extend to our friends, our family members, all the people we needed to show our appreciation to. We wanted to tell them how much they meant to us. If anything happened to one of us, or to one of them, we wanted to make sure they knew how important they were to us. We wanted the last thing we'd said to them to be an expression of gratitude.

The phrase quickly became contagious. Our friends and family started to use it too. "Love you, mean it" made it easier for people to express their affection for one another—"I love you" is a powerful statement, one that people usually reserve for a select few. Even people who might be apprehensive about expressing their emotions began to use LUMI. To us, the message was clear: Love is a gift. Share it.

5 · Ann and Ward

Ann:

That fall, when I returned from Scottsdale, I took off my wedding and engagement rings and put them away. I'd already decided that I would remove them after the anniversary.

I knew I needed to pick a time and stick to it. Friends and family kept advising me that I should wear the rings on a necklace, or have them reset, or put the engagement ring on the other hand as a cocktail ring. They told me I should lock them away for when it came time for my sons to be married. They told me I should sell them and use the money to buy something special. This was such a personal decision, and I wanted it to be my decision, not something I'd done because others told me to. And I was afraid that if I waited years to take them off, when I finally got up the courage, it would be too much of a statement.

It was hard. I'd found such comfort in seeing the rings on my hand—a reminder of how much I'd been loved, that I'd had this amazing connection with Ward, and that our bond was continuing after death. The rings gave me a degree of protection; they meant I didn't have to deal with the fact that I was single. Sometimes the sight of them on my finger would momentarily trick me into believing I was still a married woman, with all the security that confers. But after a while, I began to feel as if I was fooling others and myself by wearing the rings. I wasn't married anymore. I was widowed. And as time went by, I needed to see some outward symbol of that change.

I knew that removing my rings didn't mean that I missed him any less, or loved him any less.

In the end, the removing of my rings became a very private ceremony. I looked at them before I took them off. I put them in the ring boxes and snapped the lids shut. I placed them in the safety deposit box. I took one last look and closed the lid. I turned the key in the lock.

When you get married, there's that moment in the ceremony where the priest declares you husband and wife. But for me, there had been no single moment when I became a widow. Instead there was a long, agonizing dawning that had lasted many, many months. Sliding the rings off my finger was just another step in the slow and painful acceptance of the completely unacceptable.

WHEN I FIRST met Ward, I was not yet thirty, a recently divorced single mom with a beautiful two-year-old boy to care for. For two years I'd been living in Rye, a commuter town forty minutes from Manhattan, a place with white picket fences, detached family houses, quiet suburban streets, and good schools. At that time, I was emerging from the difficulties of my marriage ending, and coming into a good phase. It had been tough managing on my own, but I was doing it. I was beginning to believe that I could handle raising my son, TJ, by myself. I was maintaining the house, making it our home, paying the bills. I was doing well in my career, working as a financial advisor in Manhattan, earning promotions. I wasn't just handling this, I was beginning to actually succeed at it, and this gave me a newfound strength and confidence in myself.

I'd gotten engaged for the first time a few years out of college. I was twenty-three when I met him. I was twenty-four when we married. From the very beginning of the engagement I would look at him and wonder why I couldn't get along better with this man that I felt I loved. We fought a lot. Even though I had my reservations, I was so inexperienced, so swept up in the excitement of the preparations for the wedding, that I told myself, Maybe when we're married, things will get better. Besides, once the invitations had gone out, I knew I didn't have the courage to call off the big event.

Within two years of marriage, I discovered I was pregnant. I was scared, I felt unprepared, far too young. When our son, TJ, was born, we decided to move to Rye, a great place to raise a child. By now, my husband and I were arguing constantly and had no common ground anymore. When he left me, I felt humiliated; I thought I had failed. I was raised to believe that marriage was a lifelong commitment. In retrospect, I can see that by leaving me, he gave me a gift. He gave me a way out, a new life I wouldn't have asked for, but once it was mine to accept and deal with, I was better off.

He moved to a nearby town. I decided to stay in Rye. TJ was a little over two. I don't mind admitting that I went through a period where I was very lonely. Rye is very much a couples' town, where people tend to become entrenched in their existing friendships and don't feel the need to look beyond the confines of their established social circle. My parents lived five and a half hours away, in upstate New York. I was alone, but determined to make the best of the situation. I thought, I can either sit here and feel sorry for myself, or I can get up and do something about it.

I went through a period of post-heartbreak self-improvement. No more wasting lunch hours—I took classes at the gym every day instead. I attacked my work, taking on more responsibility and succeeding. I spent my evenings reading—Henry David Thoreau's *Walden* and my favorite, Ernest Hemingway. In an effort to meet new people, I joined a biking club. A friend from work introduced me to some of her friends living in the area, and an old friend from college moved to the vicinity. I started to have a social life, a newfound sense of community. I also had people to go out with in the hopes of meeting someone special.

ONE SATURDAY IN early summer, I was going on a sixty-mile cycle ride through the Connecticut countryside with my biking club. It was a great day—we cycled through the lush, rolling hills under cloudless skies. Along the way, I was meeting interesting people who seemed just as interested in getting to know me as I was in getting to know them. One of the club members invited me over for an afternoon pool party and barbecue after the ride, and of course I accepted. I stayed for an hour or two, and then had to leave early as I had promised to meet another friend for drinks.

I was running late, so I decided to stop by the bar and tell my friend to wait while I went home to freshen up. After having biked sixty miles and gone swimming, I desperately needed to shower, blow dry my hair, put makeup on, and change my clothes.

"Have one quick drink first," my friend insisted. One quick drink somehow turned into a couple of drinks, despite my disheveled appearance.

About an hour later, my friend grabbed my arm and told me she wanted to introduce me to someone. She led me over to meet a guy she was interested in. Her crush happened to be with his friend Ward. For the next half hour, Ward and I got to know each other a little bit. I remember the exact navy sweater he was wearing. He was tall, six foot, a big guy who made me feel small at five foot four. He had a great smile and a definite twinkle in his eyes. Very attractive. I remember Ward telling me he worked for a sports magazine specializing in golf and had just returned from a trip to Pebble Beach. I remember the conversation we had about my son and his brother, also named TJ. I remember forgetting about my appearance. I remember touching his arm, so unlike me, but almost an involuntary response. We each went back to our respective friends, but first found out each other's plans for the evening.

On my way home, I had a giddy feeling. I showered and got changed, selecting my outfit carefully, before calling my friend to convince her to go to the bar where I knew Ward would be. He was there. The two of us worked our way into a corner and talked. There were so many things to discuss; it was as if we couldn't say the things we needed to say fast enough. There was a naturalness, a flow to the conversation that convinced me I hadn't been wrong to hope this was someone special. But when it came time to leave, and Ward asked me to go with him, I knew it was too soon. I rejoined my friend and he left for the evening.

ABOUT A WEEK later, I was on a date in a small neighborhood pub. Ward was there too, also on a date. Within minutes, he was standing at my table, leaving his date sitting alone. I introduced Ward to my date, and without pausing to ask permission, Ward sat down right next to me in the booth. The men proceeded to talk about golf and their common interests for a few minutes. Before he left, Ward told me he'd been trying to call me but couldn't find my number in the book. I told him exactly how I was listed in the phone book.

My date was stunned. "Did he just ask you out right in front of me?"

I spent the rest of the evening trying to stop myself from smiling too broadly. My heart was soaring. I could hardly wait to get home to see if Ward had called. The minute I got in, I hit the answering machine message button and heard his voice.

We planned to meet for dinner the following Friday. Ward picked me up, and when he turned on the car stereo and my favorite Grateful Dead song was playing, we knew we shared common musical tastes. Before he pulled out of the driveway, he kissed me. A very good kiss.

"Just wanted to get that out of the way so we didn't have to think about it all through dinner."

Over dinner I learned more about Ward. He told me about his father's death, two years ago, how it had been a turning point for him, one that had helped him to define himself as an adult. He was twenty-four at the time, living in Aspen, Colorado, working as a ski and golf instructor. His father died so quickly, Ward didn't get home in time to say good-bye. His dad was only forty-eight. Right away, Ward moved back to Rye to be closer to his family.

Ward also told me about his grandfather, a man with such a positive outlook on life, and in whose footsteps Ward hoped to follow.

"Like PopPops always said, 'Life is not a dress rehearsal. . . .' That's the way I plan to live my life."

Ward grew up in Rye—his mother was raised there, his grandparents lived there, as well as his uncles. He was a gifted athelete, which meant a lot in that town. The country club remained a major component of his social life. People often referred to him as the mayor of Rye, because wherever he went he ran into someone he'd known for years.

The thought flashed through my mind—why does this handsome, confident, popular, younger man want to date me? He was twenty-six. I was twenty-nine. And apart from anything else, I didn't know anyone at the country club. I'd been too busy commuting, working hard at my career, paying the mortgage, and looking after my son to do much socializing.

But Ward did want to date me. Life moved forward and it was wonderful. My new boyfriend combined a very attractive humility with radiant confidence. Ward knew what he wanted, and didn't hesitate to go for it—even if it meant asking me out on a date while I was on a date with someone else. Even if it meant incurring comments and looks from friends and family members who couldn't immediately understand why he wanted to involve himself with a single mother and her small child. But around the same time Ward fell in love with me, he also fell in love with TJ. The bond between them was amazing to watch—instant and mutual.

Ward loved to laugh; he had an exuberance about him that was infectious. He enjoyed nothing more than instigating a gathering of friends, and people always wanted to be around Ward. I soon got to know all of his many friends and became a part of their circle. While I wouldn't describe myself as a shy person, even so, I was much more reserved than my husband. I preferred to sit in the corner during a party and have one quality conversation with someone rather than talking to everyone in the room, as Ward would do. It was Ward who reached out and made new friends. I was the one people turned to when they wanted to have more of a one-on-one conversation. We complemented each other in this respect.

Two years later, in 1994, Ward and I were married, on a sweltering July day, by the waters of Long Island Sound. TJ was our ring bearer. After the ceremony and reception, Ward and I literally sailed away into the sunset on a friend's boat. We'd planned our honeymoon around the British Open. My new husband was an eight handicap golfer—I was learning to love Ward's favorite pastime and was determined to improve my game.

. . .

FROM THE BEGINNING of our marriage, Ward and I tried to have children. I had two miscarriages followed by a year of being unable to conceive. When I became pregnant, and we discovered I was having twins, we couldn't have been happier. We'd wanted a big family, and now we were going to have two new additions at the same time.

When the twins were born, full term and perfectly healthy, a boy and a girl no less, Ward and I thought our lives were pretty close to perfect. Ward had two reactions: they were bigger than he'd thought they would be—those tiny five-pound peanuts—and they didn't have any birthmarks. They were so beautiful to look at, these physically perfect, healthy little beings. We fell in love with them instantly. Looking at the pair of them, we couldn't have felt happier or more fortunate. We named them Billy and Elizabeth.

Taking care of two newborns, however, was harder than I could have ever expected. It truly seemed to be more than twice the work of looking after one. I don't remember ever having a second to myself. I never sat down, I never relaxed, I would be lucky if I found enough time to take a daily shower. But every month brought another milestone, and it got a little easier. They recognize me! They smile at me! I can make them giggle! I can prop a bottle to feed them instead of holding them full-time! They can entertain themselves in the baby saucer!

Then it hit.

At six months, we thought Elizabeth had a bad case of gas and constipation. She was curling up her little body in pain, as if she were doing sit-up crunches. We spoke to the pediatrician on the telephone about it, and she agreed that it was probably constipation. But the following day, Elizabeth was getting more and more fussy and irritable. That Friday, I decided to take her to the doctor. I didn't want to risk going the weekend without having someone look at her.

I brought her in to the pediatrician late on a Friday afternoon. As the doctor walked into the room, Elizabeth started doing the sit-up crunches I'd previously described.

The doctor instantly revised the diagnosis. This wasn't constipation. Elizabeth was having a seizure. She made some phone calls and got us an appointment for the next morning with a neurologist. What? Doctors' offices aren't open on Saturday, but they were opening for us? Not a good sign. The pediatrician then explained that we would need to go to the hospital following the neurologist appointment, so we should pack a bag. The hospital? It wasn't even our local hospital, but the medical center and teaching hospital where there would be specialists who could help us. I needed to get home. I needed Ward to know. I needed him to make it better.

When I got back to the house, Ward was home from work, sitting in the den having a beer with a couple of friends, debating where we should all go for dinner. So carefree, so easy. It's the weekend, let's celebrate. Life is good.

I told him I needed to talk to him upstairs. We went upstairs with Elizabeth and sat on our bed. I repeated the things the doctor had told me, that Elizabeth was having seizures, she needed to see a specialist, and she needed to go to the hospital. At this stage, we still had no clue as to the severity of the situation, but we knew enough to be scared. There were tears in our eyes. How could this beautiful little baby be sick? We held each other and we held Elizabeth. How could this be happening?

OVER THE MONTHS and years that followed, Elizabeth underwent every treatment and every antiseizure drug available. It seemed that her seizures had been caused by immunizations, but we would never know that for certain. While we hoped for a miracle, we learned that Elizabeth would probably never walk or talk, and would always need to be cared for. We just wanted her better, but trying to get her better meant endless hospital stays, treatments, specialists, needles, drugs that sometimes made her worse, so many worries. As we watched her twin brother reaching the simple childhood milestones of learning to crawl, to toddle, to run, to say his first words, we were reminded of how far behind Elizabeth was falling.

As parents, we naturally wanted the best for our child. Ideally, what was "best" for Elizabeth would be a cure, but in trying to find that cure, she was being subjected to painful and harmful treatments with dangerous side effects. Elizabeth's improvement had been minimal at best. Should we keep subjecting her to these treatments, hoping for a miracle but risking her overall health? Often, we felt like our daughter was a guinea pig. We learned that her doctors were only human. They didn't know all the answers. Yes, they wanted to help, but ultimately, they could only warn us of the potentially dangerous side effects, and leave the big decisions to us.

AS THE YEARS passed, we both began to come to terms with what had happened to Elizabeth. We started to accept that our daughter wasn't going to be able to toddle, to walk, to run around, to talk, or even to cry. It seemed so unfair. I sometimes wondered, Why me? What did I do wrong? But over time, I began to realize that even if we could place blame, it still wouldn't matter. What mattered was Elizabeth. I watched as Ward became an amazing advocate for our child. I remember his words to one specialist we went to see in Boston: "I just want her to have the best life she can possibly have. I want her to be happy."

When Ward and I met, he was twenty-six. I fell in love with a man who was younger than me, who was living a fairly carefree existence comprised mainly of socializing, playing golf, and dating pretty girls. But even so, he knew he was ready to settle down. He was ready for this new phase of his life. He'd fallen in love with a divorced woman and her two-year-old son. Having lost his own father, he had an immediate empathy for TJ—he could give this child the love and guidance he longed for from his own dad. Helping TJ was healing for him.

When the twins were born, it was as if Ward expanded his own notion of fatherhood. He was looking after tiny babies for the first time, and I loved seeing him fall in love with these needy, whiny, scary little beings who needed every ounce of his attention and didn't give much back, at least at first. But Ward was caught in the realization that every new parent has—that he would do absolutely anything and everything to give his children the best life possible. It was no longer just about him; it was all about them.

When Elizabeth became ill, I watched Ward go through yet another transformation. After he accepted that she would probably never be "perfect" or "normal," he embraced her limitations and loved her all the more deeply for them. She was his little "Bumpa," his angel, and although she would never have the life he had pictured for her when she was born, he was going to do everything he could to make her life the best it could possibly be. There's nothing more painful for a parent than not being able to help his sick child, and yet Ward handled the situation with great love, acceptance, and selflessness.

The flip side of all these difficulties was that our relationship became even stronger. We were in this together. We were going to do what we could to help Elizabeth, to raise our boys. There was always such a purity about Elizabeth, this child who couldn't complain, couldn't judge, couldn't fight, couldn't be jealous, couldn't be selfish. She inspired kindness. Elizabeth made us more patient with her brothers. She reminded us to be grateful for Billy and TJ's whining and temper tantrums—they could express themselves, while their sister couldn't. Most of all, she increased our capacity for unconditional love, our ability to give of ourselves freely and to put our children's needs before our own. Ward called her his little angel because she gave him real perspective on what's truly important in life.

After his death I thought about how fortunate I'd been to see this side of Ward, the side that might have never emerged if it weren't for Elizabeth. He'd been faced with the most difficult challenge of his life and rather than let it destroy his spirit, he became a better person, a better husband, a better father.

I REMEMBER THE summer before he died being with my extended family upstate in the Thousand Islands, sitting on my cousin's dock by the river. Ward had been playing all afternoon with the children. The rest of the adults had dropped back, exhausted from interacting with eight children ranging in ages from two to thirteen. But Ward was hard to wear down. He was loving showing the children how to fish—baiting the hooks, taking the small fish off, and releasing them back into the water, over and over again. He would finish with one child's line and then go right to another. My cousin turned to me and said: "Ann, does he always enjoy life this much?"

I nodded and smiled. Ward was just as happy showing those children how to fish as he was on the golf course with his best friends, as he was coming home at the end of the long day at work, opening a beer, and watering the lawn while trying to get his sons with the spray from the hose as they raced around the yard.

. . .

THAT SEPTEMBER 11 morning, I lay in bed with my eyes closed, savoring the thought of being able to stay under the covers for a little while longer. It was my turn to sleep in today. I could hear him, though: his alarm going off, the sound of his feet padding against the floor on his way to the bathroom, the shower turning on, teeth being scrubbed, the opening and closing of his box on top of the dresser, more walking around, the clinking of the quarters being transferred to his pocket so he'd have money for the morning paper, more walking around. Couldn't he be quieter? I was determined to keep my eyes closed and go back to sleep.

"Look who's here. I brought you our little angel." I opened my eyes to see Ward standing there, holding Elizabeth, four years old, still unable to walk or make a sound. She did look like an angel, though, with her pale blond hair and fair complexion, bright blue eyes and cherubic features. I smiled. Ward put her in bed next to me, on his side, and came around and sat on the edge of the bed on my side. We snuggled and kissed for a moment, me all warm and bed-headed, and he all fresh-smelling and ready to go. We said our "I love yous" and "see you laters." As he was walking out, Ward looked back at me one last time and we smiled. And then he was gone.

Actually, he didn't just walk; he purposefully strode out, knowing it was exactly a seven-minute walk for the 7:11 train he wanted to catch. Confident, happy, and looking forward to his new job. He was on top of the world—literally. He'd started working for his new firm a couple of weeks ago, and had been excited to find that he knew most of the people on his team from previous jobs. He'd told me what a great group of guys they were and how much he liked this new position in a company that boasted the most cutting-edge technology in the business. He would call me from his office and tell me how he was looking down from the 105th floor to see the Empire State Building directly below him, even though it was thirty blocks away.

And he was still glowing from what an amazing weekend it had been. He'd picked up his new "dream" car on Friday and spent time bonding with our boys, his mother, and his grandmother, just driving around, pulling into friends' driveways to say hi and show off his new toy—I opted to wait for my turn, knowing that we were going to take a drive to Connecticut for a quick getaway, just the two of us, the following weekend. Ward's former high school football team had a big rivalry game that Saturday, so tailgating, reuniting, and laughing with lots of old friends were a given. A casual, fun dinner at our home with our closest friends completed our Saturday night—I'd made Ward's favorite meal: big, fat juicy steaks, salad with my secret-recipe vinaigrette, and garlic bread, followed by brownies with ice cream. On Sunday we couldn't complete our usual Sunday ritual—golfing together for a couple of hours on the course next door to our house—because the course was closed for renovations. Instead, we spent a few hours at the beach, together as a family, with Elizabeth actually enjoying the experience, smiling at the wind in her face and exploring the texture of the sand. Ward and I watched her—we'd never seen her do this before. It gave us hope that there might be more family outings we'd be able to take with Elizabeth in the future. That evening, we had an extended family dinner at Ward's grandmother's home—a weekly tradition that completed the weekend.

Nothing felt too out of the ordinary, but looking back, I wonder if everything was going just a little too right, a little too perfectly. I wonder if those weren't signs that our happy life together was going a little too well. Does God try to give you signs just before your world collapses?

I THINK ABOUT our last moments together. If we'd known we wouldn't see each other again, how would we have wanted those moments to be any different? Even without that dire knowledge of what was about to take place, our last moments together were so right. The unspoken bond of us as parents acknowledging unconditional love for our "imperfect" daughter, the recognition of the many gifts that she was giving us every day. The physical affection that was a staple for us, occurring frequently because it was an affirmation of our love and it just felt so good. The "I'll see you later" because I do believe—have to believe—that he is in heaven and one day I will be with him again.

After Ward left, I snuggled with Elizabeth a little longer and then got up to get Billy ready to leave. The eleventh was his first day of preschool, and I had taken the day off to accompany him and to show the baby-sitter the ropes.

A little before nine I answered the phone. "What's Ward's cell phone number?" demanded a male voice.

"Who is this?" I asked.

"Who is this?" asked the voice, not expecting me to be home from work that morning. It was Ward's biggest client and a personal friend. Once this person realized it was me on the phone, he explained. "Ann, all of our squawk boxes and direct lines have gone dead. I need to get ahold of Ward to make sure he's okay." There was a long pause. "Ann, you need to turn on CNN."

My mind went into slow motion, trying to process what he was telling me. What did he mean the lines had gone dead? What did he mean when he said he had to make sure Ward was okay? I did as I was told, switched on the news, and saw the images of Ward's tower in flames. I called his cell but I only got his voice mail. Rooted to the TV, I watched as the second plane hit. It looked like a small plane. Maybe the crew was doing some rescue surveillance or making a news recording. Maybe the pilot had a heart attack. It never occurred to me that these were purposeful acts.

I kept calling Ward's cell phone and his office, leaving frantic messages. Even though I'd taken the day off to bring Billy to school, I told the baby-sitter to take him without me. There was no way I was leaving the house. I needed to be home and by the phone to answer Ward's call.

Do something. I couldn't sit still. I was determined to believe that he was going to be okay. He just had to be. What would I do without him? I couldn't allow myself to think the thought. He was going to be fine. He had to be. Determined to act as if everything was normal, I went to the computer, synced my Palm, and printed out my schedule for the next couple of weeks. Everything had to go on as normal—it had to. Here was my schedule in black and white.

Upstairs in my bedroom, I saw Ward's dirty clothes from yesterday. The tiniest sliver of doubt entered my head—if something happened to him, I would never wash those clothes, I would want to save the smell. Unable to even begin to bear the thought, I picked up the clothes and went downstairs to throw them into the washing machine. As if I could control what was happening.

The phone didn't stop ringing.

"I haven't heard from him. I have to leave the line open. I have to go."

I answered the door to see a friend of mine, her face whitened and horrified. I didn't want to see that look. I told her, "It's going to be okay." It had to be.

Another friend arrived, bringing with her a bottle of wine. She asked for a corkscrew.

"I'm not drinking!" I told her. "It isn't even ten in the morning yet!"

"Listen, we need it. . . ."

After pouring two glasses, my friend informed me that she would go out and get cigarettes.

I looked at her like she was crazy. "We don't smoke," I protested.

"I know, honey, but we might need to."

I had my first sense that everything had fallen out of place into a surreal new version of existence.

My eldest son TJ, in seventh grade, called in tears. He had heard through the school grapevine that the towers had been hit and he wanted to make sure everything was okay. I couldn't tell him that Ward was safe, but I did explain that all communications were down and that Ward would call when phone lines became available again. TJ accepted the explanation, but wanted to leave school and be at home. A friend offered to go and pick him up.

That day, Elizabeth had several therapy sessions booked—physical therapy, occupational therapy, her speech therapy, and special education. As more and more friends arrived, the various therapists kept asking if they should just cancel the session. I told them to keep going. I was adamant that they continue, to keep the routine as close to normal as possible. These were the things I could control.

WITHIN A FEW hours, my home was full of people. They came bearing food and drinks. We needed to be together and we needed to keep the fear contained.

"If there is one person who can make it, it's Ward." "Imagine the cocktail party stories he'll tell after this one." "He'll probably walk in the door any minute, announce that he's parched and wants to know where his beer is. . . ." We were actually laughing, hoping and fooling ourselves into believing that at any moment he would walk in through the back door.

At some point that afternoon we heard Billy call out, "Daddy!" with all the excitement and anticipation of a four-year-old seeing his father at the end of a long day.

Our hopes soared. We turned to look outside at the driveway, expecting Ward. There was silence. It wasn't him. It was one of our friends, a man with a similar build and his back to us, getting something out of the trunk of his car.

Everyone looked down at the ground. No one could look at me. No one could look at Billy.

The minutes must have stretched into hours, but for me, there was no sense of time, just the waiting and the hoping that Ward would call. In the morning, I'd told my parents not to come. If they made the five-and-a-half-hour trip from upstate, I would have to accept that this was real. By the afternoon they'd told me they were coming.

Every time the telephone rang, I had hope. By now, my friends were manning the phone. Other families we knew had loved ones missing as well. We kept in touch, to share the positive rumors and give one another support.

At some point that evening, someone answered my phone and told me there was a Claudia Ruggiere on the line. Although we had never met in person, I immediately knew who Claudia was, as Ward had told me about her and her husband Bart. The two men sat next to each other at work and had known each other from a previous job.

I grabbed the phone and went out onto the back stoop for some privacy. Even though I had spoken to other families, I knew I really needed to talk with Claudia. Bart and Ward sat next to each other— whatever happened, she and I would share the same fate. Claudia told me that Bart had called her immediately after the plane hit to tell her that he was okay and that he was getting out of there. If Bart was okay, then that meant Ward was okay too. With those words, Claudia had become my lifeline. We promised to stay in touch.

The next day, TJ again stayed home from school, wanting to be with us and to be there when we heard from Ward. We all believed Ward was coming home. I steadfastly refused to accept any alternative outcome. That evening, I went upstairs to my bedroom, where Elizabeth was watching a video in my bed. I needed to escape for a few minutes from the dozens of people waiting in my home. I sat on the bed with my daughter. But instead of looking at the television, Elizabeth kept looking at the corner of the room.

Even though Elizabeth doesn't speak and has very few expressions, she often seems to understand intuitively what's going on around her. I asked her what she saw. Elizabeth looked at me and started wailing. This is a child who never cries, who only smiles and laughs and is the most content child on earth. She was crying as if she was in terrible emotional distress, a deep, painful cry coming from the pit of her stomach. I looked at her, and said, "You know, don't you? He's telling you that he is gone, isn't he?" I started to cry as well, the first opening in the door of acknowledgment.

When I finally fell asleep that night, I dreamt of Ward. He was standing at the end of my bed. The vision was so real I could have touched him. I asked him what he was doing there. He told me that he was visiting me. I told him he had to leave, that it would be too confusing for the children if he stayed. My subconscious was confirming what I knew in my heart but was unable to admit during my waking hours: that Ward was gone and now my role was to protect our children.

THE FOLLOWING DAY, TJ told me he wanted to go to school. His desire to go back to school and resume the normal routine was a clear message to me that children need their lives to be as normal as possible. I resolved that I would do everything in my powers to help mine maintain a semblance of normality. I wouldn't make their lives any harder than they had to be, and I would be there to support them.

I kept the televisions in the house switched off. I didn't want the children to see the images of the towers falling over and over and over again.

Claudia continued to check in with me several times a day, and I continued to call her. She was convinced that both Bart and Ward were alive, that they'd been injured and were in a hospital somewhere, or that they were trapped. I wanted to believe her so much, and my hope fueled hers.

Within a few days Cantor had set up a meeting and information room at the Pierre Hotel, and Claudia and I planned to meet there.

"I'll be the blonde in the pink twin set," I said, as if we were meeting for a nice lunch.

When I walked into the Pierre, a striking young woman with dark brown hair, olive skin, and bright blue eyes rushed over to me. Even though I'm blond and fair and our coloring couldn't be more different, looking at Claudia was like looking at my reflection. We were both red-eyed from tears and sleeplessness, our drained faces tense from the strain of continued hope against the odds. Even though we had come to the hotel with family and friends, we only wanted to talk to each other. Claudia was still completely convinced that there was reason to hope. She wasn't going to give up on Bart, and she told me I shouldn't give up on Ward.

But every day that passed, our chances lessened. After a week of waiting, I agreed with Ward's family to plan a memorial service.

Telling Claudia was unimaginably hard.

"Claudia, we're going to have a memorial next Saturday," I told her.

I told her I had my children to think about. I had to memorialize Ward and then begin the impossible task of continuing with our lives. I remember feeling as if I'd betrayed her, betrayed the hope we'd shared, betrayed Ward, betrayed Bart.

"That's eleven days from the eleventh," Claudia calculated. "I guess if they haven't found any survivors by then . . ." Both of us desperately hoped that I would be able to cancel that memorial.

THE TOWN OF Rye had one of the highest death tolls of any community in the country. Families had to plan memorials around one another. I went to six services in the space of two weeks. I needed to go, to feel the community of others who had also lost loved ones.

I felt that I had to plan the best memorial service I could for Ward. I wanted him to be proud of me, to have something that epitomized him. The music was particularly important—in addition to traditional funeral hymns, we were going to have one of Ward's friends sing his favorite Grateful Dead and Van Morrison songs, accompanied on the guitar. There would be Scottish bagpipes and his uncle's quartet singing "Ave Maria."

Before we left home that morning, Billy grabbed his beloved toy monkey from his bed. He was four. He had no way of fully comprehending what was happening to him, but he knew he needed that toy. He held onto his monkey for the rest of the day.

When we arrived at the church, there were people spilling out onto the steps outside.

"How bad is it?" I asked one of the ushers, wanting to get a sense of how many people were inside.

"It's not so bad," he assured me. Even so, I decided to go in the back door. There was no way I could make it down the aisle.

The church was filled to capacity. Afterward, hundreds of people attended the reception at Ward's golf club, to have a drink and use his driver for one shot off the first tee in his honor. Everyone came: Ward's family, my family, friends of Ward, friends of mine, friends of our families, Ward's coworkers and clients, my coworkers and clients, former coworkers and clients, caddies from the golf club. It seemed as if anyone and everyone whose life had been touched by Ward was there.

But the one person I sought out was Claudia—a woman I had met less than two weeks earlier. What I remember most about that day was sitting on the terrace with her. It was a gorgeous fall day. All day I had been the center of attention. I was the person that everyone wanted to speak to, like a bride at a wedding reception. I remember telling Claudia that I just wanted to run away and for this day to be over. We both wanted to know how this could be happening. We spoke about the memorial Claudia was planning for Bart in four days' time. I promised her I would be there.

IN THE MONTHS after Ward's death, the main thoughts that were going through my head were: "How am I going to survive without him?" and "How can I make all of this easier on the kids?" It was up to me to be both a mom and a dad to three children. It was my task to figure out how to get the kids to where they had to go, to pick them up, to feed them, to bathe them, to help with homework, to put them to sleep, to love them, and to protect them. And at the same time I was working full-time in the city, trying to run the house, keeping the baby-sitter happy so she wouldn't quit, and trying to figure out how to do the best for Elizabeth.

So I didn't spend a lot of time thinking about what it meant to be a widow. I was so busy thinking about how I was going to get through the day that my brain had little room for anything else. I was so forgetful back then—I would forget to return forms to the school, miss appointments that I thought I had canceled. I never knew where my keys were. I'd be on the phone and saying something and then I would have to ask the other person if I'd already told him or her that, because I couldn't remember if I'd said it before—which doesn't make for a very effective mother, friend, or employee. Everything took twice the effort to accomplish because I couldn't recall what I'd done already or what I needed to do next. Organization had been one of my fortes, but now I sometimes felt like I had lost all control, and that my life was slipping through my fingers because I wasn't able to manage the basic day-to-day stuff of a working mom.

I had to be strong but I couldn't always be strong. Driving by the local pizza shop, Sunrise, where Ward loved to stop for a slice, I'd have to blink away the tears so I could see the road ahead, my kids in the back of the car. In the supermarket, passing his favorite foods, I'd have to hold my breath to stop the sobs. The whole town of Rye was filled with memories of him. There wasn't a corner of this place that didn't make me feel like he was alive and well, and would be walking through the door when I got home that evening.

I had always prided myself on being a good parent, and I knew I had to be twice as good now. If I continued to let sorrow and despair dominate who I was, then my children would sense that, and this would make their lives even more difficult than they were already. I knew that in order to be a good parent, I had to find ways of making our home a happy one.

But I couldn't concentrate. I couldn't sleep. I couldn't always stop the tears. And this continued for months and months and months. I knew I had to maintain an even keel, had to keep getting up in the morning, had to make it to the end of every day. I kept printing out my schedule, trying to stick to the plan. I went back to work in January. Saturdays I barely had time to think. I had three kids to send in three different directions: to soccer, hockey, lacrosse, music class. Coordinating their schedules and making sure they had the right shoes and clothes for the right activity gave me no time to pause. I didn't want to stop, to have time to think, but even so, there were moments when I was so physically and emotionally exhausted, I no longer knew if I had the strength to carry Elizabeth around the house or to and from the car.

Sundays were the worst days of the week. This was our family day, when Ward and I would dedicate a few hours to be alone together. In the evening, we always ate dinner with his extended family at his grandmother's home. Now our children and I stayed home, not wanting another reminder of how much had changed. I would fill our Sundays the best I could, then spend the evening organizing for the week ahead: packing their backpacks, reviewing their schedules, laying out their clothes.

I needed to know that I had a "to do" list that was a mile long. The list and all the items on it allowed me to escape into the simplicity of tasks. Grief was unpredictable and unknowable, whereas the things on the list could be controlled. I had dozens of Post-it notes on my computer. Some I managed to eliminate quickly. I redid my will, because I was so grateful that Ward had made his intentions clear before his death. I knew that if anything happened to me, I didn't want to burden anyone, I wanted to protect my children, to make sure our affairs were in order. Friends coordinated the scrapbook of Ward's life I wanted to have as a record. But there were some Post-its that would stay on my computer for months and months to come. Changing the joint account to my name—I couldn't bring myself to have checks printed without Ward's name on them. Getting the necessary information for the estate tax return. Ordering a plot and a headstone for my husband, even though we didn't have his body to bury. I would look at those notes and be consumed with loathing and dread about such tasks.

I don't think any mother is able to sit and do nothing—there's always something to do—but it was even harder in these circumstances.

How could I sit and watch some mindless TV sitcom when I looked at my life and all I wanted to do was cry? How I could I enjoy time playing and being with my children, knowing they were going to grow up without him?

Apart from Claudia, every single one of my girlfriends was married. Any social event I attended just reemphasized that Ward was gone, and that I was one half of a whole. Even so, I always said yes when I was invited. I was terrified of being left out of social events. I'd already lost so much—my husband, my best friend, the father of my children. I needed to hold onto a social life. I needed to believe I still fit in. I didn't want to stay at home in the evenings. I wanted to get out of the house so I wouldn't have to be reminded of Ward's absence. I was never where I wanted to be—wherever I was, I longed to be someplace else. Our home, the place that used to be our sanctuary, was a place I feared returning to.

I was so worried that, along with the loss of their father, the children were losing a part of their mother. I was terrified about how this would affect them down the line. I remember TJ, age thirteen, becoming very protective of me, suddenly concerned about the future, about money, how I was going to pay the bills. I could feel him looking over my shoulder when I was getting the groceries—"Mom, can we afford that?" He'd overheard people's whispers and took them to heart. I hated it when people told him he was "the man of the house now." That comment made me so angry. He wasn't a man; he was thirteen, barely a teenager. It was heartbreaking to see a thirteen-year-old suddenly bearing the weight of the world on his shoulders. I knew I had to make him believe that I was there to take care of him, rather than having him feel it was his responsibility to take care of me.

Billy was so much younger. Even though he couldn't always express how he was feeling, it was clear he was struggling. Someone had given Billy a storybook we called the "heaven book." It was about how everyone dies and when they do, they go to heaven. I read it to Billy a lot in those early days.

One day, the heaven book went missing. I kept asking Billy where it was. I couldn't find it for three nights in a row.

I kept asking, "Billy, where's the heaven book?"

Eventually he answered me. "I hid it."

"Why?"

"I don't like that book anymore."

I asked him where he'd hidden it.

"In a really dirty place where you'll never find it," he replied.

Months later, I found the book under my bed. That at least made me smile—Billy thought that under my bed was a "really dirty place."

I stopped cooking for my family. I love to cook, but I couldn't make food because it only reminded me that I would never cook for Ward again. The baby-sitter would make our meals—we lived off chicken nuggets, mac and cheese, kid food. One evening TJ was upset, crying, telling me he wanted things back to normal. Why didn't I cook anymore, why didn't I smile anymore? "You never make that chicken thing anymore," he accused me. I realized he was right. Chicken piccata was one of Ward's favorites; I used to make it at least once a month. I was depriving the children of one of the traditions and memories they craved. If my son wanted me to cook for him, I was going to have to get over my sadness and try to give him the things that he needed. This time the solution was simple: start cooking again.

DESPITE HIS ABSENCE, Ward was making his presence felt. About a month after Ward's death, I was in my house doing paperwork and Billy was in the front yard playing. For some reason, I called to my son to come in, even though it was too early for lunch. About twenty minutes later, a neighbor called to tell me to look out of my window. There had been a robbery just down the street from our house. The thieves had stolen the neighbor's car and, in the attempted getaway, lost control of the car and ended up swerving into my yard. I went outside and saw the track marks where they'd driven through my hedge and into the yard, taking out a walkway light before plowing through the hedges again.

If Billy had been playing out in the yard when this happened, he might have been killed. The difference of a few minutes would have left me with a second loss to bear, and one that I knew I wouldn't have been able to sustain. I'd had no reason to bring Billy in. I'd just known

I wanted him inside. I felt a strong intuition that Ward was watching over us. My husband was going to find ways to continue to protect his family. Thank you, Ward.

Then there was the mystery of his watch. Ward had two watches, one that his father had given him as a graduation present and one that I'd given him that July for our anniversary. I'd looked for the watches in the days immediately after September 11. I needed to determine which watch he'd been wearing so that I could put this detail on the missing persons report. I carefully went through the wooden box where he kept his watches, his business cards, money clip, and keys. The watch his father had given him was in the box, so I concluded that Ward had been wearing the watch I'd given him and I listed it on the missing persons report.

Weeks later, I again went back to the wooden box to look through his things, to touch his belongings, and to try to feel his presence through them. That's when I saw it, right on top of the box, just lying there. Although I'd searched through that box from top to bottom numerous times, now, as if by magic, the watch I'd given him was there. Ward had found a way to leave behind two watches, one for Billy and one for TJ.

THAT SPRING, CLAUDIA and I decided to go and offer our personal testimonials to be used in the trial of Zacarias Moussaoui, the first terrorist to be indicted in connection with the attacks. This was the first time I had been involved in a "September 11" issue like this. It wasn't that I hadn't been asked. Letters would come all the time in the mail and via e-mail. From the beginning, everyone was sharing information about support groups, memorials, and charity events. Then some groups started to become more politically active, focusing on the rebuilding efforts, or on investigations into the events of September 11. I know I was so grateful to those people who were getting involved, spending hundreds of hours of their time to positively influence events, but I felt that I couldn't cope with anything else right now. I didn't want to say yes to something and then be unable to follow through. I wanted to do what I could, but I could only do so much.

With the trial, however, I felt strongly that I wanted to contribute.

The first step involved attending an interview with an attorney for the Justice Department in order to explain the "depth and degree" of my loss.

I remember the judge asking me at some stage during the interview: "Do you feel that with the Victims Compensation Fund you will be better off financially in the future than you were with your husband?"

I looked at the judge in disbelief. I thought it was a given that no amount of money could make up for the loss of my husband, or the loss of my children's father.

"Ward and I already lived well," I told her. "We had everything we needed and we considered ourselves lucky to enjoy such a nice lifestyle. And even if this weren't the case, no amount of money is worth losing the man that I love. No amount of money can bring back my children's father."

Thank goodness that Claudia was there that day and we could go through the experience together. Over the past months, Claudia and I had been in contact almost daily. Family and friends were so supportive, but Claudia and I shared a bond. When I didn't think I could go on, I would call her and she would understand. She could talk me through it. When *she* felt she couldn't go on, I could help her, and it gave me strength to know that I could help.

Claudia and I encouraged each other. We reminded each other not to overdo it. "Don't be so hard on yourself," Claudia would say to me. "Life is hard enough already."

We were in the process of healing, Claudia counseled. Judging ourselves would only make things worse. It was okay to make mistakes and forgive ourselves for them.

Then, that summer, Claudia introduced me to the girls in the WC and we agreed to go away after the anniversary. That meeting was such a turning point for all of us. Immediately, we derived so much support and comfort from one another.

WHEN WE RETURNED from Scottsdale after the anniversary, I decided I needed some kind of a new start. Not only would I remove my rings, I was going to redecorate our bedroom. I felt it would help me to know that I had taken this step to transform the only place in the house where I could escape if I needed to. To make it my own space.

Earlier in the year, I'd cleared out Ward's closets. I was having quilts made for the children from his clothes, and the children were allowed to pick out the fabrics they wanted to use—Billy and TJ chose their favorite T-shirts and sweatshirts for their quilts. Clearing out the closets became a family activity. But redoing the bedroom was something I could do for me. It was the easiest change I could make to the house because it wasn't as if I was changing anything that Ward and I had chosen together. When we'd first moved in, we'd never redone our room. Now I decided to rearrange the furniture. I chose new drapes for the windows. I created room on my side table for new photos of Ward and the children.

Also that fall, an old friend offered to set me up on a date with someone. I was so lonely and longing for a male companion, for physical affection, for a lover, for a partner, that I accepted. When Ward had died, in one sense my transformation from wife to widow had been immediate. But it didn't feel that way. The process of adjusting to this new role was slow and agonizing. It involved an enormous act of reinvention on my part. By taking my rings off, by changing my room, by going on a date, I was trying to convince myself that I wasn't some broken half of a whole. That one day, maybe not just yet, but one day, I could be a person in my own right again.

Ann and Claudia

By the beginning of the second year, the people around us had started gently encouraging us to date. Ann had already decided she would start dating after a year. Pattie and Julia weren't sure that they were ready yet—or if they'd ever be.

Claudia's mother would say to her in her classic New York accent: "Claaw-dia, maybe it's time."

Claudia would reply: "Why? You didn't."

Her mother would say, "Yes, but I regret that now."

One day in October, after returning from Scottsdale, Claudia was walking down the street with Bart's sister, Kathleen, when they bumped into an old college friend.

After they walked away, Kathleen nudged Claudia in the ribs. "Why don't you date him? He's cute."

Claudia told Kathleen she was out of her mind. At this point, the whole concept of dating still seemed extremely bizarre.

We were so worried about what other people would think when we started dating, that it was reassuring when family and friends seemed to want us to look to the future. The WC became our incubator, where it was safe to talk and laugh and cry at the absurdity of being back at a stage we'd assumed we'd left far behind when we'd met and married our husbands. Why would we want to date when we were already married?

We talked about our rings—should you take them off or leave them on? Were we cheating on our husbands if we kissed another man? Were we really going to remain celibate for the rest of our lives? And on the other hand, could we even imagine sleeping with someone other than our husbands? Was there some sort of widow word for losing your virginity the second time around?

A year ago, we wouldn't have been able to contemplate these conversations. It was too big of a step. But that was exactly what this was—a step. There were going to be so many steps we would have to take along the way, and this was just one of them. Besides, what did we risk by going out to dinner with a guy? We'd already lost more than most people could imagine. And if we didn't get along with him, we would always know we'd experienced great love in our lives, and no one could take our memories of our marriages away from us. Ann especially hoped that dating would help her begin to lessen the pain, to fit back into the "normal" couples social life she was surrounded by in the suburbs, even to find a little bit of happiness again.

An old friend of Ward's set her up on her first date. Ann was so relieved that others were looking out for her. But was she really ready to date? The reality was that she wasn't even close to being ready. On the other hand, she wasn't going to turn down *any* chance to move forward. So, in response to Ward's friend asking her if she would be interested in a blind date, the answer was "Yes, have him call me." Ned called the next day.

Ann hadn't dated since she'd met Ward over ten years ago. Even a phone conversation was cause for nervousness. But if anything, the chat was easier than she'd anticipated. During that initial conversation, Ann and Ned discovered that they had another mutual friend in common. She'd barely finished hanging up with Ned, before she was calling her friend to get the lowdown—always do your homework and be prepared. Since Ann was launching herself into the dating scene again, she figured she'd better play by the rules.

The evening of the date, Ann left the children downstairs eating dinner and headed upstairs to figure out what to wear. What *do* you wear on a first date? Since she really didn't have a clue anymore, she played it safe—black pants and light blue silk V-neck sweater, a notch above casual but not too dressy for a weekday dinner date. She made sure she was ready on time. She didn't want Ned to wait for her for one second in her chaotic house, where her kids could potentially scare him off before she'd even met him.

The doorbell rang and she answered. He was cute—very cute, with short stylish hair, casual jeans, a fitted sweater, and a brown suede jacket, definitely more Banana Republic than Brooks Brothers. This was a good start. Right away, it was easy to laugh about their mutual friend setting them up. Ann and Ned went to a great local Italian restaurant. A table for two, a bottle of red wine that he ordered, and a conversation that just progressed. They talked about their jobs, their hobbies, blind dates that Ned had been on over the past years, Ann's life, and of course, Ward.

Perhaps every time someone goes out on a date with someone new, there's that underlying question: Is he the one? So despite Ann's mature, realistic side recognizing that she probably wasn't going to fall madly in love with the very first man she dated after the death of her husband—and life would automatically become wonderful again—she still had that hope of finding love, of finding happiness, and of having a complete family again. Every time Ned and she found something they had in common, Ann would think, "This might just work . . ." "Oh, he skis . . . I ski too." "He likes Italian food; I *love* Italian food." In some ways it was like being in eighth grade again, learning how to talk with a boy, learning how to flirt, learning how to carry on a conversation without giving too much away, without revealing all the doubts and fears.

And at the same time, the date was going well. Ann was realizing, I can do this. The fact that they lingered over dinner, and then took a brief walk up and down the avenue afterward, reinforced her sense that she was interesting to him and that he was attracted to her.

Ned took her home. They said good-bye with a hug and a kiss on the cheek. It was easy, it was comfortable; there were a lot of smiles and the hope of getting to know each other even better.

But in the coming weeks, pretty quickly, it also became clear that they were destined to be friends, not lovers. No particular reason— although maybe subconsciously Ann knew she wasn't ready—it was just the lack of that spark that has to exist if a relationship is to get started.

"I guess I'm lucky to have such an easy transition into the dating world," Ann told the WC.

THEN, THAT NOVEMBER, Claudia met a friend of Ann's, Paul, at a party. Six foot, with light brown hair and gray eyes. He had been sepa- rated from his wife for two years and had two little girls. A great guy, funny and sweet. And a friend of Ann's. Claudia and Paul started e-mailing back and forth. Paul's best friend had died in the World Trade Center; he shared stories about his friend, and Claudia could talk about Bart. Paul told her how he had been diagnosed with cancer in his twenties. Like Claudia, he knew what it was like to be faced with peo- ple who didn't know what to say. Like Claudia, Paul wanted a full life and to make every experience count. Claudia knew he was one of "us."

So when he asked her out, she thought, "Okay, what do I have to lose?"

They started dating. Although it was awkward and nerve-racking at first, Claudia began to admit that she had missed going out to dinner with a man. It was nice having someone to talk to, to call her at the end of the day. One night, Paul surprised Claudia by taking her ice-skating at Rockefeller Center. When Christmas came around, they went to chop down a tree together. Paul was showing Claudia that there could be glimmers of happiness and hope, if she was willing to open herself up to the possibilities.

Pattie, Claudia, Julia, and Ann

The first Friday in January, the WC left town for a weekend trip to Vermont. We met in front of Julia's building, where she pulled up in a huge truck that she and Tommy owned—we could barely see her tiny frame from behind its giant steering wheel.

The WC's destination was Bromley Mountain, a place where Bart had skied since he was a child. In Bart's honor, and with a portion of the money raised from his foundation, the Bart J. Ruggiere Adaptive Sports Center had been established, where people with physical and mental disabilities could learn to ski with the help of trained volunteers and special equipment. Claudia wanted us to be with her for the weekend, knowing that the WC would be able to understand the mixture of pain and pride she was feeling now that the Center was open.

But that weekend, Claudia, who never got sick, ever, came down with the flu. "Hey, on top of feeling completely miserable, this is the first time I'm going to Vermont without Bart," she told us. "Is it my imagination, or is God trying to pour salt in my wounds? I don't know what I'd do without you ladies."

Even though she was ill, it still felt right to be making this trip. Bart loved to ski. He wasn't very athletic; he never worked out. At six foot one and a hundred and seventy-five pounds, he never had to worry about staying in shape. But he was a gifted skier and made sure he got out on the slopes every winter. Before she met her husband, Claudia had skied intermittently, but Bart's enthusiasm for the sport really got her focused. Bart always said his favorite vacation was in January 2001 when they went to St. Moritz in Switzerland.

"What do you mean it's your favorite vacation?" Claudia would ask him. "What about our honeymoon?"

Bart would lean over, tousle her hair, and say: "Hate to disappoint you, but . . ."

For our weekend in Vermont, Claudia had packed Bart's old ski jacket, his hat, and his neck warmer to bring her luck. No matter how sick she felt, Claudia was determined to wear them, to get out on the slopes.

"Can you appreciate the irony?" she asked. "Bart, a man who never worked out a day in his life, now has a sports center named after him."

IT WAS GOOD to be getting out of the city together, heading into the mountains. The next morning, we woke up early and headed to Bromley and the Bart Center. We found it on the ground floor of the lodge. Here we met the half dozen men and women who were going to be running the place, all of whom were volunteering their time and energies. We could see how proud Claudia felt, knowing that Bart would approve, that this was exactly what he would have wanted. It was inspiring to see the volunteers, to see the compassion and commitment they brought to their work—confirmation that there are so many good people in the world. We were all moved by their generosity and willingness to give of their time for others.

Despite her flu and the emotional nature of the visit, Claudia had her brave widow face on. She greeted the volunteers, thanked them, told them how much she appreciated their dedication. Claudia had given the center a copy of Bart's eulogy, with several pictures, and the volunteers had taken the photos and hung them alongside a plaque commemorating Bart's life. They were so pleased to show Claudia everything they'd accomplished, and Claudia kept thanking them and reassuring them that everything looked great.

One of the volunteers was explaining the range of programs they were going to be offering. Meanwhile, Claudia was looking over at the photo of her wedding day hanging on the wall. She was thirty years old in the picture; her life with her new husband was just beginning. It was just over three years ago. Bart and Claudia had gotten married in St. Patrick's Cathedral on Fifth Avenue. It was a magical day. People would tell Claudia that she and Bart had the fairy tale New York wedding. Now that fairy tale felt more real to her than the completely surreal experience of standing in a sports center named after her dead husband. The girl, standing next to Bart in the photo, wearing the white dress, she was the real Claudia. The Claudia standing here in Vermont looking at the picture was an imposter—a cold, tired, sick imposter—who didn't want to ski and didn't want to be here anymore, who just wanted her husband back. Yes, good can come from bad, Claudia knew this, but it was too high a price to pay.

SOMEHOW, JUST LIKE she always did, Claudia picked herself up and made the most of the situation. That afternoon, she got herself onto the slopes. It was probably not the smartest thing a person with the flu could do—spending an afternoon outside in the freezing cold—but we weren't even going to attempt to deter her. Claudia was skiing for Bart. It was something she had to do, and it was definitely a good thing for rest of us. In the mountains the air was fresh and the temperature was sub-zero, making our faces flushed and stinging. We wanted to challenge and invigorate ourselves—not to retreat to our beds each weekend. Instead of our usual everyday tiredness, we got to experience the satisfying exhilaration of careening down mountains, instead of just fighting to get up them.

Ann told us about how Ward had been a ski instructor out in Colorado when he was younger. Julia told us about how Tommy was an advanced skier and had skied all his life. When she met him, she was an absolute beginner, but was determined to keep up with him. Instead, she would be at the top of the slopes, making big loops down the mountain to stop herself from going too fast, and he would be at the bottom, waiting.

He would tease her. "Julia! It's called 'downhill skiing' for a reason. Point your skis *downhill.* . . ." In Tommy's honor, Julia picked up some speed.

By the end of the day, we were aching all over. But it was nothing a good massage or a cocktail couldn't cure. God knows, we knew what real pain felt like.

THAT SATURDAY EVENING, we decided to eat at a restaurant we'd driven by earlier in the day. The place was called the Perfect Wife.

"How perfect is this?" someone asked. "Four widows eating at the Perfect Wife."

We sat down at our table and started to scan the menu.

"You know, I used to try and be a perfect wife. Now I have to worry about what it means to be a perfect widow," said Claudia.

Our conversation had begun. Was there such a thing as a perfect wife?

"It never even occurred to me to try to be the perfect wife," said Pattie. "All I wanted was to be with Caz. Perfection really didn't come into it."

A good point. Did anyone really aspire to be a perfect wife? Sure, we loved our husbands, and wanted our marriages to succeed, but we were women with strong careers who were completely independent before we'd met our husbands.

"It's not like I was ever some kind of Stepford Wife," Julia pointed out.

"I wasn't exactly staying home knitting Bart sweaters," Claudia said. "He was the one who did most of the grocery shopping and cooked all the meals. He even took care of the majority of our wedding plans."

"What does 'perfect' mean anyway?" Ann added. "Life is stressful. In any marriage, sometimes your temper is short, kids get cranky, money's tight, the job isn't going so well. Stress can make you selfish. The hard parts of life make us all less than perfect."

. . .

EVERYTHING FELT IMPERFECT now. From the outside, we might look like we were complete, but we were walking around with this feeling of emptiness inside that almost never seemed to leave us.

Although we never worried too much about being the perfect wife in our marriages, now we recognized that we were spending a disproportionate amount of time worrying about being the perfect widow. Being a widow presented so many challenges. We all felt this pressure, this responsibility to do the right thing—to make our husbands proud, to keep a good connection with his family and friends, to preserve his memory, to make some good come out of such terrible circumstances, to be worthy of all the love and support we were receiving.

The problem was, we were all still pretty confused about what it meant to be a widow, let alone a perfect one.

OVER DINNER, WE tried to figure out how to live up to our own expectations and those of other people.

When you're grieving, people want to help you. Thank goodness. We couldn't have survived without the tremendous support we'd received over the past year and four months. We were grieving through such public events that we'd received an inordinate amount of attention. It felt like everyone was on our side—our families, friends, colleagues, communities, complete strangers, the whole world in fact. As a result, even in those earliest days of craziness, we still had the sanity to call ourselves blessed.

But there was a flip side to all the attention. People would see that we were in pain, and they wanted to try to make it go away. It made them unhappy to see us so distraught. On some level, it reminded them how fragile life is—that what happened to Tommy, Ward, Caz, and Bart could happen to anyone at any time. Perhaps as a result of their discomfort with the facts, their desire to help, and because they felt sorry for us, people tended to cast themselves in the role of the advice giver.

"You should move to a smaller house," people would tell Ann. "Leave the memories behind you." But with everything her family was going through, the last thing Ann wanted to do was put them through the trauma of moving.

"You shouldn't travel right now; it's not safe," people said. Claudia would think, Yeah, right, and going to work is?

"Are you going to stay here in New York now?" they said to Julia, as if New York wasn't her home just because she grew up in Tennessee.

"Thank God you were only with your husband for a few years and you didn't have children. You'll have another life." Wait a minute, Pattie would think. A widow doesn't just grieve for the years she spent *with* her husband, she grieves for all the future years lost, the family she's never going to have with him.

"You shouldn't spend so much time with your widow friends—that can't be good for you. You don't want to be around people who are going to bring you down." No comment.

"If I were you, I'd take his voice off your answering machine." Well, lucky for you, you're not me.

"All the good men are taken. You'll never meet a man as good as your husband." Thanks for the vote of confidence.

"It's really time for you to stop spending weekends in bed."

"You look tired. Are you sleeping?"

"You shouldn't work so hard."

"Thank goodness you have your work."

"You need to get out more."

"You need to stay home more."

"You look great! Keep doing what you're doing!"

"You look so skinny, you need to eat."

For the most part, we would let people give their advice, because we realized their motives were honorable. But at the same time, people telling us what to do just made us more confused. We would listen politely and then we'd listen some more, tell the person that we appreciated his or her caring, and then carry on as best we could.

Then there were the friends and family members on whom we relied, who knew how to help us—who brought food, who took us out to dinner on Sunday nights, who slept over when it all got to be too much, who listened on the other end of the line, who said they didn't know what to say. Who didn't tell you they knew how you felt, or what to do. These were the people we depended on.

SINCE THE WC came together, we'd realized it was possible to live with tremendous pain and at the same time experience surges of intense vitality, of the need to live. At first, we guarded this realization. We kept it for the times when we were together. But after a while, we began to show others that we were changing. And as a result, we found we were getting a lot of mixed messages from people. Everyone wanted the best for us. We knew that. No one wanted us to get any sadder. But even so, a widow is the keeper of the grief for everyone. If a widow moves forward and tries to make a life for herself without her husband, then it's just another reminder for others that he's gone.

"Sometimes I feel like, if I just disappeared from life, people could pretend that Ward and I were on vacation, or that we moved away," Ann explained. "They could make believe that nothing had changed. They wouldn't have to be reminded of his death. But if they see me out, alone, or on a date, if they see me smiling and laughing, if they see me having a good time without Ward, it reminds them that he's truly gone from their lives. And that upsets them. I understand their pain and their loss—I loved him too—which is why I'm not angry at their feelings. But it's so hard to live up to their expectations."

We were reclaiming ourselves, but we were fearful of being judged, of letting people down.

There was the friend of Ward's who kept encouraging Ann to go out on dates, saying: "If Ward were alive, he would be dating. It's what he would want for you." But then when Ann went out with Ned, the same friend told her, "Well, I hope I don't have to meet the guy."

There were the people who would tell us that they wanted us to find happiness again. But when we went to see them with our rings switched to the other hand, they gave us a look that said, "What does that mean?"

Even if the advice was on target, if we weren't ready to hear it, we rejected it. "In five years' time, you're going to look back on this and you'll be in a much, much better place," people would say. Another four years of this? We couldn't imagine surviving this for another day, let alone four years.

"You're damned if you do and damned if you don't," Julia pointed out.

TO BE FAIR, it was as much our own expectations we were dealing with as anyone else's. We really wanted to be the best widow we could be for our husbands. But what did that mean? We went through some of our own assumptions: The perfect widow doesn't date. The perfect widow never cleans out his closet. The perfect widow wears his wedding ring on a chain around her neck. Okay, that one really wasn't fair. Claudia, Pattie, and Ann might never have their husbands' rings returned to them.

And then there was the perfect September 11 widow. The perfect September 11 widow is on committees. She protests. She appears in front of Congress. She organizes. We'd managed none of this. Pattie was advised that she shouldn't hold a fund-raiser due to disputes over Caz's estate, and felt badly about not doing something charitable. Did that make her a bad widow?

The perfect widow doesn't change anything about her life or surroundings. Okay, we could relate to that one. We still had our husbands' voices on our answering machines, his products in the bathroom cabinets, his shoes by the door where he'd left them.

We were always fighting the guilt. Maybe it was better to pull the covers over our heads and to wish away the rest of our lives. Maybe it would be easier to conform to that stereotypical definition of widowhood, to curl up and pretend we'd died too. Maybe that was a better way to honor our husbands. Maybe that would show the world how deeply we loved him.

THAT NIGHT AT the Perfect Wife restaurant, we talked a lot about the possibility of having regrets in the future.

"I never understood the power of the word 'regret' until now," Claudia said. "Regret scares me. You don't know you have regrets until it's too late. One time, my mother and I were having a heart to heart and she said to me, 'Don't do what I did; you have to make a life for yourself.' At fifty, my mother never imagined there would be a sixty-two."

Pattie said she saw it differently. "I'm sort of the opposite. I don't want to regret a bad decision. I want to take the time to gather the information and make the right decisions for me at the right time."

By the end of the evening, we came to the following conclusion: We couldn't apply other people's advice or standards. Decisions were ours and ours alone, and we tried to do our best and accept responsibility for them. We were trying to do things that would lead us ultimately to the kind of lives that our husbands would want us to have. We were resigned: we had to do what we knew was the right thing in our hearts. We were never going to make everyone happy. We appreciated other people's advice, but we needed to be individuals and heal in our own time and in our own way.

"Maybe we have to look at our widowhood the same way we looked at our marriages," Ann pointed out. "My marriage with Ward wasn't perfect, but we always tried to do the best that we could. We had respect for each other. We accepted each other and loved each other more deeply because of our imperfections. It made for a very happy marriage and a lot of love. To me, a perfect marriage is doing your best. That's all we can do now. We just have to do the best we can."

8 · *Not the Worst Thing*

Claudia

Claudia:

In the new year, Paul, the man I'd been dating, broke up with me. He told me that he was doing it for my sake, that after everything I'd been through, he didn't want to drag me into what was becoming a very messy divorce with his soon-to-be-ex-wife.

Even so, I couldn't believe that I'd gotten up the courage to date, only to be dumped by the first man I went out with. My initial reaction was to feel let down and be angry. But that didn't last long. I remember going to dinner with the WC at The Grill and telling them, "Yes, I'm bummed, but this isn't the worst thing that ever happened to me. . . ."

In hindsight, I could see that Paul had been the perfect "transitional guy." He was kind and thoughtful and he cared about me. He helped me take that first step. He reminded me that I would rather take a chance than sit on the sidelines watching life pass by. I knew I didn't want to be paralyzed by the fear of getting my heart broken.

·   ·   ·

NOT THAT THERE'S ever an ideal time for a breakup, but Paul's timing wasn't exactly perfect. I was thirty-three. I was at that age when all of my friends were having babies. In the past eighteen months, seven of my closest girlfriends had gotten pregnant. One by one they would call me, or arrange to meet for dinner, and then they would tentatively share their good news. I would tell them I was happy for them, and I meant it. This was when I realized it's possible to feel genuinely happy for someone, and equally sad for yourself. It devastated me to think that Bart and I were never going to have a family together. But it was more than that: I didn't want life to go on as if nothing had changed. I didn't want to think about how much was going to happen in the future that Bart would never experience.

In February, I was working from home one afternoon, when I got a call from Marcella. "Claudia," I heard my sister say nervously. "I have something to tell you. . . ."

Immediately I assumed it had something do with our mother.

"It's nothing bad," Marcella reassured me.

There was no easy way to say it: She and JC were pregnant with their third child.

I told Marcella I was so happy for her. I told her how exciting it was. I asked how she was feeling. When was she due? I did everything in my powers to stay composed on the phone, and not hang up too soon.

But as soon as I put down that phone, I lost it. At that moment, I didn't want Marcella to have a baby that Bart would never know. But mostly I just wanted Bart back so that we could experience what Marcella and JC were feeling right now.

We had seven nieces and nephews who adored Bart; he could never spend enough time with them. I would watch him play with them and think how fortunate I was to be with this man who was so relaxed and happy around children. Bart and I had decided that we'd wait a few years after we were married before starting a family. We dreamed of a girl. We wanted to name her Sophia.

In the summer of 2001, Bart and I had been at my sister's for the day, and when we got home that night and were making love, in between kisses Bart told me he wanted to have a baby *right now*. I laughed at him and told him that he needed to get over it—he was in the process of planning two extravagant vacations. In addition, I pointed out, when he woke up the next morning and was *sober*, he would deny he had ever said it. Bart rolled over and grabbed a scrap of paper and scribbled on it, "I love Claudia and I want to have a child with her, and not wait a year because I love her soooooo much and we just should!!" This way, when we both woke up in the morning, I would have proof of his intentions.

After his death, I would hold that piece of paper and stare at it. What would it have been like if I'd said yes to Bart that night, and we'd had a child? How would it be different if I could look at our child and see something of my husband there?

The afternoon when Marcella called with the news she was pregnant, it was crystal clear to me that I was never going to be a mother. I climbed into bed, fully dressed, pulled the covers over my eyes, and cried myself to sleep.

What if I had that child? I tried not to go there. I consoled myself that our first year of marriage was magical. I treasured the time we spent together, and in retrospect, I was comforted that I hadn't had to share Bart with anyone.

But now that Bart was gone, did this mean I had to miss out on the experience of having a child? Did my dreams of being a mother have to die with Bart? Did I have to give up hope of ever becoming a parent? Was it predetermined that I was never going to be a mother? Even in the most unlikely set of circumstances, if I did meet someone new, I was thirty-four, my biological clock was ticking. Time might run out. Or could I adopt? Could I be a single parent? No, I couldn't imagine that.

THAT SPRING, SEVEN days before what should have been my third wedding anniversary, my mother-in-law and I were appearing before a judge in an arbitration hearing for the Victims Compensation Fund. Like most families, we had such mixed feelings about the fund. The process of awarding financial compensation was being covered extensively in the media. This left you open to judgments and assumptions from all kinds of people. I remember one of the doormen at my building asking me: "So, did you get all that money?"

I told him, "Listen. Bart and I had everything we needed. We had a great lifestyle; we had a nice car, a beautiful home; we were going to Paris on vacation in September. I don't want this money. I want my husband back."

For the arbitration, Bart's mother, Pat, and I had to appear at an office in Midtown. My attorney laid out our case before the justice, a woman from Louisiana.

In stating our position, my attorney kept using the phrases "this woman lost her husband," "this woman lost her son." Every time he used the word "lost," I cringed. Bart wasn't lost in a parking garage. He wasn't misplaced. He was at work, where he was supposed to be. He had been murdered by terrorists. I couldn't stop myself; I didn't care if it hurt my case. Every time my attorney said Bart was "lost" I corrected him: "He was *MURDERED*."

At the end of our hearing, I thanked the judge for her help. I knew that she was a volunteer, and that it must be hard to see all these heartbroken families. Pat and I were in this together, supporting each other, but not every family was as fortunate. The judge seemed fair and respectful, and I didn't want to seem ungracious.

She thanked me for acknowledging her work and told me that yes, it was very difficult, but that this was important to her: "You see, my brother was *murdered* several years ago, and I understand the difference. That's why I volunteered to do this."

LATER THAT MONTH, I decided I needed to take a trip somewhere. It had been a long, cold, depressing winter, and recently I'd been experiencing such intense highs and lows. I knew I needed to check out for a week and level off. None of the girls could take time off from work, so I decided to go away alone. I'd traveled on my own in Europe before I was married, and always enjoyed it. I'd loved that feeling of sitting in a café, at a table for one, reading a book and watching people go by. I decided to go to Santa Barbara, California, to a resort that Bart had seen in a magazine and saved in our travel folder.

In California, I would wake up in the morning and take a tennis lesson, practice yoga, and then sit by the pool and read. I hadn't played tennis since high school, and I found it challenging and strengthening. By now, yoga had evolved from a workout into a form of physical and emotional release for me. Both of these activities helped me to feel invigorated, gave me reasons for getting out of bed in the morning. At the airport I had picked up the book *Love Stories of World War Two,* which I read throughout my trip. I had developed a need to read books that brought my pain to the surface. I sat in a lounge chair by the pool, reading stories about soldiers killed in war, and cried for all of us. I knew people were staring at me and wondering. I didn't care.

In Santa Barbara, I came to a point of reconciliation with my life. I could be alone, and it was okay. I could go on vacation by myself. I could feel myself growing stronger. I was reminding myself that life was a precious gift, and even without Bart, I had to go on because he would want that. I was amazed to realize that I didn't want to leave when the week was over.

9 · Julia and Tommy

Julia:

That spring, to mark what would have been my third wedding anniversary, I decided I wanted to go back to the beach in the Bahamas where Tommy and I had gotten married. I had this idea that if I surrounded myself with places I had been with my husband, somehow it would help me to move forward. My plan was to fly out for a few days alone and then two friends of Tommy's and mine were going to fly over and meet me and I would spend the rest of the week with them.

I was happy that I was going to have a chance to show our friends the beach and all the places that we'd visited during our wedding week. I needed to share my memories with people who appreciated them. You see, the people closest to us weren't there for our wedding. Tommy and I eloped. We didn't have a video camera, and only took a few pictures. At the time, this didn't matter—it had been our plan to come here the following year, for our anniversary. "Next time we'll bring friends and family," we'd said, "so they can see where it all happened."

After we became engaged, we'd talked a lot about what kind of wedding we wanted. We had some big decisions to make. Where would we get married? In New York where Tommy grew up, or in Tennessee, where I'm from? Would we have a big or a small wedding? Who would be in our wedding party? Tommy had been best man at nine weddings—how could he choose who would stand next to him on this big day? We joked about eloping to the Bahamas, but we really didn't give it too much thought. The most important thing was that we would be married. The rest was just details.

In May of 2000 we decided to go on a vacation to the Bahamas, cruising around in a motorboat that Tommy kept in Florida so that he could use it year round. Tommy loved being out on the water. When I first met him he was studying to upgrade his Captain's license, taking evening classes and studying on the weekends, eventually passing with flying colors. He would joke that he was now a "100 Ton Masters Captain" and able to drive the Staten Island Ferry if he needed to.

I still have the e-mail he sent me when we decided to take the trip to the Bahamas. It said, "Stop dreaming, start planning!" We were going to boat around the cluster of small islands called the Abacos, just the two of us. We set out from Florida with GPS in hand, and traveled until we got to an island called Green Turtle Cay, a tiny land mass surrounded by white sandy beaches and crystal waters.

We looked at each other and agreed.

This was where we wanted to get married. It was just that simple. Although we wished we had all our family members and friends with us, this was the solution to all our questions about where and how to get married. We decided that if it proved easy to arrange to have the ceremony here, then we'd take it as a sign that this was the way it was meant to be. If it became too complicated, then we'd wait to get married another time.

We walked into town and asked the way to the Town Hall, which turned out to be a modest building on the main street. We walked through the door just as the island commissioner was walking out. When we told him we wanted to get married, the commissioner took us back inside and asked for our passports.

We waited for his verdict.

"No problem, mon," he told us in his laid-back Island accent. "I'll marry you tomorrow morning at ten-thirty. Not U.S. time; Bahamian time—so don't be early."

The commissioner told us that he was only on this island twice a week and he'd been about to leave for the day, so we were lucky we'd caught him. This was the sign we'd been looking for. We completed some paperwork and paid $25 for his services. Then we realized we didn't have wedding bands. We had to have bands! Back outside, we spoke to the woman who ran the marina and she made a phone call to someone called Shirley. We met Shirley at "Shirley's Shell Shack," where she opened her store for us so that we could pick out matching dolphin rings for our wedding bands. We were set.

That night, we went to a local watering hole, where we informed anyone within sight that we were getting married tomorrow. Everyone at the bar toasted us and promised to come to the beach to watch the nuptials the following morning. After all, they'd been at our "rehearsal dinner," so why shouldn't they be there for the wedding? They celebrated with us late into the night. Earlier in the day we'd booked a room at the resort with two single beds. This was the "night before our wedding" and we weren't supposed to sleep with each other.

The next morning, I put on a white slip dress that I'd brought to wear in the balmy Caribbean evenings. Tommy wore khaki shorts and a navy blazer. We were both barefoot.

At 11 am on the morning of May 24, we exchanged vows with our hotel manager standing in as the "maid of honor" and a fishing guide standing in for Tommy's "best man." Needless to say, none of the people we met from the night before had shown up (the Rum Runner drinks must have gotten the best of them).

After we exchanged vows, we went to the restaurant next door for champagne and breakfast. That afternoon we boated to a remote island one of the locals had told us about. The place was deserted and we spent the afternoon, just the two of us, basking in the sun and toasting each other. That evening, we went back to the bar where we'd had our "rehearsal dinner." As we walked in, the band remembered us from the night before and introduced us as "Mr. and Mrs. Thomas Collins!" We took to the dance floor. That night, we danced into the wee hours as husband and wife.

The rest of the week was spent blissfully boating around the islands. I couldn't imagine any better way for the two of us to spend our "honeymoon."

On the plane coming home from our wedding (or vacation, or honeymoon, or whatever you want to call it), I remember looking at Tommy and saying, "So do I live with you now?"

We laughed, realizing that although we were married, we still lived in separate places. Just after we returned from the trip, it was my birthday, so I took the day off work to move some clothes over to Tommy's apartment. When he came in from work, he brought me my favorite flowers and a cake with a candle. We spent the evening together, just the two of us, and it was so special to celebrate with my husband. And it felt so great to say that, "my husband."

Now, only three years later, I was visiting those same places we had visited on our honeymoon, but I was alone. After I arrived in the Bahamas, my friends called to cancel their trip because their son had become ill. I was disappointed, but understood that they couldn't leave him. I decided to try to make the best of the remainder of my time there.

I took a water taxi over to the beach where we'd been married. I don't know what I expected to find there; maybe some kind of sign that Tommy was still with me? The beach looked exactly as it had that day of our wedding: a strip of bright white sand edged with turquoise water and shady palm trees. The only person with whom I shared my wedding memories was no longer with me. We would never make more memories together. All I did was think about my husband and how much I wanted him there with me. It was unbearable. Everywhere I turned, Tommy should have been there, and he wasn't. I sat on the sand by the water for I don't know how long, it could have been hours, crying. The only thoughts in my head were: "How could he be gone? I want my life back. I want Tommy back." When I returned to the hotel, I called the WC. I could barely get my name out I was crying so hard. I called friends who lived in Florida, and they booked me on the next flight home.

. . .

I FIRST MET Tommy three years before our wedding, in the summer of 1997. I'd only recently moved to the Northeast from Dallas, relocated by the mail-order sports company that I worked for at the time. I was living in Weehawken, a small New Jersey town just across the Hudson River from the island of Manhattan. My first few months in Weehawken were pretty lonely. I knew very few people in the area, and I would work ten to twelve hours a day and then go home to work some more. I just kept telling myself that this didn't have to be permanent, that I needed to do this for my career and to hang in there. I was lucky because my company was new, so everyone was in a similar situation. Within a few months, I had bonded with some of my colleagues and began to have something of a social life.

That summer, one of my coworkers asked me if I wanted to go with her and some friends to a birthday party in the Hamptons. I jumped at the chance. After all, I had nothing else on my calendar.

I'd never been out to the Hamptons before and I remember being so impressed— "Okay, this is why people live in New York," I commented. "So they can come to this stunning place on the weekends."

I didn't know anyone at the party that night, except for my work friends. At one point in the evening, however, I became aware that there was this great-looking guy across the lawn. Something made me want to introduce myself to him. He was roaming around the party, talking to everyone, gesturing with his hands, commanding the attention of whomever he spoke to. He was wearing khaki shorts and a pale-colored polo. His huge smile radiated from across the yard. In the end, there was no need for me to make the move. Later in the evening, this man walked straight over to our group and introduced himself.

"Hi, I'm Tom Collins, shaken not stirred."

Tom Collins soon had us roaring with laughter telling us stories about going out in New York, boating with his family and friends in the Hamptons, and about his brother, whose birthday we were celebrating. Now that he was standing in front of me, I could see that he had bright blue eyes to contrast with his dark hair and dazzling smile. Something about those eyes gave me butterflies. After he walked away, I blurted out: "Oh my goodness, now he is exactly the type of guy I would love to be with." I went home that night thinking of him, secretly hoping that our paths would cross again, even as I reminded myself that it was unlikely that it would ever happen and that I needed to stop daydreaming.

In the coming week, I thought it through. I was new in town, and when I met someone I clicked with, I made a point of following up with them. I liked this Tom Collins, so why shouldn't I ask him out for a drink as a friend? A few weeks passed, and eventually I asked my girlfriend if she had his number. She gave me what she thought was his number. I left a message telling him that if he ever wanted to go out for a drink, to give me a call. Later that day, Tommy called. It turned out that I had called his brother's phone number, and Tommy thought it was hysterical that I left this message on his brother's machine. We talked for a while and decided to meet up the next week for dinner. Great, I thought, I've made a new friend in New York. I figured that he was probably just being nice to me, seeing as I was new to town (even if I was hoping it meant otherwise).

Tommy had lived in the city since graduating college, and so while I knew nothing about New York, he knew all the places to go. We decided to meet at an Italian restaurant in the Theater District that he suggested. When I arrived, he was sitting at the bar. The second I saw him, that butterfly thing happened again with my stomach. After a few drinks, we moved to a table. The evening began to swing. I don't know if I wasn't nervous because it wasn't a "date," or if Tommy put every girl he met at ease, but I didn't care. I was having a great time with this guy, chatting, laughing, sharing stories. There was no awkwardness between us. Tommy had this magnetic sense of humor. This was something I'd noticed at the party in the Hamptons, but now I was face to face with Tommy, it was clear to me. This man was just so alive. I felt his presence, not just because I was sitting next to him, but because he generated postive energy. It was invigorating and hypnotizing at the same time. During dinner we were both joking with the waiter, so much so that by the end of the evening, he asked us how long we'd been dating. I remember thinking that it would have been an easy mistake to make—there was something about being with Tommy that made me feel completely comfortable, as if I'd known him for years.

After dinner, we decided to continue the night and have a drink at the bar next door. After more great conversation, we realized it was getting late. We both had to be at work early the next morning and it was already 1 am. Tommy called a car for me, took my number, and kissed me good-bye. I think we were both surprised: I'd thought, "Dinner and home by 11 pm"; he'd probably thought he was doing a favor for someone who was new to town. I don't think either of us had expected it to be this much fun. I headed back over the river and spent the rest of the night thinking of him.

TOMMY AND I started to see each other, but very casually. We dated on and off for over a year, partly because neither of us was looking for love and we were hesitant about making a commitment. I wasn't sure if I was going to stay in New York longer than a year, and Tommy was focused on his career. Besides, we were having a fantastic time just being with each other. But the more time I spent with him, the more I knew in my heart that he was the one. I'd never met anyone like him before. It wasn't just that he was handsome—and believe me he was handsome. There was never a dull moment with Tommy: he could be serious, he could be funny, he was the most entertaining person in any room. He was successful in his work as a managing director of his investment firm. His position required him to turn on the charm with clients, but this was something that he did with genuine ease. But work didn't dominate his life. The thing was, he made the guy on the corner where he bought his coffee each morning feel the same way as his biggest client. He made people feel good about themselves, me included.

The following winter, however, when we were in one of our "off" periods, I'd gotten some film developed from the summer before and wanted to send Tommy a photo of him with a friend from a weekend we'd spent on Long Island. The photo was a great shot and I knew he would want it, so I wrote him a note and put it in the mail with the picture.

Tommy called to thank me. He asked how I was. He told me that he had been thinking a lot about "us." I asked him how things were with him. He told me that he'd just spent the last three days with one of his closest friends whose sister had died unexpectedly. The experience had affected him deeply. He told me that watching his friend in so much pain was almost more than he could bear.

Toward the end of the conversation, Tommy asked me if I wanted to go out with him and some clients who were in town and whom I'd previously met.

I told him no. I'd made up my mind. I couldn't do this on again–off again thing anymore. I knew by now that I loved him, and that I couldn't open myself to getting hurt again. I needed to move on. But Tommy being Tommy, he persuaded me to go out with him. After that night, the relationship became serious.

I didn't mind that it took a while for our connection to solidify. I think it was good for both of us to assess the situation and make sure of what we were getting into. I decided that I loved being in New York and wanted to stay here. Tommy decided that he was ready to take a chance on this relationship. While many of his friends would joke that he would never settle down, only the people closest to him knew the real reason he was cautious. Tommy took marriage very seriously. He didn't want to enter into such an important bond without making sure the relationship was right.

Tommy was thirty-two years old when I met him, a native New Yorker who'd grown up in a close-knit Irish-American Catholic family in suburban Long Island, the eldest son. I'd spent my childhood in Chattanooga, Tennessee, the second of five children, your basic Southern Baptist upbringing. Although our backgrounds were somewhat different, we had a lot in common. We were both natural entertainers, loving to be the center of attention at any gathering. We were the owners of our own karaoke machine. We scoured three stores to find it, like we were shopping, not for some electronic toy, but for a house. We finally found the perfect model, a machine that had dueling microphones— there was no way the two of us would be able to share one mic. We both had a competitive streak. In high school and college, he was a lacrosse player; I'd been a cheerleader at college for four years. We were both athletic, loved to work out. We both loved to dance—at weddings, we were always the first and last on the dance floor, Tommy flipping me over his shoulder in our own version of swing dancing. We both appreciated downtime too, spending evenings at home during the week, ordering in, watching a football game or the Discovery Channel on TV. People say that "opposites attract," but we were very much alike.

Tommy proposed on St. Patrick's Day 2000. We'd been hanging out after work at an Irish bar across the street from Tommy's apartment. He still had his business suit on and asked if I would run across the street with him so he could change his clothes.

"No way," I told him. "I'll sit here and wait for you while I finish my Guinness."

But he was persistent, and I finally gave in.

As we walked into the apartment, he went straight to the coat closet and pulled out a ring box, placing it on the counter in full view.

"W-w-w-what are you doing?" I asked him, my heart beating out of my chest.

He got down on one knee with the box in his hand and opened it up. Inside was a stunning emerald-shaped diamond ring.

"Will you marry me? I have only one condition."

"Oh my God, what's the condition?"

"I get to keep my walk-in closet."

I grabbed him, hugged him, and honestly thought my heart would explode with love.

Tommy had a deal. Now we'd always have two reasons to celebrate St. Paddy's Day.

AFTER OUR IMPROMPTU wedding, Tommy and I started planning for the future. Although I'd always wanted to have a family someday, I'd never taken it for granted that it would happen, which made it all the more amazing when I began to let myself dream that this was something Tommy and I would do together. Now we were ready. I'd recently been offered my dream job, working for the National Football League. Tommy was thriving in his field. We went into "let's get serious and try to make a baby" mode. Each month, I would wait and wait to see if "it" would happen. Month after month, my period would arrive and I would get more and more disappointed.

Tommy would hold me. Then he would look me straight in the eyes.

"Julia, what would be so wrong if it's just you and me? Would that be so bad?"

I often think back to his words. No, it wouldn't be so bad. Now I would give anything for that to be the case.

I'll never forget the time Tommy woke up in the morning, sweating and obviously shaken from a dream he'd had.

I looked at him and asked him what was wrong.

"Are you okay?"

"Yes, but I just had a dream that we had three daughters and they all wanted horses. What am I going to do?"

I hugged him and said, "Don't worry, honey. Let's just work on the first baby, and we'll worry about the horses later!"

It was something he wanted as much as I did. He was thirty-six; the time was right. Tommy had already tracked down our family's second home on Long Island. The idea was that we would stay in our apartment in New York during the week and live in the house on weekends, until we both were ready to leave Manhattan. The house was perfect, with a wraparound deck and mooring rights. Tommy had spent the summer of 2001 restoring an old boat for us that had been sitting in the backyard of his parents' house for years—it was his mission to get this boat back in the water. And he did it. A week before Labor Day he made the inaugural boat run with his brother. We were just starting due diligence on the house in August of 2001, so excited about being homeowners for the first time together.

And at the beginning of September, we both went to our doctors to get tested to see if there was a reason why we couldn't conceive. My test came back and I was in the clear. We were just waiting for Tommy's results.

THE WEEKEND BEFORE September 11, Tommy and I were visiting my family's home in Tennessee. We hung out with my parents and siblings, we went to my college alma mater football game, and we went hiking around the waterfalls. It was great that my husband was getting to spend time with my folks when they lived so far away. On Sunday, we drove to Nashville—I was staying in Nashville on Sunday night to attend a Titans football game with clients; Tommy was heading back to New York for work on Monday morning. I drove him to the airport and let him out at the departing flights area. Usually I would have kissed him good-bye in the car, but this time, for some reason, I turned the ignition off, got out of the car, went around, and hugged and kissed him good-bye. He turned around, waved, and walked into the airport.

I remember thinking I couldn't wait to see him on Tuesday night. It was just like us to be going ninety to nothing—we both traveled frequently for work. We often joked with each other that one day our ship would come in and we would both be at the airport. Lately, we were planning our trips at the same time so that we could be home together more often. Unfortunately, it wasn't the case for this particular business trip. After the Titans game on Sunday I had to be in Denver for the first Monday Night NFL game of the 2001 season.

I spoke to my husband one last time just before boarding my flight home from Denver the following Tuesday morning, in the rental car bus heading to the terminal. It was 6:30 am mountain time, and I was exhausted after my long business trip and a great night out with my clients. It was 8:30 am in the East, and, as usual, Tommy was at work already. He always arrived before 7:30 am. I told him about the night before, about how we were out very late and I was totally exhausted.

"Julia, you're married now, you can't be gallivanting and staying out all night!" he joked. We laughed and I agreed with him. I told him I couldn't wait to get home and see him. He suggested that I meet him for a workout, and then we would have dinner with our good friend Tim Byrne. I was looking forward to coming home to see Tommy and having dinner with Tim, who always entertained me and kept me laughing.

It was a perfect blue-skied September day, and my flight took off with no delays. After a light breakfast, I stared out of the window and then drifted off to sleep. I woke up when the captain made an announcement.

"The FAA is having all planes land as soon as possible. We're headed back to Denver. A plane has hit the World Trade Center and it's a clear day in New York like it is outside your window, so I'll let you draw your own conclusions."

What? What did he just say? Did I just hear that right? I got up from my seat and headed to the back of the plane to ask the flight attendant for more information and explain to her that my husband worked in Tower Two. What kind of plane hit the building? Which building? Within a few minutes she returned and told me to gather my things, that she was moving me to first class. I asked her why and she said it would be easier to get information to me and I would be more comfortable. It didn't make sense. Why were people looking at me? Why did a woman stop me on my trip up to first class to say she would be praying for me?

As I arrived at my new seat, I was told that when we arrived in Denver, two airline representatives would be on the ground waiting for me. This confused me even more. Why was everyone acting so strangely? Not once did I think that something might have happened to Tommy.

As I exited the plane, two people were standing there to meet me. They tried to explain the situation, but I was having a hard time understanding what they were saying. They told me it was one of their planes that hit the building and that both buildings had collapsed and they were not certain of any survivors. Then I collapsed.

I remember being in the Admiral's Club, trying to contact Tommy, his family, and friends from his company, anyone, but I couldn't get a phone line out. The staff from American Airlines assured me that they would take care of me and make certain I got home as soon as possible. By now, the Denver airport was shut down. I stayed with a good friend in Denver, who took care of me that impossible night.

I was in contact with family and friends whenever I could get a phone connection. I stayed glued to the television, convinced I would see Tommy giving an interview to Katie or Matt or Barbara about how he'd carried people on his back down the 104 flights.

My employers at the NFL assured me that they would do everything possible to get me home, but because all air travel was suspended, they were not sure how soon it would be. On Wednesday morning, September 12, the COO of the NFL called and put me in contact with the Denver Broncos head of security, Bill Malone. Mr. Malone called and said he would come to where I was to make sure I was doing all right. After he arrived, we were talking about the events of the past twenty-four hours when his cell phone rang. After a brief conversation into the phone, Mr. Malone looked at me and said, "How soon can you be ready?" I responded, "I'm ready." He drove me to a small airport, where I boarded a jet owned by Robert Tisch, one of the owners of the New York Giants football club, who had flown his private jet to Denver for the Monday night game. Mr. Tisch had been granted permission to fly a group of FEMA personnel to New York, one of the only flights that took off that day. At that point, I didn't even know that FEMA stood for Federal Emergency Management Agency. I only knew they must be important people and they were headed directly to New York to help with the rescue. I described Tommy to them and gave them my phone number, just in case. I told them about his big blue eyes, his small muscular frame, his infamous scar on his forehead.

I remember looking out the window of the plane, not being able to wrap my mind around what was happening. I was doing my best to remain positive. I thought about how I couldn't wait to tell Tommy about this plane ride. I knew he would be the first to make me retell this story over and over at parties. I could hear him already: "Hey, you've got to hear this story about the owner of the Giants flying my wife back to find me." I knew he would soon start embellishing: "Did you hear? The entire football team came with her to look for me."

As we were flying into Teterboro Airport in New Jersey, the sun was setting. The pilots asked me if I wanted to come into the cockpit to see a view of New York City. As I hesitantly walked up to the front of the plane, the sky beyond the windows had turned to shades of deep red and orange. From the cockpit, I could see a cloud of smoke above the city, making it unrecognizable. What had happened? Where was he? I needed to get off the plane so I could check my messages. I needed to get to my husband.

A car was waiting to take me directly to Long Island to be with Tommy's family and our friends—I couldn't think about going to our apartment without him. As I approached the exit off the Long Island Expressway, I realized I couldn't remember how to get to Tommy's parents' house. Where was I? I had been here a hundred times and I had no idea where I was—Tommy always drove and I couldn't remember where to go. I called my brother-in-law and he guided me.

I arrived at his parents' to find over fifty friends and family standing out on the front lawn. I sank into the arms of the people I loved. I was finally home.

THERE WAS A steady flow of people at the Collins house over the next few days, bringing with them flowers, drinks, food—so many people wanting to hear from Tommy. My family soon arrived. Friends in the city were posting missing signs all over downtown. We knew Tommy would be coming home. We just knew it. In the meantime, I refused to sleep in any other bed but "Tommy's" bed in his old family home.

On Friday night, my brother-in-law and I decided to get out of the house for a while. We went over to a friend's restaurant to have a drink. It was here that I received the news that a friend whose brother worked for the NYPD had called. The officer had located a "Tom Collins" in one of the makeshift morgues that had been set up around the city.

This information was not acceptable. Tommy had survived the bombing of the World Trade Center in 1993; he would survive this time. There was no way that he was gone. We were going to grow old together, to have children together. It was not possible. He couldn't be dead.

My friends and family were responsible for getting me through the next few days. Everything was happening too fast. The wake took place on Sunday and Monday, and the funeral took place on Tuesday, exactly one week after Tommy was killed. The funeral home told us they had never seen so many people for a wake. I've been told that there could have been as many as a thousand people in the space of two days. I'm also told that I stood for five hours at a time, talking to each one of them, that the line of people waiting to give me their condolences snaked through the funeral home and into the parking lot.

At the funeral, as I walked down the aisle, I held onto the casket, as if I could hold onto my husband. The church was filled to capacity. The eulogy was read by one of Tommy's best friends. He delivered it with such passion and love and composure. As I sat and listened, I turned to see Tommy's closest friends—now his pallbearers—in the next pew, heads hung low, eyes glazed. Whenever I'd been with these people, we'd always had so much fun—to see them like this was incomprehensible to me. When the eulogy was finished, even the people standing in the back waiting for mass afterward clapped like they were at a concert. I've never seen so many people clap in church. I've also never seen so many people cry.

After the funeral, we went out and caused a tremendous traffic jam on the way to the cemetery. At the cemetery, I attempted to do my best Jackie Kennedy, but I just couldn't go on. I went back to the car, where I sat and let the sobs come.

IN THE COMING days, my head felt like it was going to explode. I would listen to people talk, but it was as if their conversations were taking place somewhere far away from me. My head hurt, my throat hurt, my lungs hurt, my body ached. I couldn't comprehend how my heart kept beating. At times I could barely breathe.

I didn't go back to our apartment for another week. I just couldn't go. When I finally did, friends and family came with me.

At the apartment, I'd begun going through my mail, when I saw a letter from the doctor's office. My heart skipped a beat. I opened it. Tommy's test results. He'd been given the all clear. Something clicked in my head. Maybe we could still have our baby after all.

At last, a ray of hope. He'd just been tested the Thursday before he was killed. Just maybe I would still be able to have Tommy's child. I called my friend Caryn and she went straight to the doctor's office and waited there for hours to speak to the doctor. Finally, when the doctor saw her, she told Caryn that they didn't give out that kind of information, that I would have to call.

I called the doctor.

She told me that they didn't keep the test unless you had previously arranged it.

"Are you sure?" I pleaded with her.

"Yes, I'm sure," she told me. "I'm so sorry."

My only ray of hope had vanished.

THE DAYS ROLLED by. I had no idea how or why. I relied on others to tell me what to do and where to go. I was so far from my own family that I depended on my friends and Tommy's family. That first month, a friend would sleep with me every night so I wouldn't have to sleep alone. There was always someone at my apartment. My phone never stopped ringing.

I wept constantly. I slept; I couldn't sleep. I didn't know where I was or who I was. I kept asking people, "What should I do?" I didn't want to be around people; I would only bring them down. I couldn't be left alone.

I had always considered myself strong, independent, competent, but now I couldn't complete the simplest task. I was so incredibly sad; it had sucked out every bit of life from me.

Every day there would be a mound of letters and cards in the mail for me. I was keeping the USPS going. I saw my mailman in the lobby of my building one day and he hugged me and told me how sorry he was. He'd asked my doorman for my story, as he couldn't believe how much mail I was receiving. Those cards and letters were so important to me. I looked forward to them each day. They reassured me that there was so much good in the world and that people cared. My mailbox would continue to be full for the next two years. I replied to every single one of those letters and cards, or I hope I did. That's how I would spend my nights—writing, writing, writing. I have no idea what I said in my replies. I only know that I wanted to write an individual and inspiring message to each person, even if in reality I probably sounded like a rambling idiot. I'm sure I addressed letters to the wrong people.

Writing gave me a focus, especially as I was beginning to have problems speaking. There was a tremor in my voice. I didn't seem to have any other symptoms of a cough or cold; it was just that I couldn't get a full word out. My voice sounded like a bad connection on a cell phone. I went to the doctor. As I sat filling out the form, I got to the section marked "status." The options were "married," "single," or "widow/er." At that moment my brain had to process the concept that my status had changed. Everything had changed, and at the same time nothing had changed. I was still Mrs. Thomas Joseph Collins, and yet, according to this form, I was a widow. I was no longer married. There had been no divorce, no separation, and yet I wasn't married. I had to force myself to move the pen and check the "correct" box.

The doctor told me I was under a lot of stress and to relax and that the voice problems would go away. I was given breathing exercises. I would sit at home trying to breathe, gasping from the effort. What was wrong with me? Eventually, after visiting a string of doctors, I was diagnosed with spasmodic dysphonia, a rare neurological disorder that affects the vocal cords and that's often mistakenly diagnosed as a symptom of stress or nervousness. SD has no cure, although some treatments can offer temporary relief.

What was going on? I was the cheerleader, the yeller, the conversationalist, the joker, the entertainer, the karaoke girl. I lost my husband. I lost my personality. I lost my voice. I lost my means of communication. I lost it.

I started taking muscle relaxants to help with my vocal cords. The pills were a lot like Valium. I would become immediately drowsy, but remain awake. I loved taking them. The emotional pain didn't go away, but I became amazingly lethargic. I was sad, but I was in a haze. I took the medication for a few months. Then I went to a specialist who thankfully found another treatment for me.

ABOUT A MONTH after Tommy's death, I decided to go back to work. I needed to fill my day. It was too depressing to sit home in the apartment. My employers told me to take as much time as I needed, that there was no rush for me to come back to work. But I needed to do something. When I arrived back in my office, I was greeted with a bouquet of flowers on my desk and a stream of visitors who would check on me every day. At the beginning, I would work for a few hours and then have to leave midday. It would be another six months before I actually worked a full day. My employers were unbelievably patient and understanding. With everything I had to worry about, I know how fortunate I was not to have to worry that my job would be taken away from me too.

Around the time I went back to work, my friend Caryn told me she wanted me to meet another widow who lived on the East Side. Caryn had heard about this woman through her friend Maureen Fontana, one of Tommy's ex-girlfriends from years ago. Maureen grew up next door to this woman's husband. At this early stage, I didn't have a mind of my own. If Caryn told me to call this person, I was going to call this person. Caryn gave me Claudia's number.

"Okay, let's meet."

Claudia and I decided to meet on Halloween, at a restaurant near to where we both lived. I'd brought candy for Claudia. I remember seeing this stunning dark-haired woman walking toward me.

I held out the candy and asked, "Trick or treat?"

Then I stood up and we hugged, and kept hugging.

I was so meek that evening. I was still having such difficulties with my voice that I was very quiet. But Claudia wasn't meek, and she certainly wasn't quiet. As we started to talk, it was such a relief to hear someone being so vocal and honest about our situation.

"How screwed up is this?" Claudia asked. "How are we widows? What the hell are we doing here?"

We actually managed to laugh about how crazy our lives were.

Claudia was sad; she was depressed and pissed off—and she didn't mind admitting it.

We talked about Tommy and about Bart. Our memories of them were so vivid. They weren't even memories yet; they were still "now." It was only a month and a half ago. We sat in the bar and cried together. Like me, Claudia was so in love with her husband. We were both newlyweds, only married a year and a half.

A few weeks later we arranged to meet again, this time with some other friends. This was when Caryn, the woman who had introduced us, met Claudia for the first time.

Claudia was her usual forthright self: "Life sucks. This all sucks."

I nodded, saying, "Right!"

At one point that evening, Caryn pulled me to one side. "Julia," she said, "I don't know if it's a good idea to spend time around Claudia. She seems like she's really angry."

But there was no way I was going to stop seeing Claudia. I knew that Caryn had the best intentions, but I was already crazy about Claudia.

Claudia was the voice I no longer had.

BETWEEN THE TWO of us, Claudia and I had so many people supporting us. Even so, we would call each other almost every day and see each other whenever we could. Claudia would call and leave a message: "Hey, I haven't gotten out of bed in three days."

I would be right by the bed, so out of it I wasn't able to pick up the phone. Then I would call her back.

"I couldn't pick up because the phone was out of reach. It was a foot away from me."

"What did you do today?"

"I got up to go to the bathroom."

"You did?"

"Oh."

"This sucks."

"Yeah."

"I think I'll go shower."

"Okay."

Other times we'd both be weeping so hard we ceased to make any sense at all.

Claudia was my widow hot line. As long as I could stay connected with her, I felt like I had some kind of "in." I trusted that if anyone could pull us through this, Claudia could. She was so honest and determined. She might be going under, but she wasn't going down without a fight. It was the blind leading the blind, but it was like Claudia was the blind person who'd figured out how to get the dog and the white stick.

ON NEW YEAR'S DAY 2002 I started keeping a journal. I dedicated it to Tommy.

I would write in my journal every day. The words would sometimes be different but the message was always the same: "Please come back. . . . I can't go on. . . . I miss you. . . . I love you. . . . Things are so different now. . . . I still feel you're with me. . . . It's just that you're away on a very long trip. . . . I still think that you've joined the CIA and will come back in a few years. . . . Some days I want to die. . . . I love you. . . . So much to tell you. . . . I don't think I can do this by myself. . . . People take things for granted. . . . I need to start over. . . . I must survive. . . ."

I was a widow who kept believing her husband had just gone away for a while. When strangers would see my rings and ask, "Where's your husband?" I would often tell them he was out of town on a business trip. This, for me, was what it meant to be a new widow—it meant failing to believe that I was a widow, no matter how many times I had to check the "correct" box.

I wasn't a widow. A widow wears black, a widow is old, a widow never forgets her husband. I wasn't wearing black, I wasn't old. But the last part—about never forgetting—this was true for me. In my head, I would make myself remember every bit of Tommy, over and over again. I would remember everything we'd done, everything we'd said, everything we'd planned. I kept remembering as if my life depended on it. If I stopped thinking and remembering, then it would be like I'd stopped keeping faith with Tommy. He would think I had given up on him, and I would never do that.

Months later I would still sit in meetings at work glazed over. Pretending to care was an ongoing struggle. I couldn't understand how people could focus on a circulation list, or what the catalog cover should look like. "Do you know what happened to Tommy?" I wanted to say to them. "Don't you know that three thousand people died? Shouldn't we be mourning that? Forever?" My colleagues were doing anything they could to help. People covered for me. They told me, "Julia, you do what you have to do. We'll be here." They helped draw up my schedule for me, reminded me where to go and what to do. At home, my friends had to pay my bills for me; otherwise I'd forget to do them. I couldn't balance my own checkbook.

I kept all of Tommy's things as he'd left them in his walk-in closet—after all, that had been his "condition" for marrying me. I refused to move or change anything. I would sit in that closet for hours just to be near to the clothes that had touched his body. There was one dirty shirt of his that I would sit with, clutching it and inhaling what remained of his smell. In the bathroom his washcloth was hanging on the shower holder. I couldn't bring myself to move it, let alone wash it. There was the empty Post Raisin Bran cereal box in the kitchen cabinet, my husband's favorite, maybe even his last meal. I was never going to throw the box away.

Tommy's little phrases and jokes, the things he used to say, were never far from my thoughts. Every time I was coming back into the city at night and saw those two massive gaps in the skyline, I would think of one of his recurring jokes whenever he saw the towers after dark:

"Damn, I left my office lights on." I carried on a continuous one-way conversation with Tommy in my head. I asked him constantly for his advice, I told him about my days. The first time I figured out the route to his parents' house on my own—getting from the Fifty-ninth Street Bridge to the Long Island Expressway—I actually picked up my phone to call him and tell him that I'd done it. It was like I'd come up with the answer to a math problem and I wanted to yell out the answer. Why couldn't I call him anymore? Why couldn't he e-mail me? I would call his work number over and over, only to get a busy signal.

Walking into my apartment to darkness, I'd call out, "Hi, honey, I'm home!" Then I'd go straight to our bedroom, take my clothes off, get into bed, and switch on the TV to drown out the silence. I'd watch hours and hours of mindless TV, reruns of shows I never wanted to watch in the first place. I'd call friends and sob into the phone, talking and talking but never hearing the one voice I needed above all others. I'd do this until I took a sleeping pill or managed to sleep without one, which was a rare occurrence.

I started asking Tommy to answer me by sending me signs. This didn't always work. Mostly, all I could hear was the sound of my own questions, pounding inside my brain. But more than once, when I asked my husband for a sign that he was with me, it worked. Waiting to cross the road, I'd see it right there in front of me. A moving truck with the words "Collins Brothers" on the side.

SIX MONTHS AFTER Tommy was killed, I was having a particularly bad day. All days were bad, but this was truly the worst. I'd left work early because I felt so terrible. I opened the door to the apartment and went straight to the couch to fall asleep, hoping that just maybe I would wake up from this horrible nightmare. A few hours later, when I did wake up, the sun was setting over the terrace of our apartment. I decided to open a bottle of red wine that we'd bought together at a vineyard in Napa. I thought about that trip, about how wonderful it had been, before remembering that we would never go away together again.

I had a few glasses, pacing around the apartment, trying to figure everything out. I was trying to retrace his steps that horrific day. How far did he make it down the stairs from the 104th floor? How far had he gotten when the tower fell? How close was he to escaping death? I couldn't get those images of stairwells and flames out of my head. That's what you do when you're a widow, especially when you're a September 11 widow. You retrace and retrace his steps. You try to figure out his last moment on earth. You rack your brain trying to come up with answers to questions that will never be answered. You think about this as if your own life depended on it. I went out onto the terrace. How could this happen to Tommy, to my husband, to my best friend? Why had this happened to him? How could I ever recover from this? In my heart, I wished that I'd been killed that day instead of him. I loved him and I'd do anything for him. I would die for him if that meant he could live.

I looked over the terrace railing, trying to figure out how to put an end to this nightmare, so that I could finally wake up and be happy again. Our apartment is on the top floor of a nineteen-story building, and it looked like a long way down. Which way would I jump? If I jumped on this side, I would land on the sidewalk and I might hurt someone. If I jumped the other way, I would land on top of a lower building and I might not be found for a few days. I'd have to pull myself over the railing and then push my body off the edge if I didn't want to crash into the apartments below.

What was I thinking? I went back inside to fortify myself and to attempt to get these crazy thoughts out of my head.

I decided to go through Tommy's things again—almost everything that he'd had on him that day had been recovered from Ground Zero. The only thing I knew was missing was his wedding ring. I pulled out the box and sat down in our favorite chair, where, only a few months ago, we would sit, legs and arms wrapped around each other, watching a movie together. The smell that came up from that box as I opened it made me reel back—a raw, acrid smell of smoke and dust. Here was his leather Day-Timer, still intact; his calculator, smashed but still hanging together by a thread; his credit cards, battered but with his name legible; his wallet, only slightly dented; the cash from his pocket, his cell phone, his briefcase, his laptop—everything covered with ash. There was dust and rubble in the box that contained these items, but these things existed. They'd been found. They had survived and Tommy hadn't. It was impossible to comprehend this.

The Day-Timer, which he never went without, was in almost perfect condition, not at all burned, just a little crushed. I started flipping the pages. I loved seeing Tommy's handwriting and going over things we had done that he had marked in the calendar. As I traced his handwriting with my finger, I was sobbing. I asked him to give me strength to go on without him, because I really didn't feel as if I could do this alone. I asked him for a sign telling me what to do, to please help me.

When I came to the day of September 11, I pulled the somewhat crumpled pages completely apart so I could read every word describing what he was going to do that day. That's when I noticed something behind the first of the three silver rings holding the binder together. My heart stopped.

Tommy's platinum wedding ring.

I'd thought that his ring had been lost. It was the only thing that hadn't been recovered from his body, or so I'd thought. I knew that it wasn't in our apartment. I'd wondered whether it had somehow flown off when he was running to escape the building.

Now here it was.

The one thing that I wanted so badly had been with me all this time, hooked onto the ring of the binder. I remembered that Tommy would sometimes take it off and play with it, spinning it between two fingers—he must have clipped it into his Day-Timer. I'd looked through that book so many times, and I had never seen it before. Somehow, Tommy knew I needed to find it that day, that moment, in order to be able to take the next step. He'd given me the sign I needed.

I called Claudia, crying so hard that it took me a while before I could communicate the story. I told her that finding that ring had saved my life.

The next day, I took the ring to a jewelry store to have it resized and inscribed with Tommy's name on the inside. I was going to wear it forever.

. . .

THE FOLLOWING SPRING, after I returned from my awful trip to the Bahamas for my wedding anniversary, there was something else to add to my misery. My fortieth birthday was looming. This was not a birthday I was looking forward to. I was getting older, I was childless, and I knew that, with every year, my chances of having a child lessened.

What if? What if I'd been pregnant? What if I'd been carrying Tommy's child when he died? What if I'd been able to see my husband's smile, his laugh, his eyes in our baby? We'd been trying so hard to get pregnant. Why hadn't this happened for us? It felt like I'd been doubly punished. Not only did I not have children, but also I had this grief that made it impossible to imagine having a child with anyone else in the future.

I looked in the mirror and wondered: "Does everyone see what I see? Does everyone see the old lady that I've become?" My eyes were always so sad and there were wrinkles creasing around them. I knew that I had aged. It was as if I'd gone through a hundred lifetimes in only a few years. My birthday was just another reminder that more time was passing without Tommy. All I could think about was how I would have spent my birthday with him. What would Tommy have thought up this year? What would we have done?

Tommy wasn't here to mark my fortieth with me, but now I had the WC. One of the unwritten rules of the club is that we will always make birthdays special. We can understand how difficult a birthday is to deal with, so we try to alleviate that by buying a thoughtful gift, going out for an exceptional dinner, or throwing a party. On that first trip to Scottsdale we'd pulled out our Palm Pilots and agendas and punched in everyone's key dates: our birthdays, our husbands' birthdays, our wedding anniversaries. We did this because we knew how hard those days were for us and we wanted to be there for one another when they came around. Between the four of us there were a bewildering number of dates that we marked: three memorials and two funerals; the dates of our first meetings with The Boys and our engagements; and that was before you factored in Thanksgiving, Christmas, and New Year's. In our former lives, these dates were reasons for celebration. Now our year was divided up into days that we knew we dreaded. We would feel apprehensive about them for weeks beforehand, and then, once we got through them, we had to face the fact all over again that nothing had changed.

This particular year, I definitely didn't want a party or an elaborate gift. All I wanted was a weekend at the beach with my three friends. I told them what I wanted more than anything was to put together a scrapbook of the cards, letters, and memorials that had been sent to me after Tommy's death. Even though the WC kept insisting we have a party or invite a lot of my friends out to dinner, I was adamant that I didn't want a big fuss. The girls honored my birthday wishes and agreed we would spend a weekend at Pattie's beach house, and I was grateful.

Instead of just focusing on the negative, we had decided to turn my birthday into a positive, as best we could.

Ann, Claudia, Pattie, and Julia

Julia and Ann drove out on Friday afternoon for the birthday weekend, and met up with Pattie at the beach. Claudia would join us later.

Pattie wanted to share with us one of her favorite rituals with Caz—having a glass of wine at the end of the day, sitting on a beach chair covered in a blanket by a bonfire, as the sun goes down and night falls. She had already packed firewood, a shovel, picnic basket, wine, and real wineglasses. Caz always said it wasn't proper to drink from plastic, even on the beach. Ann, Julia, and Pattie stopped at the store and got some snacks and a pack of cigarettes too.

Pattie got the shovel out of the truck, dug a hole, and strategically placed the logs so that the oxygen would help the fire to catch. It was something she'd done a hundred times with Caz, and she was determined not to forgo the pleasure of the experience, especially with people who understood its meaning. We got cozy under the blanket and opened a bottle of wine. The three of us were all beginning to understand how important it was to enjoy such feelings of well-being when we could. For hours huddled under the blanket we shared our stories, our sadness and joys. We indulged in wine, tortilla chips, and smokes, declaring that we had "all the nutrients a girl needs!"

The sun slipped below the horizon and the colors of the beach began to fade. The firelight created a glow in the new darkness. Our eyes adjusted, and despite the oncoming cold, huddled in our fleece pullovers, the blanket covering us, and with the heat from the fire Pattie had built, our bodies became accustomed to the temperature. It was so comfortable, this sharing and being together.

Something about the closeness and simplicity of this made us feel young again.

"I guess you're only as young as you feel," said Ann.

Julia loved *that* thought.

By now, it was getting late, so we decided to head off to the Palm restaurant, where we'd arranged to meet Claudia, who was driving in late from the city. The Palm was Pattie and Caz's home away from home on Friday nights in the off-season; a place to catch up with friends and share stories. Claudia arrived and we stayed until the early hours, talking, toasting Julia, commemorating.

THE NEXT MORNING, despite the urge to stay in bed, we decided to go out for a run. Okay, to be honest, it was primarily motivated by Julia—it was her birthday weekend, so she could get us to do anything she wanted.

Personal Trainer Collins was back—"C'mon, let's go for a run. It will make you feel better."

As we jogged, Julia and Ann showed us the punches they'd been perfecting in their new boxing class. We'd all found that working out helped maintain our sanity—when we were running, we would allow all the angry, painful thoughts to pass, imagining we were stomping on them until the thoughts gradually dissipated and we could begin to relax. With boxing, Ann and Julia explained, it was the same effect but multiplied. Boxing was one of the best releases of pain and tension either of them had ever experienced.

"You get to hit and pound away at the thoughts with your fists against the bag," Julia told us.

"It's like this is your chance to punch away at the unfairness of life," Ann described. "Here's one for the terrorists. Wham. Here's one for the unfairness of doing this all by myself. Wham. Here's one for having your entire future stolen. Wham."

As we continued to run, the sun broke through the clouds; summer was on its way. Windows were opening; there was the smell of honeysuckle in the air. Pattie took us along one of the most picturesque roads in the area, Gerard Drive. We were running through the middle of a narrow peninsula, stunning views of the bay on one side, the quiet expanse of the creek on the other. Lola followed behind us like a sheepdog herding.

This was a place that Pattie knew she might never have experienced if it weren't for Caz. Before she met him, she was very anti-Hamptons—she was put off by the scene, the parties, the obvious wealth. But Caz showed her the natural beauty of the place. His priorities were very different from the people who came here to dress up, go out, and be seen at parties. Caz came here to escape from the city, to work in his garden, to spend time in the ocean. Thanks to Caz, Pattie was now especially attuned to the incredible colors of this landscape, the quality of the light—vibrant blues, greens, and whites, shades creating a pure luminosity.

BACK AT THE house, we started work on our birthday project—helping Julia with her scrapbook. We settled into loungers by the pool. Julia started opening up shoe boxes and bags filled with letters, cards, and keepsakes. We sat on the deck and began sorting through them. As we started to work, so many memories from those first weeks were rekindled, and along with the reminders of such destruction came the flooding kindness of so many people. Here were the letters and cards from Julia's friends and family, and we started to read some of them. They spoke about their own pain, but also their need to make sure Julia was going to be okay. When she first received these letters, Julia wasn't in a fit state to be able to grasp their full power. Now, reading them over a year and a half later, the meaning of them resonated. This time she could appreciate how thoughtful these people had been, especially at a time when they were experiencing their own grief.

Julia had notes from students in grade school, paper doll angels that children had sent her, programs from memorials held all over the world, letters from people who didn't even know Tommy.

Ann started reading Tommy's eulogy. She read about Tommy's genius for friendship, his kindness, his generosity, his energy. The words hit hard. Ann began to cry, but at the same time she realized that the birthday project was going to be difficult enough for Julia without others breaking down too. Ann walked into the house to finish reading the eulogy, letting her tears come without having to stifle the full release of sorrow. As Ann was recovering, Pattie came into the house and asked her if she was okay. Ann knew that Pattie understood. It wasn't necessary for them to explain anything to each other: it was important to stay strong so that they could help Julia.

While the feeling of cohesiveness and closeness never dissipated, we began to work independently. Pattie went back to her gardening, pulling up weeds, with Lola at her heels. Ann began her own project of framing photos for her home—it was something that she had put off for too long—photos of Ward, of the kids, of the WC, and of The Boys. Claudia picked up Tommy's eulogy and began reading part of it out loud:

"Tommy excelled at snow and water skiing, wrestling and lacrosse during his years at high school. I'll always remember during one particular lacrosse game when we were losing to a rival team, our coach, with great drama, lay down in the middle of the huddle and, in an emotional moment meant to motivate the team, implored us to 'just walk all over him.' Without missing a beat, Tommy stepped into the middle of the huddle and took a giant step over our shocked coach. I knew that Tommy was a leader right then and there."

Claudia was laughing, crying, and wishing she had known him.

Then, every now and again, Julia would share a letter, article, or photo. We were all doing something different, but at the same time we were together. We'd often spent time like this with our husbands, just coexisting, and now we realized how much we'd missed the feeling. It was rare and precious to be able to experience solitude but with one another.

· · ·

THAT NIGHT, WE made a special birthday meal for Julia. Pattie took control of the grill. She and Caz loved to entertain guests. Every weekend people would come over for dinner. She had her system down: when to light the grill, when to boil the water, when to make the salad. The division of labor happened so seamlessly when Pattie was with Caz, and now it felt great to have people here to help. In a good relationship, it's natural for couples to work as a team, and roles tend to split between the two of you. With him gone it was up to Pattie to pour the charcoal, to get the fire started, to figure out the right temperature for the meat. For her, being here with the WC, making this meal to celebrate during such a tough time for Julia, was the turning of a tide— this feeling, of being part of such a well-coordinated team again, was vital. There was such a good energy between us.

Taking our lead from Pattie, we all kept busy making salads, preparing the vegetables, setting the table, lighting candles. When everything was finished, we photographed the table—the settings, the food, the plates—we were so proud of our Herculean effort. The menu was made up of Julia's favorite foods and flavors. The finishing touch was Pattie's homemade mint chocolate chip ice cream, made with mint from her garden. Martha Stewart had nothing on Pattie. And any guilt we would have had about the calories in our past lives was irrelevant in this new appreciation of food, friends, conversation.

Claudia pointed out that we needed to be grateful for birthdays, that our husbands would have given anything for the opportunity to turn forty. So we toasted to that.

OVER DINNER, THE conversation turned to motherhood. Claudia, Julia, and Pattie were always amazed by Ann, how she managed to stay strong and survive the intensity of this grief with three children to care for.

"When you have kids, you have a focus," Ann said. "There's that responsibility to someone other than yourself. You have to get out of bed in the morning. You don't have a choice. You have to keep functioning."

Ann told the rest of us how much she admired us for our strength and determination to make the best of our lives when we *didn't* have children.

"My children have been a huge blessing. I knew right from the beginning that I had a part of Ward that would live on. It did make it easier. I can see it in Billy when he outwits me with a joke. It's in TJ's desire to equal Ward's sports records and in Elizabeth's smile. I know I always have a part of him."

But, as with everything, Ann explained, there was a flip side. When she looked at her children—whenever they succeeded at school or reached a new stage in their development, made a joke or did something memorable—all she could think about was everything that Ward was missing and how much they were missing without him.

The rest of us talked about how we were going to move forward in the future, about how the ticking of the biological clock was keeping us up at night.

"Is there any way I can still have a baby?" Julia wanted to know.

"Definitely," we told her.

"Okay, because I'm thinking about asking some of Tommy's friends to donate their sperm. And then I could pick one of the samples so I don't know who the father is but I know it's someone Tommy loved and I love too."

"Kind of like a sperm lottery."

Julia broke into laughter. "Exactly!"

"Why not do it the old-fashioned way? Go out, find some cute guy, and have your way with him," Claudia suggested.

"Hey, Julia, remember you can borrow my kids anytime you want," said Ann.

AFTER DINNER, PATTIE made a confession. For the past few weeks she'd been carrying on a phone conversation with an attorney who worked for her accountant's office, named Stanley.

Stanley was aware that Pattie was a widow, and she was aware that he was single. As she explained to the WC, he was definitely "geographically desirable"; not only did he live out of town, he was from out of state, which, as every New Yorker knows, meant he was pretty much from another planet. Although she was a client, if they didn't get along, it wouldn't cause her problems because she would rarely see him and could avoid talking to him.

"He's perfect," said the WC.

What's more, Stanley had already told Pattie he was coming to the city for a meeting she was going to be attending the first Tuesday in June, next week.

"That's definitely perfect."

Pattie's mission, should she choose to accept it, was to ask him to have drinks with her.

"Can you believe we're even having these conversations?" someone asked.

"When you said your wedding vows, did you think you'd ever have to talk about this again?"

It was like we were pedaling backward when our friends were moving forward, buying homes, having children, becoming grown-ups.

"How did we end up here?"

Pattie:

The beach house was such a special place for Caz and me. Each Friday morning, as we opened our eyes, the first thing Caz would say was "We're going on vacation." It was Caz's house before it was ours, but he shared it with his usual relish and enthusiasm.

Caz and I spent our last weekend together at the house. The renters who'd inhabited the place over the summer were gone. It was a great weekend of blue skies and bright sunshine, warm enough to spend all our time on the beach. Caz loved everything about the sea; he loved the smell, the air, the salt. He would boogie board for hours in the ocean or go crabbing in nearby Georgica Pond. That weekend, as always, Caz was flopping around in the surf, waving his arms, begging me to come and join him. I'd go in with him until my fingers turned blue and wrinkled from the cold. While I returned to my book and beach towel, Caz remained in the sea, bonding with strangers who soon became good mates. After warming up in the sun and watching him frolic in the waves, I would periodically join him for more fun.

After his death, I'd ask myself over and over again why I didn't stay in the water with him longer, why I didn't understand the preciousness of those moments.

That same weekend, on Sunday, September 9, 2001, leaving the morning service at the church in East Hampton, the same church where we'd been married, the same church where we would later have his memorial, Caz stopped me in the churchyard. He took my hands.

He looked me straight in the eyes.

"Love, let's stop and reflect on what we accomplished in our first year of marriage."

I laughed and told him—"Love, Lola, laughter, and no loans!" That year, Caz had spent months tracking down the perfect Border terrier, our baby, Lola.

I didn't want to hang about in the churchyard. I was antsy that morning, eager to go home and change so we could get to the beach. The sun was shining; the waves were waiting; I didn't want to waste time. I assumed Caz would always be there and that there was all the time in the world to talk, that we could reflect on our first year of marriage when our anniversary came around three weeks later. I didn't take the time to share properly.

Later that scene in the churchyard would return to haunt me. Why didn't I take the time to stop? Why didn't I relish the moment? Why?

In the car coming home that weekend, we had a silly argument. Caz always did everything in excess, and I was trying to persuade him that 105 degrees in the hot tub at the beach house was too hot, that it was wasteful and probably bad for his health. It was a stupid discussion, and I was having a little sulk about it from my position in the passenger seat.

"Hold my hand," Caz told me.

Stubbornly, I said no.

"Love, grab my hand right now," said Caz.

I still refused.

"Love," he insisted. "Someday that hand might not be there."

I grabbed. We held hands all the way back to Brooklyn.

. . .

MY STORY BEGINS in 1988, the year I graduated from college and moved to New York City. I was twenty-one and a product of suburbia, convinced I wanted to live in the big city, drawn to its glamour and energy. My parents were skeptical at first, but because I'd found a good job, they supported my decision and drove me into the city, dropping me off on the corner of Third Avenue and Eleventh Street with thirty dollars and a suitcase. Turns out, I had forgotten the bag with my shoes in it, and had to go to Woolworth's Penny Store during lunch hour the next day to purchase my first pair of work shoes. Today my closet is full of all kinds of heels, but they have nothing on those $10.99 classics.

After a couple of years of sleeping on friends' futons and in shared apartments, I was able to afford the rental on my own apartment in SoHo, a two-hundred-square-foot studio. I didn't care that it was the size of a bread box; I was thrilled to be on my own in such a hip neighborhood. I spent my weekends walking, exploring, discovering, learning the city. I joined the public gym for $35 a year, went to free concerts in Central Park, cheered at comped Yankee games, wandered into art gallery openings. I was convinced the movie screens were wider in New York—the streets certainly looked like movie sets. The food tasted better, the people were more interesting, the buildings more spectacular. Coming from a small town, I loved the feeling of being a little fish in a big pond. New York seemed the perfect place for me to lose myself and then to figure out who I was and what I wanted out of life.

Looking at photos of myself back then, I see an uncomplicated, eager, and optimistic young woman, a glass-half-full type person. Although I had friends who were cynical and sarcastic, and I enjoyed their humor and outlook, these were not things I had in common with them. I grew up in a protected environment, shielded from hurt. Even my adolescence had been relatively painless—I was pretty much unaware of what others thought, and therefore immune to the usual tortures of being a teenager. Now, in my twenties, I was a wanderer, discovering life through art house movies, literature, music, and travel. I bought a single seat for a season at the New York City Opera; I took Italian classes in the hope of one day moving to Italy; I became a mentor to an underprivileged nine-year-old girl from the projects of Brooklyn. Travel became a priority. I visited England, Ireland, France, Spain, Hungary, Poland, and Czechoslovakia on trips with my brother or with friends. I went fly-fishing in Montana and skiing in Colorado, and white-water rafting in the rapids of Wyoming and Utah.

I dated sporadically, but it was never my focus. I wasn't looking for a husband. I was looking for new experiences and sensations.

Then, the summer before I turned thirty, I met Caz. Jeremy "Caz" Carrington was a proud Englishman and successful Wall Street broker with an insatiable energy and love of life. He blew into my universe with a force that swept me off my feet and was unlike anything I'd experienced before.

CAZ AND I met at the beach in the summer of 1996. I'd always been against the flash of the Hamptons, turning down offers to join group beach houses. But summers in the city were beginning to take their toll. I'd spent the past few years studying for a series of intense financial exams and I was beginning to burn out. This year, I received a call from my college friend Susie, who had one more spot to fill in her summer share and wanted me to join.

"It will be fun, promise," she said convincingly.

I looked down at the IRS refund check that had just arrived in the mail. The amount was the same as the amount needed to pay for a share in the house.

"Okay," I told Susie. What did I have to lose?

As it turned out, the weather that summer was far from perfect, and downpours were frequent. One washed out Saturday over the July 4 weekend I was out at the house with Susie, her boyfriend, and my brother. We decided to simply stay at home and relax. I was reminded of rainy days of youth and suggested a game of cards.

"Good idea," said Susie. But the house didn't have a deck. "Let's drive over to Caz's house; it's close and I'm sure he has a pack."

I said I'd come along for the ride. Susie had dated Caz for a couple of years after college, and after an amicable breakup they'd remained good friends. Although I'd run into them on the street once, I'd never properly met Caz.

By now, the sun had set, and the rain made the evening seem even darker. Caz's house was on a hill, hidden from the street. The lights lit up the surrounding trees as we crawled up the steep drive. The house came into view, a white modern structure—an adult house. Susie and I let ourselves in and went upstairs to the living area, where we greeted Caz and his friends.

Standing in front of me was a handsome man with a big smile, barrel chest, and sparkling blue eyes. Instead of being one of those guys who denied he was balding, this man had shaved his head to dramatic effect. I'd always said that I would probably end up with someone who was balding or salt and pepper, as both always seemed a sign of sophistication to me. Caz immediately asked us if we wanted a drink, some food? Anything? He exuded hospitality and had a charming English accent to top it off. After fixing us some drinks, Caz sat, surrounded by friends, cuddling a guest's dog. My first impression was of an extrovert, dominating the room with his tales and exuberance. He carried himself as if he was lord of the manor.

We told him we had to get back, said our good-byes, and promised to stay in touch that weekend.

As soon as we got to the car, I started peppering Susie with questions. Was Caz dating?

"Yes, seriously close to engagement," Susie informed me. "But please don't let that stop you. She's a witch, to tell you the truth."

"Would you mind?"

"No," Susie shot back. "I would be grateful."

On the drive home, Susie told funny stories about Caz. She clearly still admired him, even if the relationship hadn't worked out. We arrived back at the house, and although Caz remained on my mind, we really didn't speak about him for the rest of the weekend.

THE FOLLOWING SATURDAY, it rained again. Caz called Susie to find out what we were doing for the day.

"Not much . . . ," Susie told him.

He asked if he could come over and watch a movie. A few minutes later, the door burst open and Caz had arrived. Right away, the topic of food came up. What were we going to eat while watching the film?

Apparently this was a very important question. Susie and Caz went back and forth as if they were planning an elaborate dinner with the Queen of England. In the end, Susie agreed that Caz was the most qualified to choose the menu and procure the snacks. As he was walking out the door, Caz asked me if I wanted to join him.

"Sure," I said and followed him out the door.

We headed over to the "secret deli," a little spot off the beaten track with a decadent yet old-fashioned array of bakery items. Watching Caz pick out "sweets" and "savories," as he called them, was like watching a small child in a toy store. We bought ham, pâté, cheese bread, *and* cheese. As I was deliberating as to whether to buy myself a cookie or a cupcake, Caz solved my dilemma.

"Get both," he instructed me. "Don't deprive yourself of something so simple. You can always have half of each." Later I would discover that this statement epitomized his attitude to life.

Before heading back to the house, Caz suggested we go to the beach to see the waves. We drove up to the parking lot on Main Beach and watched as fifteen-foot waves crashed onto the sand, frothing white foam rising from the steel blue waters. As the rain pounded against the windshield, I realized I was more attracted to this man than I had ever been to anyone before.

When we got back to the house, as planned, we watched movies and consumed our delectable snacks. Caz and I took the same couch. He spread out on one end and I was on the other. My feet were curled up along the side of his body. No doubt about it, something was happening.

Later that week, Caz called to see if I wanted to go to a movie with him. As I was still unsure of his dating status, I was reluctant, but he assured me he was doing nothing wrong by taking me out. After the movie, over dinner and drinks, we talked for hours, Caz dominating the conversation. I couldn't get a word in edgewise. Even so, I was enthralled. He walked me home and we agreed to spend time together that weekend.

CAZ DISENTANGLED HIMSELF from his prior interest and we started seeing each other. Although this was my first experience of true love, it felt natural. I soon felt that I couldn't live without him. We were inseparable. For the first time I was sharing my existence with a partner, establishing the foundations of our life together.

Caz was fascinating to me. He was from a background that was completely different to mine. The product of an English military father and a mother with a Scottish background, he lived as a child in Northern Ireland, Hong Kong, Singapore, and Cyprus, before at the age of seven going to boarding school, where he was taught to be a proper Englishman and quickly perfected humor as a survival technique. He spent weekends with his beloved maternal grandmother, Nanna. He was thirteen when his parents separated and Caz became the "man of the family." He remained incredibly protective of his mother and his sister. He'd had to grow up fast, but when he told his story, it was without a trace of bitterness. No "Woe is I." Caz had a stoic Scottishness about him, inherited from his mother's side; he would rather get on with things than stop to complain about them. Caz left school at eighteen and started a career in finance, moving to New York at the age of twenty to work on Wall Street.

It was a background that couldn't have been more different from mine, growing up in a very happy, apple pie, God-fearing New England family, the youngest of four children, my parents still together. Caz meanwhile wasn't exactly my parents' idea of the perfect match for their daughter. He was outlandish, he was noisy, he was spontaneous. He was the first to admit that his career was volatile. Some years brought good financial rewards, but there was always the chance he could be out of a job the next year. He smoked cigarettes back then. He had a missing front tooth from playing rugby—he liked to pop out his retainer and show off the gap. He was English.

When I moved in with him before we were engaged, it sent my parents for a loop. I loved them dearly, but I was confirming my independence, doing something that went against the grain of my upbringing. If my parents had pictured me with the all-American boy, then Caz was far from it. But after a surprisingly short amount of time, he won them over, charming my mother with his jokes, listening with genuine fascination to my father's life stories. Underneath the showman was a gentle soul. Caz just wanted the people around him to be happy. My family sensed this and accepted him into their midst.

Perhaps they saw how much Caz and I complemented each other. Whereas he was extravagant, I was more circumspect. Once we were buying limes for a recipe that called for two. Caz bought a dozen.

"Why twelve?" I asked.

"Why not?" he replied. "Just in case! Limes are cheap. . . ."

Rolling my eyes, I agreed that, yes, limes were cheap, but why did we need an extra ten?

"We might have guests!" It was true. Caz loved to entertain, and those limes were soon transformed into a large round of margaritas.

Once, in passing, I made a comment about "not really feeling like I'd made it in New York until I had my own washer and dryer." Very few people in the city have the luxury of washers and dryers in their apartments because of lack of space and access to power.

The next day, Caz was already conspiring with someone at his work to buy her old washing machine. A few days after that, I walked into the apartment and saw a big Sears box and Caz coming toward me with a bottle of champagne and a huge grin on his face.

"My dear," he said, flourishing the bottle and gesturing at our new washer *and* dryer in the hallway closet, "you have made it!"

Caz was expansive, and sometimes exasperating, but passionate and never ever boring. He was flamboyant; I was steady. I loved to laugh; he loved to joke. He'd always been the giver in a relationship—now he allowed himself to take. We fit; we worked. I'd always been so independent that it was refreshing for me to have someone in my life so full of support and encouragement. When I was frustrated at work or feeling insecure, he'd simply say: "Why are you worried? You're much smarter and more charming than any one of those people. Carry on and do your best."

Caz was someone who knew something about everything. Partly because of his English education, and partly because of his natural curiosity, he was well versed in a seemingly endless number of subjects: the constellations, the Latin names of plants, why the tides came in when they did, why phosphorescence glows, the phases of the moon, bird names and bird calls, how to sail and how to fish. This was a guy who could knit, garden, play rugby, cook a meal, define any word, and most importantly, make people howl with laughter. I loved to listen to him describing the world to me.

. . .

WE WERE MARRIED out at the beach on an Indian summer's day in September 2000, four years after our first meeting. Caz loved his wedding day, loved being the center of attention and sharing his happiness with others. The photos from that day say more than I could ever hope to express. Caz's radiant hopefulness and confidence are barely contained within the stillness of the photos. In one of them, he's on the beach, looking up to the heavens, holding one of my hands while his other arm stretches out to the sky. In the photo he's so alive, filled with a sense of wonder at the world.

We were going to spend the rest of our long, healthy lives together. Our first year of being husband and wife passed quickly, an exciting and romantic time. In July, I went to Korea for four nights on a business trip. How were we going to make it? Caz explained to me that he made a body out of pillows so he could pretend that I was there, because he couldn't imagine life without me. I had a fax in my room and he faxed me a letter every day, along with a call in the morning and the evening. He sent me flowers, as he did each time I stayed alone in a hotel. We made plans to go to Vietnam and Cambodia on vacation, leaving September 23. Caz had his sights set on two little nippers to make our family complete—a girl, then a boy. Our first anniversary was approaching. Life was full of possibilities.

Then just as dramatically as he entered my world, influencing it on so many levels, Caz exited with even more power, changing me forever.

THAT MORNING, CAZ got up first to walk our dog, Lola. I stayed in bed, waiting for him to leave, which was my cue to get up. After returning from the walk, he plopped Lola on the bed and carried on getting ready for work. Before leaving, he came over to the bed to kiss his girls. Tanned from the weekend, he was looking quite dapper in khakis, a white shirt, and loafers. He picked up Lola by her four legs, like a pig at a pig roast, and then nuzzled her belly. He gave me a kiss and hurried out the door, saying that he loved me.

A few minutes later, he raced back into the room because he'd left his work pass in yesterday's pants. He was muttering that he was going to be late.

He came back to the bed for another good-bye, coming over to cuddle Lola one more time and wish me a good day. Another kiss on the lips and he scurried off, telling me he would call me later.

I got up, showered, and got dressed in a blue pin-striped pantsuit. The usual train ride to work, a stop at the coffee truck, and an elevator ride to the sixteenth floor of my Park Avenue office building. As I entered my office, the phone was ringing. I took the call. It was my friend calling from London asking if Caz was okay.

This was the point at which my life began to unravel.

I had no idea what my friend was talking about, but I assumed it was a small plane that had gone astray. I thanked her and let her know that I would call Caz as soon as we hung up. I did. I got a rapid busy signal. My heart began to beat a little faster. I walked out of my office to ask my coworker if he knew anything. His brothers were police officers. "Yes, I do," he told me. "I'm trying to get as much information as possible." My phone was ringing off the hook—my boss, family members, friends were calling. My friend Kia rang and said she would be right down.

"Why?" I asked her.

"Because . . . ," she replied.

I kept trying Caz's number. Busy. A rapid busy signal.

My boss came running in.

"Are you okay?" she asked with concern in her eyes.

I told her I was going over to St. Patrick's Cathedral to say a prayer. She agreed to join me for the walk two blocks away. When we got to the cathedral's steps on Fifth Avenue, we looked downtown and saw plumes of smoke billowing from the towers.

"Oh my God," I said, my knees buckling beneath me.

There was a policeman guarding the steps. He refused to let us pass.

My boss let him know that my husband worked in the Trade Center and that I just wanted to say a quick prayer for his safe sprint down the stairs.

This was the first of many doors that opened for me in my new position of "privilege."

I walked through the vast doors of the cathedral, thinking how strange that people were being prevented from entering a religious building in the middle of a crisis. I said a prayer to God to give Caz the strength to get down those stairs as quickly as he could and into my arms. I talked to both Caz and God. I remember repeatedly telling them how much I loved them both.

When we got back to my office building, we ran into Kia, who was just arriving. Her face was marked with worry. She hid what she knew. Up we went in the elevators, silently.

When I got back to my office, my neighbor was calling. He offered to go over to my apartment to set up base and take any calls. By now, communication was erratic. Sometimes you could get through; sometimes you couldn't. I managed to get hold of Caz's mother, his sister, his father, my brother-in-law. The more people I spoke to, the more questions were raised. I didn't have any answers. I had to stay glued to my desk so I would be there when he called. News was random and confusing. My coworker informed me with trepidation that Two World Trade Center had collapsed. What? My mind was racing, desperately trying to keep up with what was happening, panic mounting with every second.

In an attempt to control my anxiety, I announced I was heading back to St. Patrick's. Kia and I walked over together, but as we turned the corner onto Fifth Avenue and looked downtown, nothing was there. There was nothing in the sky, only smoke. This wasn't possible. Somehow, Kia got us through the doors of the church. We lit a candle. Dear God, please, I beg you, bring him home safely. Get him down those stairs. I calculated 105 stories in my head, about twelve steps a floor, that's about 25,000 seconds, less than an hour. He could make it. Please, God, please.

Back at the office, Kia's husband was waiting. What should we do? I wanted to be there for Caz when he called. But maybe we should go to him. We called my neighbor back at base. Has he called? I looked to my coworker. He did his best to be upbeat, but his expression gave him away. He was distraught.

We decided to go and look for Caz. I changed my outbound message to tell him we were on our way, then repeated, I love you, I love you, I love you.

We headed back to Fifth Avenue. Again I looked at the smoke and empty sky. Those towers were such a part of my landscape. We were residents of Brooklyn Heights, the neighborhood just across the river from Lower Manhattan. I saw those buildings every day. "I don't get it," I kept muttering to myself. I kept comparing this to 1993 when Caz escaped from the bombing of the World Trade Center. I was calculating the stairs and the minutes.

We headed downtown, walking in the middle of the avenue, detouring around the Empire State Building. Ahead, I could see people covered in white-gray soot, dazed survivors trudging home. Please, God; please let Caz be walking home over the Brooklyn Bridge. Another call to base. "Any word?" I checked my work phone. I prayed.

We headed toward St. Vincent's Hospital, where empty stretchers lined the streets and people craned their necks as ambulances arrived. When the ambulance doors opened, they were empty. There were no injured inside. At the hospital, we registered Caz as missing. In the Emergency Room, people who had escaped from the towers were awaiting treatment and sharing information. What floor were you on? Which tower did you work in? Okay, they were on lower floors, but it increased my hope. Caz could do it.

Volunteers were giving blood. I suggested we do our part. My friends looked at me like I had three heads. This was the beginning of "the looks." These looks were founded in love and support, but what they communicated was "Does she know what's going on?"

Ring, ring, ring. Did he call, did he call, did he call?

We had learned nothing at the hospital. We headed over to another location to register his name on a citywide list. People knew nothing. Everyone wanted to help. Quiet chaos. By now more friends had joined us, and I agreed to go to a nearby bistro, as no one had eaten or drunk a thing that day. I couldn't eat. I took a sip of a drink but then felt immediately sick. Where was he?

We headed off to find the triage centers. Perhaps he was there and didn't have access to a phone.

EVENTUALLY WE GOT to Houston Street. The barricades were up and we were told that no one was allowed south. We begged our way through, identifying my connection to the towers—that "privilege" again. Crossing Canal Street, we pleaded to be allowed to pass. We were deep in black smoke, the poisonous smell burning our nostrils. Trash was scattered everywhere. Humvees were crawling the streets. We had entered some kind of war zone. At Chambers Street, again we were told that no one could pass. This time the policeman—almost comatose with shock and sadness—wasn't in the mood for negotiation. He suggested we make our way back to the Manhattan Bridge and cross over to Brooklyn there. Beyond him we could see the orange smoldering of flames.

On the bridge, I turned to look at the city behind me. Were we really here in New York? Was this actually happening? Could he really be hurt?

Back at the apartment, my neighbor was in control. He had compiled a list of over a hundred calls expressing concern, arranging the list into three columns—names, phone numbers, comments. But we were only looking for one call. Where was that call on the list? Where was Caz?

I picked Lola up and held on for dear life. I allowed a few of my first tears to come. I sat down. Someone handed me a glass of wine.

More waiting. After a while we walked half a block, to the end of my street, the beginning of the Brooklyn promenade that overlooks Lower Manhattan. Ahead was a street sign I'd never noticed before: a yellow caution triangle warning of a DEAD END. Another sign right behind it said END. Gray, thick smoke filled the air. Papers were littering the ground, black with soot. We sat on a bench, staring at the smoldering sky. People had tied flowers and photos to the posts of the railing. There were candles.

Back to the apartment. We made lists of emergency services, of hospitals over the tristate area, of contacts at Caz's firm, Cantor Fitzgerald. Endless calls. Dial, busy. Dial, busy. Dial, no, sorry, we have no one by that name here. All through the night we sat on my bedroom floor, calling. I was not taking a break. I would not give up. Fighter planes roared overhead. Dial, busy. My brother finally reached me from France, where he was with our parents. Oh God, if we'd joined them,

Caz wouldn't have been at work. Hurry home, I told my brother, stay positive, we need you.

I didn't sleep during this time, the longest day of my life. The calls continued throughout the night and into the next day. I went to church the following morning, gray with emptiness. Where was my consolation? At home, people stopped by to offer help. We gave each other updates. No television was on. No one spoke about death or loss, and yet it was palpable. Calling, calling, calling.

That day the rotary phone broke and someone was dispatched to buy a new one.

I wouldn't give in to sleep. Kia suggested half a sleeping pill.

"Please, Pattie, you need your sleep, you've been up for thirty-six hours." Although I did as I was told, I fought the pill as it began to take effect, forcing myself back to consciousness when I heard the phone ring. Finally, as painful as it was, I let myself go under.

On Thursday, my sisters arrived. That night, my sister slept in bed with me. In the dead of night came the storm. Crackling thunder, white lightning—heaven speaking. Sitting up in bed, I held Lola, who was panting with fright. Was he out there, in the wind and the wet, exposed to the elements? The next morning, as I woke up, the stench of burning metals and rubber hit my nostrils. The rains had made the smell even stronger, the wind blowing east toward Brooklyn, infiltrating the apartment.

That morning, I took a call from the brother of one of Caz's colleagues. He told me he had spoken to his brother minutes after the plane crashed into the building.

"He said good-bye, told me he loved his family, that he wasn't getting out of there."

I tried to keep myself composed—this was someone I didn't know so well. I managed to hang up before I collapsed.

I called the wife of another colleague. Did you speak to him before the towers went down?

"Yes, he was scared. He told me that he loved me and that he didn't think he would be able to get out."

Oh God.

I hung up. Began wailing. Couldn't breathe. Didn't want to believe. Not possible. Caz wouldn't be scared. He would have taken control. He would have been strategizing. He was a leader. He had to be okay. Trembling with fear. Hyperventilating. I still couldn't believe. Why would anyone fly a plane into a building to deliberately kill people?

Shock prevents belief, protecting us against the unbearable nature of information. It's nature's way of giving us a chance to absorb the awful reality drip by drip rather than in one giant deluge, impossible to swallow.

IN THE AWFUL weeks afterward, those days leading up to our first wedding anniversary on September 30, my brother, sisters, parents, friends, and coworkers were doing everything they could to help me. I had known Kia and Sandy since college days, and since the eleventh, they had barely left my side. They took turns, tag teaming with my brother and neighbor—encouraging me to eat, forcing me to go to bed, making me get out of bed, doing my laundry, sorting through paperwork, taking messages from the hundreds of calls we received every day from friends, family, and virtual strangers. It was a heartfelt outpouring of love and support, but I didn't want to talk on the phone. I was too sad for words.

Kia coped by cleaning. She cleaned and scrubbed; washed, folded, and ironed. One morning, she was folding a fresh batch of laundry pulled from the dryer. I looked at her and my face dropped.

She knew immediately.

"Oh God, I washed his shorts." She had washed his blue shorts. The last pair he'd worn, still containing the shape of his body. I would never have washed them; I had to retain every last trace of him.

"Oh God, I'm sorry, I'm sorry, I broke your heart all over again."

That weekend, I walked into the kitchen and witnessed my father opening the bag of potato crisps that Caz had just purchased from the English grocery shop in Greenwich Village.

"How could you touch those? They belong to Caz," I told my father. I knew I was being irrational, but at this stage nothing in my life adhered to the laws of rationality. I had to hold onto what was possible to hold onto.

Unable to call Caz or speak to him, I would write long notes, telling him that I loved him and missed him and that I was thinking only of him. I was retreating into a cocoon of the past. In order to protect my sanity, I couldn't expose myself to the present. The writing became my safe haven. It was the time when I could breathe. I kept a memory log. I didn't want to forget how he walked, how he danced, how he brushed his teeth. I wanted to remember how he put his Chap Stick on (lips pinched together, rubbing between the two, until the Chap Stick became a point).

I wanted to rewrite the dictionary. There weren't words to bring enough weight to my grief. The word "loneliness" meant nothing. It wasn't huge enough to describe the missing of him. Words were tiny compared to the vastness of my feelings.

My family and friends began tiptoeing around me, walking on eggshells. They couldn't predict what might trigger my distress, or what they could do or say to help. What was there to do? They could feed me, they could pay my bills for me, they could do my laundry, but they couldn't bring him back to me.

I couldn't connect. I was a robot. Even a simple task like walking Lola became a challenge: "Biscuit, bag, leash, keys," I had to remind myself when leaving the apartment, so that I didn't lock myself out.

The days and nights revolved, one arriving after the other, each one needing to be endured. In mid-October I went back to work. I believed that if I could just keep my head down and stick to my routine, then I would be able to "make it," without ever knowing where "it" was or what the hell I would do once I got there.

I was a widow in possession of my husband's death certificate with the word "homicide" on it. And I still couldn't believe that I even knew someone who'd been murdered, let alone Caz.

I KNEW I wasn't ready to have a memorial. When friends and family began urging me to do so, I held my ground. I wasn't delaying having a memorial because I didn't have a body, I was delaying because this was a milestone I wasn't ready to pass.

Everyone had an opinion, but I knew Caz would want me to do what I had to do. I was in control, and I didn't want anyone to misunderstand that. First we would hold a service in the U.S., and then we would go over to England for a memorial there in December. I worked with his family to coordinate the timing, to make sure this worked for everyone. We chose the readings, printed a program, appointed eulogists, arranged for the music. I spoke with the priest, selected an outfit. We did everything to take our minds off what was actually taking place.

We held the memorial in the same church in which we'd been married. I sat in my pew and stared at the spot where we both stood for our vows. A single bagpiper played outside the church as people filed in. The organ music began. It was bad, uninspiring Catholic music. Sorry, Cazza. I am so sorry, love, that it's not strong, proper Church of England music. I wanted to make things right for him on this day that was already so wrong. There were five eulogies, each one celebrating his life, each from a different perspective.

The reception afterward was at a restaurant on the marina. A mild rain began to fall as we arrived. Inside, I saw the faces of all the people who'd made such an effort to be there, traveling from all over the country and from England. He would have loved the crowd. Why couldn't I share this with him? We played a video that we'd prepared of pictures of Caz throughout his life, set to music. The mixing of love and sadness in the room was stinging. Then, when the film ended and we tried to eject the tape, it refused to come out, so we directed the video at a blank spot on the wall and it played all day. We took it as a message from Caz, a man not easily switched off. Partway through the reception we stepped out onto the deck of the restaurant as the sun began to set, in time to see spectacular oranges and pinks radiating over the harbor.

The day after the memorial, my father informed us that his health problems had returned—he'd been diagnosed with and beaten colon cancer three years ago, but now it was back. Why, God? Desperate to keep busy and not to think, my family and I went out into the backyard of the beach house to rake some leaves. Caz loved his garden, tending it endlessly, taking pride in his robust rosemary plant, bragging about his butterfly bush, babying his Montauk daisies. He loved cutting armloads of long, tall gladioli for me, returning every Sunday to Brooklyn with flowers for the week.

It was late fall already, and the borders were showing stripped twigs and browning leaves. The bank of hydrangeas, filled with rose-colored flowers in the fall, had long since shed their blooms. But there, in the middle of the row, one bright blue head of flowers stood out proudly. One blue head in November. A sign, a blessing, allowing me to sense Caz's presence as I set out on the arduous road to comprehending that he was gone and that his absence wasn't just temporary but forever.

WHEN KIA AND Sandy announced that they wanted to take me for a mini-break in Florida after the memorial, and just after Thanksgiving, it was very hard to say no. They had done so much for me already; it was as if by agreeing to go, I could do something for them. I was sensitive to the fact that they were hurting too. At the time, Kia was separating from her husband. Sandy had just ended a relationship of ten years. As with so many people, the shock of September 11 had made them reassess their priorities. Life was too brief and precious. Neither of them wanted to be in a relationship that wasn't meaningful anymore. And they were grieving for Caz too, missing him too, heartbroken for me. This trip was for all of us. It was a chance to be together and support one another, while getting some sun on our faces in the middle of winter.

"What do you think? Just the three of us?" they asked.

My first thought was: What will I do without Lola?

Of course, I knew I could leave her with my neighbor. That wasn't the issue. I didn't want to leave Lola. She was my best friend, my buddy. She was intuitive, sensing when I needed her to be close. When I cried, she licked my face until I smiled. I needed her just as much as she needed me.

When I wasn't talking to Caz, I was talking to Lola. I was convinced that she could communicate with her daddy. A twitch of the ear, a wink of the eye.

"But what will I do without Lola?" I protested to Kia and Sandy.

"You'll be fine," Kia replied. "Lola's a *dog*!"

My friends made everything easy for me, booking the flights and the room at the hotel, making sure that—under the circumstances—this was the best trip possible. But even on the plane out, I was already imagining being home again, already out of sync with my surroundings, even with my beloved friends.

"Well, here we go," said Kia as the plane rumbled toward takeoff. "The spinsters. Just like old times. The Golden Girls . . ."

I flinched. I definitely was not a spinster. I was not single. I was married to Caz, the man who had given me the rings on my finger. Kia and Sandy were alone because they'd decided to be alone. For me, there was no divorce; there was no decision to separate. Caz was the man I wanted to spend the rest of my life with. And while I knew Kia and Sandy understood this, that they were trying to be kind and make me feel included, how could they relate to my situation? It was impossible for *me* to relate to my situation.

As the plane climbed higher and higher, I focused on looking out of the window, scrutinizing the sky above the clouds. I always looked up when I talked to Caz, and now I was here, in the middle of "up." Where was he? Where was heaven? I believed it existed, but I couldn't figure out where it was located or how heaven worked. Was it a place with defined parameters? How old were you in heaven? When I got to heaven, would I be so much older than Caz? Did children grow up there? What language did they speak in heaven? Were there English accents or just a heaven accent? Was he with Churchill or Lincoln? Did he see me? Was he injured? Was he safe? Was he being looked after up there? Did he have a dog in heaven?

Outside the window the clouds formed into inscrutable mountain ranges, wide and white, their edges lit by the sun as if from within. I turned to my book, *Grief Observed*, by the English writer C. S. Lewis, about his grieving after the death of his wife. I could only read books that were relevant to me.

AT THE HOTEL, I had a strong feeling that I wanted to stay here for the duration of the trip. I didn't want to go anywhere else. I had come this far—this was adventurous enough. Getting ready for dinner, in my mind I was already preparing to come back to my room, to get into bed, to go to sleep again.

The following day, we made it as far as the beach, and settled into three loungers, all in a row, Kia and Sandy on either side of me.

The waves were sliding in, turning the golden sand a deep brown until the water shrank back out again, letting the heat burn off the wet.

On the loungers directly ahead there was a group of women from New York. You could tell they were New Yorkers. Maybe it was the way they carried themselves, or the *New York* magazine and *New York Times* being passed among them. They were chatting away, basking in the sun, ordering cocktails.

I knew I shouldn't have come. My skin, exposed, felt hot and prickling. This was wrong. I wanted to be home in New York where it was cold. I wanted to see Lola. I wanted to be where Caz had been. The thought of Caz, and my need for him, sent such a heavy pain through me that I imagined my body sinking even lower into the soft sunlounger, slipping down and down, deep under the sand until I was somewhere dark and cool where everything was over. I hated being here in this frivolous playground. By coming, I felt I hadn't been loyal to Caz or the thousands of others who had been killed that day.

"Ugh," Kia said at one point that afternoon. "I can't believe that girl is wearing my bikini."

I forced myself to look up. It was true. One of the women from the group of New Yorkers ahead of us—a strikingly tall and attractive blonde—was striding down to the water wearing a purple leopard-print two-piece just like Kia's.

And there were other reasons to notice these women. Another member of the group was pregnant. At some point her cell phone rang and I heard her having a heated discussion with someone on the other end of the line. Then she snapped shut her phone, announcing that her husband had just put in a bid on a new house on Long Island without her seeing it first.

"Can you believe it?" she asked the others. "How could he do that? There's no way I'm moving to a cul-de-sac near my parents in Port Washington!"

I remember thinking: "This woman's husband is alive. She's pregnant. They're buying a house. Who cares if it's in Port Washington on a cul-de-sac?" Although I never envisioned myself as a suburban mom with 2.2 kids and a Ford Explorer, I was jealous as hell. I still couldn't even begin to deal with the fact that I would never have children with Caz.

I could see that the group of women were reading out loud from one of the "Portraits of Grief," the profiles that the *Times* ran every day, of those who'd been killed.

Suddenly, it occured to me what the women were doing here. "What do you want to bet that one of those women is a widow?" I asked Kia and Sandy.

"Perhaps," they agreed.

Later, after the group in front of us had packed up their things and returned to the hotel, I decided to at least attempt to care about my health. I laced up my sneakers, started walking toward the water, then changed my pace to a slow sprint, heading north along the beach. To my left were the long lines of beach loungers and the pastel-colored tower-block hotels of South Beach. To my right was the water, a brilliant translucent blue with white cresting waves.

I thought about how this same ocean stretched all the way from here to England, where Caz was born, how it reached up around the coast to New York, surrounding Long Island and the beach house. As I ran, I came as close as I could to comfort, knowing that this same body of water connected me to home, bringing me somehow nearer to the man I loved so much, whom I kept reaching toward but who had gone someplace where I could no longer follow him.

ON THE PLANE returning home, I gave up trying to peer out of the window for signs. It wasn't working. Caz was not going to write me a message across the skies. Besides, who was to say that heaven was "up"? Maybe heaven had no parameters, maybe heaven was surrounding but not contained. Maybe Caz passed on through people, through our memories of him, through nature. I thought about the beautiful crescent moon in the shape of a C that I'd seen in the weeks after his death, and my conviction that it was his initial. The storm in the days afterward, the cracking of thunder, the single blue hydrangea in the garden—this was him; this was his way of communicating. The big things I used to care about—my jobs, my goals, my plans for the future—all of these were insignificant to me. But I could find meaning in a picture falling inexplicably from a wall at the exact moment I asked for some word from him.

I returned home to Brooklyn with relief, Lola waiting, yelping and leaping in her excitement to see me. New York in wintertime was better suited to my frame of mind—the iciness, the stripped trees, the familiar brownstones of the neighborhood. Christmas was coming. I felt very fortunate that Caz's mother would be joining my family and me for the holiday; sharing the Carrington traditions and stories would help get me through. That year, so many people gave me presents—I'd never had so many Christmas presents in my life. My brother put together a Christmas box for Caz, filled with thoughtful goodies—a crepe pan, grill accessories, a fireplace lighter, his favorite Stilton cheese, a bottle of port. Opening the box was one of the more joyous moments I can remember in four long months of sadness. It was the gesture that meant so much; the thoughtfulness was the gift.

I'd made it through our anniversary, Thanksgiving, my birthday, and Christmas. Now I had to make it through New Year's Eve, and then the holidays would be over. A group of my friends, including Kia and Sandy, were going on the midnight run in Central Park. I agreed to join them, as they really didn't want to leave me alone.

But on December 31, when the temperature dropped below zero, I backed out: "I'm not doing a 5k when it's twenty below!" I told Kia and Sandy. "I have enough pain in my life already!"

The following day, New Year's Day, we were having brunch together. I would see them then. So at around 9 pm on New Year's Eve, I climbed into bed and flipped through a travel magazine, numbly awake. Half an hour later, tissues on the pillow, I went under the covers and wept my way to eventual sleep.

The next morning, I dragged on my clothes and headed out across the river to Manhattan, the skyline flashing between the iron web of the Brooklyn Bridge, the two empty spaces in the sky glowing in the morning light, vast and powerful in their absence. Three thousand loved ones, two hundred and twenty floors, 1360 feet of building in each tower. Vanished. Still impossible, still unthinkable.

The cab cut across the island and dropped me off at Pastis, a popular bistro in the Meatpacking District. Pastis was my choice of venue. I'd had four o'clock champagne and cheese here with Caz on Labor Day the summer before. The bistro was familiar ground, and I knew how little I liked venturing out of my comfort zone.

Squeezing in through the crowds at the door, I found Kia. Then Sandy arrived. Soon after, Chrissy, an old friend of Caz's, hurried in, at her side a raven-haired woman with bright blue eyes. Chrissy had been incredibly supportive over the past four months, and now she wanted me to meet another friend of hers whose husband, Bart, had also been killed in the towers.

This was Claudia.

Up to this point, I only wanted to be around people who knew me and who knew Caz. Although I'd been reluctant to come today, I knew that Chrissy was trying to help and that I should let her do this for me. After all, I never had to see this Claudia woman again if I didn't want to.

Claudia's first words to me were "Bloody Mary?"

"Bring it on." I managed to smile. "I still feel like hell even without a hangover. . . . So how was *your* New Year's Eve?" I asked, letting Claudia know from the tone of my voice that I didn't expect her to say, "Fine."

"I spent the day in bed crying," Claudia replied. "Then I went to our friends' apartment but on one condition, that no one mentioned New Year's Eve or tried to celebrate in any way. I got there, we ordered Chinese, I cried my eyes out, made it to midnight, and took a cab home."

"Hey, you did better than I did, I was in bed by nine, flicked through a *Travel + Leisure* magazine, and then pulled the covers over my head."

"What would you do that for?" Claudia blurted. "It's just too depressing to look at that magazine and think of all the fabulous trips I'll never take with my husband."

Good point. But it wasn't like I was actually taking in the words or the images on the page. I was numbly flicking, praying that the time would pass so that I could finally close my eyes on the day.

Then Claudia admitted that, as much as she couldn't look at travel magazines, she *did* need to get out of town whenever she could. She needed to escape. Most of her friends were married or having families, but if she could ever find someone to go away with on a weekend, she'd jump at the chance.

"At least when I'm out of town I can maintain the illusion that Bart is at home waiting for me . . . ," Claudia explained.

"I guess I'm the other way around," I admitted. "I hate being anywhere but home. I need to be around Caz's things. Our place, our dog, my familiar routine. Kia and Sandy took me away last month, and I hated being in Miami. I just wanted to get home as soon as possible."

"That's funny. I was in Miami last month," Claudia said. "When were you there?"

"Right after Thanksgiving. How about you?"

"The first week of December. Where did you stay?"

The first week in December Claudia had been at the same hotel with Bart's sister and three of their friends. I'd been there the exact same time with Kia and Sandy.

"Wait a minute," I asked. "Were you with a woman who was pregnant?"

Yes, Peggy was five months pregnant.

"And I remember your pregnant friend yelling at her husband on the phone," I told Claudia, "and your blond friend had the same bikini as Kia. You were reading the 'Portraits of Grief' out loud. I tried to make a bet with Kia and Sandy that you were a widow!"

Now I wanted to know: "Did they get the house in the cul-de-sac?"

"No, they're moving to Connecticut."

Claudia explained that when Peggy got so angry with her husband—apart from the fact she was five months pregnant and totally hormonal—it was because of her grief for Bart. How could her husband want to buy a house in Port Washington? This was where Peggy and Bart had grown up next door to each other. How could they even think about leaving the city without Bart knowing? Everyone in the group had this same feeling of wanting time to stand still. Nothing should be allowed to move on without Bart knowing about it.

Amazed at the coincidence, we described our trips and everything that had been going through our minds that weekend and in the past months. Claudia and I both sensed that this was more than a coincidence, it was a sign. Life was full of signs.

"A bird sitting outside my window is Bart," Claudia said. "The light on my bedside table flickering—Bart. While I'm driving, I'll say to myself, Bart, if you're with me, make the light turn green. Sure enough. . . ."

I told Claudia I knew how that felt. I told her that I'd spent a lot of my time trying to figure out what Caz was up to in heaven. Claudia told me she pictured Bart skiing on a beautiful day in St. Moritz. I told her I imagined Caz being welcomed by Winston Churchill, his hero. We both agreed that our two Boys had probably found each other up there and were hanging out drinking heavenly Bloody Marys. Would there be cocktails in heaven? Absolutely . . .

When we said our good-byes after brunch, Claudia asked me if I wanted to attend her weekly therapy group for widows. People had been trying to persuade me to go to therapy, but I kept saying no. It just wasn't my style. But when Claudia asked, I said yes. If nothing else, it would give me an opportunity to spend time with her. Although I couldn't define it yet, there was something about Claudia's outlook that made me want to see her again.

I felt such a kinship with this woman. We had both lost what we valued more than anything. Just as with me, grief had changed Claudia beyond recognition. She was stumbling to find her feet in a new world she no longer understood. Every morning Claudia woke up and faced the same challenges as I did, yet I sensed that her approach was different. Claudia had a determination unlike anything I'd ever encountered before. She wasn't going to let this beat her.

We started meeting every week to go to our group therapy and then would spend the evening together afterward, having conversations that were just as therapeutic as the sessions beforehand. Being with this woman was a huge eye-opener for me. Claudia knew she didn't want to give up on life. She had made a decision not to die alongside her husband. She had made a conscious choice: to continue, to go on, to live.

THAT WINTER, I went almost every weekend to the beach house by myself. I hibernated, needing that quiet time to try to heal, to regenerate and process my thoughts. I would stare at the fireplace for hours on end and walk the beach in all kinds of weather. I read every book and article about how and why our system failed to prevent the events of

September 11. The days and months crawled by, every minuscule change in the season another sign of time's cruel passing.

As spring crept in, the lime green new growth of leaves on the trees surrounding the house appeared, affronting my eyes. I would have done anything to stop that brave vibrant showing of life. But I kept going back to the house. I would sit for hours, often alone, staring into space and crying. As the sun began to break through, I'd sit outside on the deck, watching the trees and the birds within them, crying still.

That spring, I got a promotion at work. It should have been a cause for pleasure, and yet I felt so empty. I couldn't call Caz to tell him the news. I called Claudia, sobbing. I told her about the last promotion I'd received, how Caz had thrown me an impromptu party, about how proud he was of his wife, "the vice president of a bank." How I couldn't bear this, I couldn't bear it.

Summer arrived like an unwelcome guest. Out at the beach I surrounded myself with family and friends, giving myself reasons to open the pool, to make meals, to live life. I felt truly lucky not to have to rent the house or sell it. I couldn't bear to think of anyone else in our home. And besides, if I rented it, someone might move something. They might throw out the wedding cake slice that was still in the freezer or they might find the Terry's Dark Chocolate Orange hidden in the back of the refrigerator. The beach towels would have to be washed. I was determined to keep everything exactly where it had been the last time Caz left it. I stubbornly maintained the house on my own. I wanted to be the one to mow the lawn, to weed the flower beds, to make the repairs, to clean the pool. It was one way I could continue to show my love for him.

That summer, I met Claudia's friends Ann and Julia for the first time, and a strange alchemy took place between us. When we were together, we were able to bare our wounds, to make jokes, to howl with tears and howl just as loudly with laughter. Meeting these women changed my life. Until I met Claudia and the WC, I was going to be the stoic widow forever. I was always going to wear the rings, never going to date, never going to move his things in our apartment, never going to move forward. This is what the WC brought me, this sense that even though I couldn't control what had happened to me, my reaction to the circumstances was within my dictates.

I kept going out to the beach, immersing myself in nature. I needed to experience the change of the seasons, no matter how much pain that brought me. Fall succumbed to winter again; a shrinking back that corresponded with my mood. Spring was painful, just as it was the year before. Another new beginning without him. I invited the WC to come and visit for Julia's birthday, and found myself taking actual pleasure in sharing this world that Caz had left in my custody.

With every trip to the beach, imperceptibly, the repetition, slow and agonizing, built my reserves bit by bit. The first time I drove out to the beach house alone, I didn't think it would be possible to live through the experience twice. But I did it again, and again. The more I drove that Long Island Expressway, the more I experienced navigating the road alone and not as a passenger next to Caz, the more I lived, the more I knew I could live. In the same way that saying "widow" over and over finally convinced me that this was the case, the more I did, the less afraid I became. I began to realize that I could do it, and slowly I wanted to do more and more.

12 · *Lola to the Rescue*

Pattie's dog, Lola

By the time Julia's birthday weekend at the beach house was over, the WC had decided. It was time for Pattie to take control. She was going to ask Stanley the attorney out for a drink. Up until now, Pattie hadn't dated; she hadn't felt the desire to date. Was she ready to date? No, she wasn't even close to being ready—even thinking about another man felt like she was being unfaithful to Caz. But with the support and encouragement of the WC, Pattie knew this was something she had to "accomplish." She was thirty-six years old, and the longer she left this dating thing, the higher the hurdle was going to become. This, like everything else, was a matter of surviving and continuing to live fully. It was something Pattie felt she had to do in case she never got up the courage to do it again.

Pattie already knew Stanley would be in town for a Wednesday meeting at her accountant's office. Monday morning she e-mailed.

When you're in town and free tomorrow night, how about a quick drink?
Let me know . . . P.

Sure, why not. My train gets in at eight. Let me know where and when.

Pattie was all business. She had a mission to accomplish. She buzzed him back.

How about the bar at Brasserie at 8:15?

See you there . . .

That Tuesday evening Pattie worked late. In the old days, she couldn't wait to switch off the computer and head home, where Caz would be waiting—as soon as six o'clock came around, the phone calls would start: "When are you leaving? When are you coming home? Hurry! Lola and I want to see you." These days, if there was the slightest reason to stay at her desk—another memo to write, an extra e-mail to send—Pattie volunteered. Better to stay at the office, to avoid going home until it was time for Lola's evening walk.

Tonight was different. At around seven-thirty, she received an e-mail.

My train is delayed a half hour. Do you still want to do this?

Pattie detected some hesitancy there, decided to ignore it.

Sure, let's meet at nine. Same place.

Pattie decided to call Kia to fill the time. This was perfect—if the guy turned out to be in any way weird, Kia would be her escape.

"Sure, I'll be your wingman," said Kia. Not for the first time, Pattie thanked her partner in crime.

She remembered Claudia's joke at the weekend—"Hey, Pattie, it's going to be tough getting lucky with that giant rock on your finger!" Pattie looked down at her engagement ring and wedding band, firmly next to each other on her left hand, the stones sparkling. She loved those rings. No way was she taking them off—they were going to bring her luck.

. . .

PATTIE AND KIA perched themselves at the bar at Brasserie, ordered martinis, talked. Kia commented on how calm Pattie was, how unperturbed she seemed by this new step.

"After everything I've been through? This is nothing," Pattie explained.

At nine o'clock Stanley walked up to the bar. Even though Pattie had met him before, she'd never seen him outside of work, and he looked a little out of context. You could tell he wasn't from New York; he didn't have that edge. It was clear that he was a little confused to find himself in a bar with a woman he didn't know and her friend. Kia stayed for the drink, took part in the polite conversation until she was sure that Pattie was going to be okay, and then made excuses about needing an early night.

"Thanks, Kia," said Pattie. "I'll call you in the morning."

And then it was just the two of them. They carried on chatting. They stuck to the classic questions: Where did you grow up? Any siblings? Where did you go to college? It turned out that Stanley had only graduated a few years back, literally, but although Pattie was obviously older and savvier than him, they chatted easily. Pattie reminded herself that she hadn't asked Stanley here to make idle chitchat. She stood up to go to the bathroom and to think things through, but as she got up, her hand slipped from the bar as she went to steady herself. Sweetly, Stanley reached out to stop her from falling into his lap.

This was when Pattie realized she was definitely tipsy.

In the ladies' room, she squinted in the mirror. Her hair had come halfway out of her ponytail and was hanging in strands around her ears. "No. Don't back out. Straighten up. You look good, girl!"

Pattie marched back out to the bar and announced that it was time to go home. Stanley looked surprised, and maybe even a little hurt. Pattie got the bill, and signed the credit card slip with a flourish.

Luckily, Stanley caught that she'd added an extra zero and was about to tip the bartender $100.

They stumbled outside. Out on the sidewalk, swaying slightly, Pattie let three empty cabs pass as they began to make awkward good-byes.

"Okay, so, I guess I'll see you tomorrow," Pattie said.

"Well, okay, I guess," he started. "See you tomorrow!" No, this wasn't the way it was meant to happen. Pattie knew she had to kiss him. She had to awaken feelings that she had chosen to ignore for nearly two years.

"Lean over, just do it. What are you scared of? That he'll reject you? Of course he's attracted to you! He should be lucky to kiss you."

Pattie made her move. She kissed Stanley hard on the lips in what definitely could not be misconstrued as a peck, and hung in there. But it was difficult to tell if he was responding, so she drew back to see if he was okay. He had the look of a deer caught in the headlights.

"Oh God, I'm sorry," Pattie said immediately, putting her hand to her mouth.

"No, don't apologize." Stanley looked confused, but not completely horrified. "It was . . . nice. I guess, I mean, if you wanted to come back to my hotel for a drink . . ."

Pattie definitely did not need another drink. What she needed was to get home to walk Lola. Usually, Lola got her walk at 9 pm, and it was 11 pm already. Pattie's poor doggie would be crossing her legs, her nose pressed up against the door, waiting for her mistress to come home.

"One more drink it is!" Pattie said.

They linked arms, Pattie leading the way, along Fifty-third Street.

AT THE HOTEL, they didn't make it to the bar. Pattie suggested they go straight up to Stanley's room. He opened the door, and Pattie went and perched on the end of the bed. Stanley came and sat down next to her. They kissed. Pattie attempted to close her eyes and to enjoy it, but it was hard to comprehend what was going on. "What am I doing? Who is this man? Why am I in a hotel? Am I having an affair?" Pattie could hear a phone ringing. She managed to register that it was her cell phone. Why was someone calling her so late? Better check.

"I'm sorry, excuse me."

There was a message from her neighbor saying that Lola was barking frantically and could she please come home and take her out.

"I have to go," Pattie announced. "I'm sorry. My dog is barking and my neighbor's worried. I have to leave."

"Well, if you're sure . . ."

"I'm sorry, I have to . . ."

"So I'll see you tomorrow at the meeting," he said.

"Oh God, the meeting. Okay, see you there." Pattie didn't want to imagine what kind of shape she was going to be in tomorrow.

When she finally arrived back at her apartment, it was almost midnight and Lola was yelping and clambering at her leg. She staggered out into the moonlit summer's night, Lola in tow. Saved by the dog. "Thanks, Lola. You have rescued your mistress from her late-night exploits. Us girls will have to stick together."

THE NEXT DAY Pattie attempted to pull herself into shape, despite bloodshot eyes and a pounding head. Between waking and arriving at her accountant's office, she drank about a gallon of coffee. Stanley was there first, looking hungover too, but, Pattie had to admit, looking pretty good. Afterward, he slipped her a note. She peeled it open under the table. It said: "Had a great time last night. Can we hang out some more?"

Okay, that didn't sound so bad.

Stanley called that afternoon. Could they grab a drink before his train home this evening? Pattie was meeting Claudia but invited Stanley to come along, excited for her friend to meet the man she'd been talking about the weekend before.

After Stanley left, Claudia told Pattie that he seemed like a good guy. A little young maybe, but friendly and definitely cute. Claudia's overwhelming impression of him was that he seemed eager to please. He was nothing like Caz, had none of his charisma, or sense of humor, but maybe that was okay—Pattie wasn't looking to replace her irreplaceable husband. What's more, Claudia could tell he was really into Pattie, which, after all, was the most important thing.

"He might just be the perfect TG, your transitional guy, someone who could help you open up to the idea of being in a relationship again."

After Claudia's experience dating Paul, she could see that in many ways it was harder for men to date widows than it was for widows to date men. We love talking about our husbands; we aren't guarded about introducing them into conversation. We have pictures of them in our brag books and all over our apartments. Their voices are on our answering machines. More than that, we had the WC. We were already at a stage where we didn't need to be emotionally dependent on a man, because we had one another. That might be hard for some men to take, but it wasn't putting Stanley off just yet. So Claudia gave Stanley the thumbs-up. It takes a strong man to want to date a widow.

THIS WAS ALSO the evening that Pattie first brought up the subject of her friend John.

"He's a buddy of mine who's back in town after living in Hong Kong and London for the past seven years," Pattie explained. "He's a great guy—funny, very good-looking. And single."

Only the week before, Cheryl, Claudia's therapist, had suggested she needed to get back in the saddle after Paul and that a crush might be a good diversion.

"Sounds good," said Claudia to Pattie. "But I don't want to have any expectations. After getting burned by Paul, I'm not ready to put myself out there just yet."

The way Pattie saw it, John and Claudia were two people that she knew and loved, and hopefully they might hit it off. Pattie was sweet about it, making sure Claudia didn't feel pressured but, even so, insisting that they seemed like a good fit.

13 · A Truly Perfect Moment

Claudia

Claudia:

I first met John on the evening of my thirty-fourth birthday. Pattie decided to surprise us both. She had told John that the WC was throwing a party for me and to come along. What Pattie hadn't told John was that we were having a small gathering at a restaurant—and that the other guests were all women. For my part, I had no idea that John was coming. On the way to the restaurant, it was pouring rain. I felt fat, old, and cranky. There was no way this birthday could be worse than my first birthday without Bart—which I'd spent in a bar with Pattie, crying my eyes out—but even so, I still wasn't in the mood to celebrate.

Pattie and I were the last to arrive. John was already there, looking a little confused—he'd been expecting to have a few drinks at the bar. Instead he found himself at a sit-down dinner with ten women, two of whom were heavily pregnant. Right away, the WC put John in charge of looking after us, giving him the title of our "cabana boy" and telling him to make sure that there was a bottle of wine on the table at all times.

Every now and again you would hear someone around the table say: "Hey, cabana boy, my wineglass is empty, you're slacking!"

John went with the flow and charmed the table. It turned out to be a great evening: fabulous food, lots of laughter, everyone clicking.

Pattie made sure John and I sat next to each other. John told me about walking over to the restaurant, through the southern reaches of the Lower East Side, one of the grittier neighborhoods in downtown New York. Along the way, he was looking for a birthday gift for me, but the only places he came across were bodegas. He'd contemplated buying me a can of Goya beans.

Later that evening, when Pattie asked me how I liked my birthday surprise, I admitted that I thought John was adorable. The minute I walked in, I'd noticed his big smile and bright blue eyes. He could hold his own in conversation and had everyone around the table in stitches. What's more, I noticed that he was wearing shoes made by Cole Haan, the company I work for. A good sign.

But by the next morning, I'd already convinced myself it was the wine talking. Then I got an e-mail from John:

Claudia, it was a pleasure/honor to celebrate your b-day. You're a blast to go out with! I owe you a b-day dinner and/or joke gift. We'll get the band back together for a gig. Take care xxoo jd

Hmmm. "xxoo." Even so, I wasn't ready. I put John to the back of my mind.

I'D BEEN INVITED to a wedding over the Fourth of July weekend. I'd agonized over whether I should go or not. Could I handle it? Would I have a meltdown in the middle of the ceremony? I'd turned down so many wedding invitations in the past two years. But after a little encouragement from the WC, and hearing "It would be wrong not to" for the thousandth time, I decided to go for it. In the back of my mind I could hear Bart saying, "The only things in life you regret are the chances you don't take."

I was beginning to discover that the buildup to whatever thing I was dreading was usually worse than the event itself, and I actually had a great time at the wedding. I came home feeling refreshed and strong—that is, until I opened my front door. While I was out of town, I had left my AC on and there had been a flood. My floors were buckled. I was standing in the middle of a roller coaster. Back to reality. Bart wasn't here; my floors looked like shit, and just when I thought there was a glimmer of hope, along came a reminder not to get too comfortable, that life isn't ever what you think it's going to be. So I did what any self-respecting member of the WC would do. I turned off the lights, locked the door, and went to The Grill to meet the girls.

This was the first time that the other members of the WC were going to meet Stanley, and I didn't want to miss it. But when we arrived, a work colleague of Pattie's happened to be eating at The Grill. The WC went into a huddle. Pattie felt she wasn't ready to be seen in public with Stanley. Coincidentally, Pattie happened to know that John was in the neighborhood, so we changed venues and went to meet him.

The second time around, John made an even stronger impression, but I was too frustrated that evening to let myself get excited.

Pattie was having a clambake on the beach that Friday, so she suggested that John and I drive out together. Although I sensed the obvious setup, I didn't read too much into it. He evidently needed a ride and I had a car.

As it turned out, neither of us could make it out to the beach. I was swamped at work and John was just moving into his new apartment. Even so, John e-mailed and asked if I wanted to grab dinner or drinks Saturday night. I told him to call me Saturday, all the time keeping my expectations in check—not because I didn't like John, but because I was starting to have confidence in myself again, that I was going to be okay on my own.

That Saturday, I was visiting Marcella in Long Island. It was a beautiful day and we took her kids to their pool club. I was in the pool playing with my niece when the phone rang. Marcella answered, heard the voice of a strange man asking for Claudia, and tossed me the phone.

"Hey. . . . Yeah it's me," I said. ". . . I'm on Long Island with my sister and her kids. . . . Oh, yes, we are. Okay, I'll get out of the pool and dry off—what time?" I could see Marcella and my mother listening to every word I was saying. When I got off the phone, they both looked at me and said, "You're going on a date!"

But I insisted it wasn't anything of the kind. John had just moved back to town and didn't have many friends around.

My mother said: "Claaaw-dia, it's a Saturday night and you're going out alone. With a man, in New York City. It's a date!"

I told them they were delusional. If I really had a date at 7 pm, there was no way I would be in the pool on Long Island at five. Even so, I realized I better get going if I was going to meet my just-a-friend at seven.

I drove back into the city, still determined not to have any expectations. What to wear? No, I wasn't going to worry about that because this was not a date. I threw on a pair of jeans, black strappy high heels, and a cute top. I looked in the mirror and thought "Casual chic." Good, but not trying too hard.

WE MET AT the Savoy in SoHo. I walked in and John was sitting at the bar having a cocktail—looking, I have to say, quite handsome. Also, I noticed he was wearing his second pair of Cole Haan shoes. I ordered a drink and we started to talk. This was easy, because John was relaxed and we had so much to talk about—the conversation had its own energy. Because I was convinced this wasn't a date, I told John all about Bart. I remember telling him that I was worried that someday I might forget what Bart's hands looked like, so that they were always the first thing I looked for in pictures. Bart had incredibly sexy hands— they made me feel safe; they touched me; they were where I looked to see his wedding band.

I told John about how my father had died while I was in college, and the effect it had on me. John told me about his mother, who had died of cancer also while he was in college. He remembered how some people would feel so awkward bringing the subject up with him. That was when he learned that you have to address death, he said.

"You can't pretend it doesn't exist or be self-conscious talking about it. If it's a major factor in someone's life, how can you not address it?"

We were having a great conversation, baring our souls one minute and laughing the next. John casually mentioned that he had made dinner reservations for us somewhere else at nine. Okay, maybe he was thinking this was a date. No, let's just eat here at the bar, I told him. There was so much to talk about—all of the places we had both been and all of the places we both wanted to go. We'd both traveled all over the world. We recounted all the places we'd visited, before realizing that neither of us had ever been to the Statue of Liberty. We talked about books we were reading. The next thing I knew, the place was closing.

John's apartment was just around the corner and he invited me inside for a nightcap. John could tell I was hesitant and promised, "Claudia, don't worry, I won't make a pass at you." Okay, I'd been right not to get my hopes up—we were going to be just friends.

When we got upstairs, my new friend suggested we sit out on his fire escape. Great, I told him. I had lived in New York for over ten years, and I had never been on a fire escape.

As I was getting ready to climb out the window, John said: "Here, hold these," handing me two wineglasses. With my hands thus occupied, John leaned in and kissed me on the lips.

Okay, so this was a date after all.

I climbed out of the window. John put on some Chet Baker.

Chet was singing, there was a half moon suspended above the apartments across the street, water towers on rooftops were silhouetted against a deep blue night sky. Between the wine and the music and the moonlight it was an unbelievably romantic moment. We kissed again.

Despite the enormous pain and sadness I've experienced in my life, I was wise enough to recognize the beauty of the moment. I'd had moments like these before, but until now, I'd had no idea how perishable they were. Now I stopped to take a snapshot of the scene in my mind, so that I'd always remember it.

Being kissed by John on the fire escape was one of those truly perfect moments.

John was a total gentleman and we kissed for a little while and then I went home—glowing. The morning after our date there was an e-mail in my inbox.

Hey most adorable thing ever, thinking about you . . .

John called me that day and asked if he could see me that evening.

Julia and Ann

Ann:

This summer was a turning point for me, but of a very different kind. I made the decision to go back into therapy. I was still meeting with my widows' support group in Rye, and of course with the WC, but I needed more than that. I was going through what I can only describe as a mini-breakdown. This was something that I hadn't foreseen—I was doing everything I could to keep getting better and stronger, to keep moving forward—and now I was suddenly and inexorably being dragged backward. I felt like I was moving through quicksand—for every step forward I was sinking deeper, unable to haul myself out.

My breakdown was precipitated by an event that's very hard for me to write about. Although it was a lot more than this single event that caused my need to go back into therapy, it was definitely the trigger for so many fears, so much doubt, insecurity, and sadness to come tumbling out of me.

In the early summer, an old friend of Ward's had been in town and we met one evening for dinner with a group of friends. The evening had run late, and this person told me he needed a lift home.

I know that I can be naïve sometimes, and I know that I can be too trusting. I never thought anything of his request. I didn't have a clue, not an inkling that there was anything more to it than helping out a friend. After all, he was a married man who was a friend of Ward's.

As we were driving, this friend asked me to pull over because he wanted to tell me something. Without thinking, I found a spot and parked, wondering if he wanted to talk about Ward, or about his wife. As soon as we stopped, he unclicked his seat belt and put his hand on my thigh. I was shocked to find him touching me, but rather than immediately pull away, I didn't protest. He evidently needed to talk and I wanted to be there for him. I didn't want to hurt his feelings by pushing him away. I could never have predicted where this was heading. Before I knew it, he had moved his body to my side of the car and had his hands and his weight on me and suddenly he was kissing me. I did not want to be doing this. Things had already gone too far. Why was this happening? Okay, enough. I pushed him away and told him to get out of the car and walk. I drove away, furious about what had happened. I felt violated.

The next morning, the events of the night before started to sink in. I began to feel a growing sense of disappointment and disgust with myself. I'd been so naïve and foolish. I hadn't been strong enough, and as a result I had let him take advantage of me. How could I be so weak, so stupid? I was ashamed of myself, not only for my children and me, but more so for Ward, and his memory. This was a friend of Ward's. He had taken advantage of me, and I had allowed it to happen.

IT WAS THIS event that prompted me to unravel. I went into pretty intensive therapy. I was scared; I was depressed. I was letting my life get away from me. I was terrified that I wouldn't be able to get back on track. I wasn't sure what being on track even meant! I just remember crying so much—I missed Ward. This would never have happened if he were alive. Just another thing to add to the never-ending list of "If he were alive, all the rotten things I have to deal with wouldn't be happening anymore." My feelings of shame about what happened prevented me from telling anyone but the WC and one other friend, but all my other friends could see that I was floundering. There were so many more emotions under the surface that I wasn't acknowledging, let alone dealing with, in my determination to be a good parent and to make a happy life for my family. The mini-breakdown left me shaken and uncertain of myself.

Around this time, I remember going to meet the WC in the city—Pattie had won tickets at a charity benefit to see Conan O'Brien and was treating us. As we were standing in line, my cell phone rang—it was my baby-sitter calling. Elizabeth had hit her head, and the small gash on the top of her head wouldn't stop bleeding. At the very best, it would be at least an hour and a half before I got home in rush hour, and she needed attention now. My heart sank to my stomach. I hated this. I hated it more than anything—the inability to protect her from things like this, the inability to make her better, the inability to get home from midtown Manhattan to suburban Rye in an instant. And no Ward to step in. The pull and the guilt of wanting to be a good mom and have a career and have a life for myself—the hypocrisy of waiting to watch Conan O'Brien and laughing and smiling with my friends while my daughter needed medical attention. Sometimes it felt like no matter how hard I tried to have a positive attitude, this was God's way of saying, "Don't get too happy, don't become too comfortable, remember that life is hard and maybe you need a little more suffering right now to remind you of that."

When Ward was alive, we were a unit, a team. Ward was a hands-on dad. I remember when Elizabeth was about three, I was traveling for work, and happened to be working in New Haven, Connecticut, about a forty-five-minute drive from home. I'd forgotten to turn off my cell phone and it rang while I was with a client. I don't even know what made me answer it, because normally I would have just turned it off and gone on with my meeting. But instead I answered it and it was Ward telling me that everything was going to be okay, but that Elizabeth was in the Emergency Room for a seizure episode that just wouldn't stop. The doctors had given her some intravenous drugs that would halt the seizures, and Ward kept assuring me that everything would be okay. His last words were "Please, please drive safely." There he was dealing with Elizabeth in the Emergency Room and he was worried about my safety. Even back then, I understood the full meaning of his words. He needed me to get there, but the thought of something happening to me was more frightening to him than dealing with Elizabeth's situation alone. We needed each other to get through these hard times.

The night of the Conan O'Brien taping, Elizabeth was with my baby-sitter and a nurse who worked part-time looking after her, and they assured me it was just a tiny cut, but it was still bleeding. They told me that this was a minor incident, nothing to worry about. Then they asked me whether or not they should get stitches for her. I told them, "I don't know! I'm not there! I'm not the nurse! How am I supposed to make these decisions?" I called a friend, who drove over to my house. I wanted advice and needed someone to help. My friend called me back and reassured me—it was nothing. Even so, I told the nurse and the baby-sitter to go to the hospital. Better safe than sorry.

I was miles away from my daughter, with no husband, trying not to cry. Even though I had done everything I could to put my family first, I was failing. I couldn't be everything to them. I didn't have Ward to save the day anymore. I needed to find myself and find some happiness so I could be a good mom, but I was so depressed and powerless to make everything right again.

The WC looked on. They were there for me, but they knew they couldn't fix this. I didn't know how to fix this either. I just wished it weren't so hard.

"When will it get easier?" I asked them. "Please let it get easier. . . ."

In the next few minutes, I got another call from the baby-sitter. She was at the hospital and there really was nothing wrong. The doctor said the cut didn't need stitches and told them to go home. But the anxiety, the having to parent all alone, the fact that I was "it" for these kids, just added to my intense uneasiness at that time.

Over the course of the summer, things did begin to improve. By talking it through with my therapist, I was able to see my way forward. We talked a lot about how I'd been so determined to get better, to heal, to make my life happy again, and to be the best mom I could for my kids, that I'd hadn't allowed myself the time to fully acknowledge and accept my loss. One of my friends told me that over the last few years I'd reminded her of the football player atop the Heisman trophy—I was running as fast as possible, head down, one arm around the football protecting it for dear life and the other stretched out to push aside anything in the way. I was desperately in search of the goal, at the expense of taking the necessary steps to reach it.

With the help of my therapist and the WC, I realized that as much as I wanted to be a good mother, I couldn't always be invincible. I had to break down every now and again, to let myself be sad and to feel incapable.

I also came to the realization that what had happened with Ward's friend wasn't my fault. He had abused my trust, as well as abusing his relationship with Ward. I wasn't going to let one bad apple ruin my opinion of people in general. I began to realize that he had his own issues to do what he did. I learned to forgive myself. Going backward, retracing my steps, seeing what had been going on under the surface—this had the eventual effect of making me stronger.

Julia:

One Thursday afternoon, in the middle of July, I was standing outside my office, chatting with a few of my coworkers, when the lights flickered and went off. Everyone was confused, and we started asking one another what could be wrong. People were calling out, saying that their computers had gone down. I walked back to my desk and realized the phones were also out. A voice came on the loudspeaker and repeated several times: "The building has lost its power. There is no reason for concern, but please evacuate." Everyone decided to leave the building. One of my coworkers who's also a close friend came over to my office to see if I was okay.

I didn't understand what the rush was, but my friend convinced me to get my things together: "C'mon, Julia, we're all leaving. . . ."

Only as we began to head down the stairwell did I start to panic. I wasn't worried for my own safety, not at all. It was a rush of recognition that caused the panic—I was in the stairwell of a building that was being evacuated. I was doing what Tommy and so many others had been doing that day. I began to relive the sequence. Was he in the stairwell when the plane hit? How far did he make it down before the building fell? I turned to my friend.

"This is what Tommy was doing . . ." She gave me a look that said, "It's okay," grabbed my hand, and we continued to walk down the stairs as calmly as possible, following in a line with hundreds of other coworkers.

No one mentioned the word "terrorism," but of course, it was on everyone's mind. This was new for me. I wasn't here that day; I hadn't been one of the thousands of New Yorkers experiencing firsthand the fear, shock, disbelief, and anxiety of being in a city under attack—I was trapped in Denver. For me, this was a glimpse into how things must have been in New York on September 11.

When we got to the street, there was a mob scene. People everywhere. The traffic lights were out. Cars had come to a standstill on Park Avenue. Total confusion. I kept trying to call the WC, but I couldn't get through on my cell. I had to find out where they were. I needed to know if they were okay. If anything happened to any one of them, well, I couldn't even think about that.

The WC had actually talked about what to do in case of an emergency—without our husbands to turn to, we agreed that we would find one another. Even if we couldn't get hold of one another, we would go to Pattie's in Brooklyn if the disaster was uptown and to my apartment uptown if it happened downtown. I was also desperate to find one of my coworkers, whose wife had also been killed on September 11. I knew how distressed he must be feeling.

Suddenly, in the crowd, I saw him. We embraced and didn't have to say a word. We each knew what the other was experiencing. We decided to go into the Waldorf-Astoria Hotel to see if we could find any additional information about what was going on. This was when we discovered that there had been a massive blackout, not just in New York, but across the entire East Coast. The blackout was a blackout, not a terrorist attack. My WC was going to be okay. We decided we should make our way home. The Waldorf was giving out flashlights, so I took one, knowing that I hadn't seen a flashlight in my apartment, ever. This was something Tommy would have known where to find. I, on the other hand, had no idea.

My coworker said he would walk me home, so we started up the East Side. I was glad I was with him. We'd worked for the same company for years, but never met until the events of September 11 brought us together. He had been married for only three years when his wife was killed, and he was always so grateful to have finally found his true love. My heart breaks for him every time I'm with him. It's like his body is there, but his spirit died with the woman he loved.

The crowd was quite dense, so it took a while even to go one block. Fortunately for me, I live twenty blocks from my work, but others were walking miles, to Harlem and the Bronx. We chatted to others as we went along. Despite the degree of inconvenience, the atmosphere was lighthearted. Now that people had been assured this wasn't another attack, they saw this for what it was: an inconvenience, but not a real problem. There were stores selling all their refrigerated goods on the street, people snatching up beers, waters, and ice cream. At every intersection there were regular civilians who had taken it upon themselves to stand and direct the traffic. For the most part, people were laughing, smiling, and talking to one another. As we continued along the avenue, a kind of walking party began to form.

Outside my building we told each other to stay in touch and if we needed anything, just to call or come by. The elevators were out, so I took the stairwell, carrying my handy new flashlight up nineteen flights. As I finally reached my floor, I ran into one of my neighbors. She told me that the blackout had been caused by a transformer and it might be until tomorrow before we had electricity again. She invited me down for drinks—we would grill some hamburgers to pass the time away. Perfect! I knew I didn't have any food, and that I wasn't desperate enough to walk down and back up nineteen floors for groceries. As I opened my door, my house phone rang and it was Ann. Thank God. She said she couldn't get home to Rye and could she stay with me? Are you kidding? Of course! We'll have a slumber party!

Like me, Ann was also at work when the lights went out. Pretty quickly, she managed to get through to her mother-in-law and asked her to go and check on the kids and the baby-sitter. Once Ann had taken care of the children, now she had to think of herself. Worst-case scenario, she could spend the night on the floor of her office—there were bathrooms, and she wasn't going to starve to death. But amazingly, Ann managed to get through to me on the phone, so she walked over.

THAT EVENING, WE hung out with my neighbors and cooked up a great dinner on their grill. Out on the terrace, surrounded by candlelight and the darkened skyscrapers, I was making friends with people I'd lived near for years but never gotten the chance to know until now.

For this one evening, everyone had come out of their boxes; we were all forced to get up from our couches and to leave our TVs. Down below, you could see people strolling behind the beam of their flashlights, walking their dogs, chatting on street corners, huddled around battery-powered radios. There was barely a car on the avenue. Without the orange glow of the street lamps, we could look up and see hundreds of stars. There was a feeling of safety and security, and of peacefulness. This was an adventure. There was a confidence that we would get through this, that a power outage of the whole East Coast wasn't a big deal in the scale of things, that nothing could bring us down.

Without the contrast of September 11, would this festive mood have been possible? We would have been complaining about the heat, the lack of transport, no telephone communication. Instead, the overwhelming reaction was one of relief and even joy. This is easy, we can do this, we've known much worse. Let's celebrate the chance to spend time without our usual distractions.

Late into the night, Ann and I stumbled upstairs (only one flight this time), with flashlight in hand, to my very warm apartment. It didn't bother us. We put on T-shirts and lay in bed with the windows wide open. I remember waking up to a slight breeze. Ann got dressed and headed home. I had planned to take the Friday off work anyway, and yet, like everyone, I had this feeling of playing hooky. No one was going into the office when the electricity still wasn't working.

LATER IN THE morning, the lights and appliances in my apartment buzzed back on. I started going around the house changing clocks and checking the lights. That's when I noticed that my answering machine was blinking. I sat down on the floor and attempted to figure out how to fix the flashing light. That's when I realized that the outgoing message wasn't responding. I kept pressing the button, wanting to check that I could hear Tommy's voice on the message, but nothing played back.

When I moved into the apartment, it was Tommy's suggestion that we change his message to say "we" instead of "I." We practiced saying the message together a few times, but there was no way of getting through to the end without laughing too hard and messing it up. Finally, we decided to go with Tommy's voice: "We're not home right now, leave a message."

Now the message was gone. I was going to leave his voice on the phone forever. I would never change it. Never! How many times had I called our number just to hear his voice? How many hang-up calls did I receive over the course of the last two years, from friends who had done the same? The power was back on, but Tommy's voice had gone. I sat on the floor and wept for the loss of the message that was not my husband but at this exact moment felt like my last point of contact with him.

In the weeks after the blackout, I couldn't bring myself to record a new message. I just left the machine off. Finally I did manage to record my voice on the machine. I knew that when friends called, they would think that I had purposefully changed it. I worried they would think I was trying to erase the past in order to move forward. In their voices when they left messages, I thought I could hear that they were taken aback at the sound of my voice. There would be a long pause and then, "Uh, uh, Julia, call me back."

Many times I'd thought about recording the following message: "Hi, you've reached the Collins residence. I didn't replace Tommy's voice on the machine. I would have never done that. There was a power outage and the message was deleted. Yes, I am crazy, so leave a message at the tone." Beeeep.

I came to the conclusion that the blackout was Tommy's way of saying, "Stop freaking people out by leaving my voice on the machine!" Maybe he knew that I wouldn't be able to erase it myself. Maybe he had to create the biggest blackout in New York since 1977 to make it happen. I was prepared to believe anything. Tommy was just the kind of guy who could pull a stunt like that.

Pattie and Claudia

In the coming weeks, Stanley and Pattie spoke on the phone frequently. Their premise for talking was business, but business was definitely not as usual.

Stanley was coming back into town for another work meeting toward the end of June, so Pattie decided to invite him out to the beach for the night. It was a bold move, but—as Pattie told the WC—oddly one that she didn't feel at all worried about. Stanley seemed like a nice guy and she wanted the company. She felt so secure in her love for Caz that somehow this protected her—there wasn't room for anyone else in her heart yet and so there was no chance her heart could be broken. The WC took the attitude that Stanley was a good thing and should be treated as a silver lining. Pattie agreed.

The night of his arrival, Pattie cooked dinner and they began to talk. Pattie had assumed that because of his youth, Stanley might not be mature enough to empathize with her situation, but instead he was impressively compassionate. It was a surprisingly enjoyable evening, with each of them taking the time to get to know the other. Although Stanley was supposed to leave early on Saturday morning, he ended up staying the rest of the weekend.

That summer, Stanley came out to the beach often. Slowly, Pattie began to introduce him to her friends out there, people who had known Caz. She found that it wasn't as strange as she might have expected, incorporating this new man into her life. Pattie kept grieving, she kept up her dialogue with Caz, she kept her life, while Stanley stepped in and played the part of her boyfriend for a while.

Pattie knew that her friends looked at her and thought, "Why him?" Several people shared those feelings with her. But Stanley was exactly what Pattie wanted at this point in her life. He was a special person who cared about her, and he was truly trying to help in any way he could.

A very few of her friends wanted to know, "How could you do this to Caz?" Pattie remained resilient. It was natural that they would react like this, and Pattie didn't blame them. Only a few months ago, she'd taken it for granted that she would never so much as kiss another guy as long as she lived. But then, with the support of the WC and her true friends, she began to understand her own need to experience this new relationship. Pattie needed to believe she could love, and be loved, again.

MEANWHILE, THINGS WERE progressing with Claudia and John. Every morning when Claudia got to work there was a sweet, tender, witty e-mail waiting for her. On their second date, he brought her a miniature Statue of Liberty—a reference to the conversation they'd had on their first date—and they agreed they had to go there together. They spoke every day and saw each other as much as they could. Claudia felt herself being swept up in this whirlwind romance. She just wanted to be with John, and for the first time in her life, she let go of her naturally cautious nature. Claudia knew this felt right, and she had the sense not to fight it.

John was thirty-eight, and ready for a commitment. He was considerate and passionate, funny and wise. He already knew Pattie so well. He got along great with the rest of the WC from the word go—he'd fallen in love with the group, and they'd returned the compliment. John had such a comforting self-assurance about him. He knew that what was happening was real. Claudia found she could talk about everything with him, that she didn't need to hide her grief from her new boyfriend. Loss was a part of her, and therefore had to be a part of this new love too.

John understood Claudia's need to spend time with the WC and with her extended family. Although her calendar was already jam-packed, she found ways of making John a priority. Saturdays and Sundays, the couple would throw beanbags out on the fire escape and do the *Times* crossword together. The simplest activities felt so right, as long as they did them together.

There were definitely times when Claudia was scared and overwhelmed, and she would share this with the WC. But it wasn't because she was worried about opening her heart to John. Mostly, she was overwhelmed because she didn't believe this could happen twice in a lifetime. For two years, Claudia had been saying the same phrase over and over again, "Life isn't ever what you think it's going to be." Now when she said the words, she found they had a different meaning. Maybe there were still some good surprises left in store.

Perhaps the hardest piece of the puzzle to make fit was that Claudia met John in the summer, a time when her apprehension about the second anniversary was already beginning to build. It wasn't easy for Claudia to balance the excitement about this new relationship with the date of September 11. How could she be happy when it was August?

What's more, John's birthday was September 5. Claudia was trying to be a good girlfriend who wanted to celebrate her new boyfriend's birthday, but it was tough to find the right balance. His sister was throwing him a birthday party and Claudia was going to meet a ton of his friends for the first time. At the best of times it can be stressful being the new girlfriend. But the party was taking place less than a week before the anniversary, a time when Claudia felt incredibly guilty talking about anything other than September 11.

The WC was there the night of John's birthday, and kept coming over and checking on Claudia.

"What am I going to do?" she'd ask them. "Every time John introduces me to someone, I keep wanting to tell them I'm a widow."

MONTHS LATER, CLAUDIA asked John if any of this was ever weird for him. "At first," he admitted. "Right at the beginning, I remember thinking that the last thing I needed was to get involved with a widow, let alone a September 11 widow." John described the WC husbands as being like star athletes dying in their prime. "It's like Roberto Clemente," he said. "You only have the good years to look back on. No losing a step, or low batting averages before retirement." Who wanted to try to compete with the memory of a hero?

But then there was that first evening together, which John described as being like "Date Concentrate."

"All the meaningful things that you usually reveal slowly over a string of dates, we discussed in a single night," he explained.

Then, in the weeks that followed, the relationship had an inevitability and energy of its own. It wasn't something you thought about; this was something you just went with.

John admitted that in the early days, coming to Claudia's apartment and seeing all the photos of Bart was a little strange for him.

"But I just wanted to spend as much time with you as possible," he explained, "and after a while, nothing else mattered."

THE DAY BEFORE the anniversary, Claudia received a poem John had written and sent to her in the mail:

Of all the kisses I have showered on you,
I wish there was one to wash away your tears today,
But my lips cannot help, for it is given by my heart.
My hugs may comfort for a moment, but my deep love for you will
*   help bear this hurt.*
For all the summer joys we've shared, there will at times be rain.
Yet, knowing our hearts and souls are one will help us through the pain.

Claudia acknowledged that from now on, she would be moving forward with parallel lives. She had two different types of loves coexisting within her. Bart was a part of her as much as her eyes were blue. She would always love Bart deeply and mourn for him; and she would continue to fall madly in love with John. She was amazed at the capacity of the human heart to love so intensely, not just once, but twice in a lifetime. It was something she might never be able to fully explain, except to reassure others that it's possible. Claudia's heart had been broken, but miraculously it kept on beating. She didn't know what she'd done to deserve this new love with John; she only knew that she was constantly thankful for it.

Bart

Caz

Tommy

Ward

Just as we began to sense ourselves becoming stronger, the anniversary came around to knock us off our feet again. The dread of the day had begun weeks before, draining us of any hard-won resources. We'd imagined that because we'd been here before, it would be a little easier. But two years later, the reality of how much had been destroyed was only just beginning to sink in. We were less numb, more aware of the ongoing reality.

Meanwhile, the city was regenerating itself—the subways nearest to Ground Zero were back in operation; the posters and pictures of the missing that had once filled bulletin boards had long since faded or been removed; most of the site was shielded from view because of construction. And yet here we were. It was another blue-sky day in September and we found ourselves in this crowd of thousands, all of us inexorably drawn back to the last place our loved ones had been.

Standing in the crowd, it was impossible not to be struck by the utter quietness and respectfulness of so many people gathered together. For the second anniversary, the children of the victims read the names, the sound of their voices as they spoke their mothers' and fathers' names rending the heart. The unbearable knowledge that they would grow up with that vital person always missing, the devastating intensity of the ceremony, the deluge of emotion, overtook us, along with the fight not to buckle under it.

Again we made our way down into the pit. Would this be the last year we could do this before major construction began? We'd all brought pictures and flowers this time. Standing there in the scarred earth, faced with the desolation, we looked up at the empty sky.

As far as we'd come, as hard as we'd tried, we were back where we'd begun. At Ground Zero, twenty-four long months disappear into thin air. Two years ago became yesterday. People always say that time heals. But when it comes to the anniversary of September 11, time is immaterial.

Part II

✦

September 2003 to August 2004

For myself I am an optimist—it does not seem to be much use being anything else.

— WINSTON CHURCHILL

Julia, Claudia,
Pattie, Ann

The day after the anniversary, we left New York to travel to Cabo San
Lucas, Mexico, for our second annual trip together. Always our travel
connoisseur, Claudia had found the resort, a place on the southernmost
tip of the Baja Peninsula, a cluster of white villas overlooking the ocean.

We agreed that we could have easily slept for a week, but instead we
packed our bags, took taxis, caught our flight, kept moving. As we arrived at the hotel, someone took our bags and the four of us walked
along a stony path and through a whitewashed entrance hall facing a
tranquil blue ocean. Above our heads, star-shaped lanterns twinkled in
the sunlight, as if we were entering another world. Our rooms were in
little white villas with views of the water and bright sandy beaches.
That night, ocean breezes kept us cool, while the sounds of the waves
lulled us to an early sleep.

The next morning, we woke up to Julia, our trusty alarm clock. As
she reminded us, we were on a mission. In the afternoon we could rest.
But in the mornings, we were busy.

Our first task was to fulfill Pattie's New Year's resolution: we were going to learn how to surf.

Pattie:

When I told the WC about my resolution for 2003, they were pretty impressed I even *had* a resolution. Only a year ago, I'd barely been able to drag myself out of bed to meet Claudia for New Year's brunch. And now I was talking surfing. . . .

In fact, I made my resolution the summer that I'd met the girls, back in 2002. I spent most of those winter weekends alone at the beach house. But when summer came, I began to invite others to join me. This particular summer weekend I invited a girlfriend and her two children.

That Saturday morning we prepared for a long day at the beach— packed umbrellas, food, drinks, and beach chairs. On the beach, as usual, I found myself gazing out at the water. The light that day was radiant, glinting off the waves, and there was just enough of a breeze to give you goose bumps and keep you from sweltering.

"God did an extra special job when he landed here," Caz and I used to say when we were at this spot.

The sun was bright. I shaded my eyes with my hand. Directly ahead of me, I could see a little girl, about eight years old, at the water's edge, wearing an orange swimsuit. She was with a guy with dreadlocks, in beach shorts, and they were both carrying surfboards. First the man showed the little girl how to lie flat on her board so she could practice paddling with her arms, and then he demonstrated how to jump upright, knees bent, arms to the sides. The little girl was fair-haired and round-faced, and I was reminded exactly of childhood photos of myself playing on the beach. My next thought was that this was what May Carrington would have looked like. May (short for Mary Grace) was the name that Caz and I had both chosen for the daughter we dreamed of having together. I liked the name because I thought it was beautiful, but Caz chose it in honor of his beloved grandmother, his Nanna.

Now I couldn't take my eyes off this vision of May. It was so impressive to see how quickly she mastered the techniques her teacher was showing her. She was agile and athletic. She was brave. When she was toppled by a wave, she would bob right up again, shrieking and smiling. Unbeknownst to the little girl or her teacher, I spent the next hour watching and imagining a life for May Carrington, a family full of love and support, with the world's most devoted dad.

When my friend happened to look up from her book, I shared my thoughts. I began to describe how, if Caz had been a dad, his daughter would have been just as courageous, just as confident as the little girl paddling around on the board out there.

"With Caz for a dad, May would have believed she could do anything in the world," I told my friend. "Anything and everything. That was Caz's way. He made you feel invincible."

"Oh, you're right," she answered. "Caz's daughter would have had no limitations, but she would probably have been slightly obnoxious because of it."

Here I was fantasizing about this happy, carefree, confident little girl and my friend was imagining an *obnoxious* child?

Her response took the wind out of my sails. The comment was inexplicable and hurtful. There was no daughter. There was no husband. The dream was only a dream. I would never find out what kind of person little May would have been. I sat in my chair quietly confounded.

There and then, I decided to turn the tables. Okay, so I cannot have this perfect little girl with my perfect husband. Okay, fine. But I am not surrendering. I am not giving in. I will *be* that little girl. I will learn how to surf.

THAT FIRST DAY in Cabo San Lucas, we put our bathing suits on and marched down to the beach, ready to take on the waves. We were so determined. We were the WC. Nothing was going to stand in our way.

Which is how we learned our surfing lesson number one: surfers need waves. Unfortunately, the ocean that morning was as flat as a pancake. Defeated yet determined, we decided on a good alternative— ocean kayaking and snorkeling. It turned out to be the best snorkeling any of us had ever done, thousands of jewel-colored fishes glimmering only inches below the surface. We didn't get to do what we'd planned, but it turned out to be a blessing in disguise.

Then, on the second day, we woke up to see beautiful big waves crashing on the shore.

Good to go. Another WC phrase, often abbreviated "G 2 G" in e-mails and inspired by Julia's cheerleader attitude, meaning: ready when you are, count me in, be spontaneous, let's do it now. When we said it to one another it became an affirmation of our approach to life. No time like the present!

Lucky for us, our instructor was adorable, the picture of a handsome surfer. He had salt-matted dark brown curls, soft brown skin, and a washboard belly. On land, he was gorgeous, but in the water, he was a god, riding the waves as if he was walking on water.

We, however, were definitely mortal, laughing and shrieking as the waves knocked us under and swept us back to shore over and over again, with none of us managing to stay up on our boards for more than a second. The surf was so strong that when the waves threw us down—our surfboards lashed to our ankles—we came up reeling and gasping for air, checking ourselves for signs of concussion.

After only a few minutes our arms burned from all the paddling. We'd thought that the hardest part of surfing would be standing upright. But none of us could have predicted how tough it was just getting far enough out to begin surfing at all. If you saw a big wave coming, you were supposed to do "the turtle." Our instructor made it look so easy. You held tight to your board and flipped yourself over until the board was on top of you. The idea was that the wave would rush over the board and then you would emerge on the other side and flip yourself back over. But if you missed the moment to flip—which you usually did—you and your board went flying, crashing back onto the beach where you'd come from. Ugh.

We were all pretty terrible at surfing. It didn't matter. We agreed that we'd never been so bad at something and yet had so much fun in the process. We actually wanted this to be hard and to be challenging. We'd spent two years battling so many invisible demons. Raging against the murderers who stole our husbands. Mad with God for not intervening. Fighting our own inabilities to move on. Fighting to hang onto our husbands. But these waves were something we could truly fight against, and although they seemed insurmountable at first, if we focused all our energy, eventually we made our way through them. Any pain we experienced while doing this was practically a relief.

. . .

IF YOU'D TOLD Ann when she was twenty that she would be surfing at forty, she never would have believed you. As she paddled out against the waves, she just kept thinking, "If my kids could see me now. Mother of three, in a tankini, belly down on a surfboard . . ." She had a raw graze along the side of her right leg from where a wave had thrown her onto a bank of sharp rocks. The salt was stinging her leg like crazy. But a little sting couldn't compete with the pain she'd been through the past week, the past two years. It was nothing compared to what The Boys must have been through that day. It didn't stand a chance against her new levels of tolerance.

Paddling against the odds, Claudia thought about how much her life had changed: if Bart were alive, the two of them would be sitting by the pool ordering margaritas right now.

As Julia pushed the board out for the hundredth time, she couldn't believe how much energy she still had. She kept thinking about Tommy's competitive spirit. She'd heard so many stories from his friends and former teammates about how Tommy had always pushed them to realize their full potential. "Okay, Tommy, I'm going to do it this time," she told him. There was no way she was going to let the waves defeat her.

Pattie was out as far as she could go without drowning. She thought to herself, "I'm going to do this if it *kills* me." She tensed every muscle, waiting for the moment when the wave began to curve, gripping her board at the front. Ready. Okay. *Now!* And then she was on her feet, her hands stretched out on either side, and the water was rushing and her blood was racing. But she was still balancing, flying, and for those seconds it felt like the force of the entire ocean was behind her.

Victory!

The rest of us were cheering like crazy, and the waves were rolling in and roaring like a round of applause. Pattie was breathless, hair plastered to her face, unable to speak from the thrill of accomplishment.

And before the end of that session, Claudia, Ann, and Julia got up on their boards too, and experienced the sheer crazy rush of it. In those precious moments, we felt like eight-year-olds, invincible and innocent; as if anything was possible, even surfing.

. . .

MUSCLES ACHING, EXHAUSTED but exhilarated, we headed back to the pool for lunch. Pattie, Ann, and Julia discovered that at some point during that lesson, the same question flashed through each of their minds: why keep on paddling out while the ocean kept pushing you back toward land again? After all, it would have been much, much easier just to slip off the board, go under the next wave, and never come up. The water was so warm, clear, and inviting. We agreed that, at times, the temptation to stop fighting was just as strong as the will to fight. There were always those moments when we wanted more than anything to give in.

At one end of the hotel's pool there was a bar you could swim right up to, with stone seats and tables in the water, and this was where we gathered for our lunches. The bartenders were so friendly, the service impeccable, the drinks delectable.

"Good afternoon, ladies!" they called out as we swam toward them. "So how was your morning?"

We told them about the waves, and our successes on our surfboards. Julia jumped up on her bar stool and demonstrated her surfing moves for the bartenders.

It was time for our toast.

"To The Boys!"

"Wish they were here."

Over lunch we imagined what it would have been like if the eight us had been there together . . .

HOWEVER, THERE WAS one other small trouble in paradise. At the resort that week there just happened to be nine—yes, nine—honeymoon couples.

We tried to be tolerant. What else should we have expected in such a romantic place? Besides, we could travel to the other side of the world and there would always be some reminder.

"Don't look now," Julia warned us, as we finished off our lunch and moved to lounge by the side of the pool, "but here comes our favorite couple."

This was the couple that we had singled out as being somewhat more annoying than the others. Everywhere we turned, there they were—smooching by the pool, strolling hand in hand along the beach, whispering to each other over lunches out on the terrace. Which probably wouldn't have bothered us—*really,* we were happy for them, *honestly*—except that whenever they saw another honeymoon couple, these two had to start discussing their wedding in *really loud* voices.

By now, we knew that our favorite couple had chocolate cake at their wedding and another couple had tiers of frosted vanilla cupcakes. She had white lilies in her bouquet; another woman had orchids. They had a church wedding; the others got married on the beach.

At least we got to amuse ourselves doing impersonations of them: "Oooo, what time did you have your ceremony? Ours was at four. . . ." "What were *your* hors d'oeuvres?" "Cheers! It's our one-week anniversary!"

At one stage, Julia got so tired of their endless wedding chitchat that she threatened to stage an intervention.

"You know what I'm going to do?" she announced. "I'm going back to my room, I'm going to put on one of my Tommy T-shirts and go and stand there in front of them and say, 'Hey, take a look at *my* husband! Who, by the way, is dead. Wanna hear about *my* wedding . . . ?'"

From the various charity events that were held in his name, Julia has a large collection of T-shirts with photos of Tommy on them. We dared her to do it. Of course, she didn't have the heart—after all, it wasn't their fault this had happened to us.

WE SPENT THE rest of the afternoon talking and crying, then sleeping, then waking to talk again. The last time we had been together for this long was a year ago in Scottsdale. Since then there had been so many months of hard work—so many emotions kept at bay by the daily grind, the pressures of our jobs, the endless mechanical doing and functioning of life. We had struggled so hard to put ourselves back together. Now, in the long afternoons of sunshine, with nothing else to do, we allowed ourselves to come apart again. When we were alone, we didn't always want to do this. It could feel too dangerous, like we might go crazy and never return to a place where life would be manageable again. But here we could let ourselves go. There were four of us. We would pull one another back again if we sank too deep. We knew that there was a bottom, and we reminded one another of it.

We were passing around a copy of *O* magazine, reading and rereading one of the articles inside, by the writer Anne Lamott, contemplating life in her forties:

> I have survived so much loss, as all of us have in our forties. My parents, my dear friends, my pets. Rubble is the ground on which our deepest friendships are built. If you haven't already, you will lose someone you can't live without, and your heart will be badly broken, and the bad news is that you will never completely get over the loss of that beloved person. But this is also the good news. They live forever in your broken heart that doesn't seal back up. And you come through. It's like having a broken leg that never heals perfectly—that still hurts when the weather is cold—but you learn to dance with the limp. You dance to the absurdities of life; you dance to the minuet of old friendships.

The writer's words leapt off the page: by the time you get to this point in your life, loss is an inevitable. Loss is universal. If you hadn't experienced loss yet, you were in the minority. Before, when people told us that there was a positive side to loss, we weren't always ready to hear it. But now we had begun to sense that there *was* good news, that what hadn't killed us *had* made us stronger. No matter how much we missed our husbands, we were starting to recognize that it's a gift to learn what's truly important at such a young age. The other side of the coin of death is life. Because if there's anything that teaches you not to waste a day, it's coming face to face with the hard fact of mortality.

WHEN WE LOOKED around again, the honeymoon couples were packing up their things, saying they were going to get "dressed for dinner." We knew what that meant—they were going to their rooms to make love after lounging around in the sun all day. We longed for that feeling, warm all through from the sunshine, making love in a hotel room with the man you adored. But since we didn't have that option, we decided to get in a last swim of the day, gathering at the far end of the pool to watch the sunset, the sky turning deep orange at the horizon and deep blue above.

Ann told us that there was nowhere else in the world she wanted to be right now, and since she couldn't be with Ward, there was no one else she'd rather be with. As the sun slipped down behind the horizon, we counted our blessings and agreed.

THE FOLLOWING MORNING, we were ready for our next challenge. We had booked ourselves to go out on all-terrain vehicles, or ATVs, those machines that look like a cross between a dirt bike and a small truck, with four massive wheels and pretty powerful engines. None of us had ridden an ATV before, or even thought about riding one, for that matter. Ann remembered being at a wedding on a ranch in Texas where the host had provided ATVs for the guests.

"All the guys went out on them," she recalled. "Ward was away all afternoon, riding around in the dirt. He came back with his face all covered with dust and a huge grin. He loved it, of course."

"So what were you doing while the guys were out on bikes?" we asked.

"Well, I stayed back at the ranch with the girls, catching up on the gossip over a nice round of cocktails. . . ."

A whole universe had changed since then.

Now, wearing long pants as instructed, so that the engines wouldn't burn us, we made our way down to the beach, the heat of the sand coming up through our sneakers. It was another cloudless day in Mexico; the surf had flattened off and the water was calm again.

Parked on the beach, in the bright morning sunshine, were eleven ATVs, their huge chrome engines smeared with grease, red chassis spattered with dust. Two of the honeymoon couples and another couple from the hotel were already there, as well as the man who was going to be our guide. We were told to each take a bike. Eleven riders, eleven bikes. But the wives in the group quickly made excuses and climbed on the back behind their husbands.

The WC members assumed our positions. We were going to be riding solo on four ATVs of our own.

Once we figured out how to work the ignition, played around with the acceleration, and tested the brakes, we were off, determined to leave the couples in the dust. We'd been given red bandannas to put over our mouths and noses, like four widow bandits.

Pulling away, we braced our arms against the handlebars, stuck our necks forward, and went for it, riding at the front of the line, behind the guide. We were low to the ground and only had so far to fall, and anyway, there was soft sand to catch us if we did. So we kept pumping the accelerator, letting the dunes and the ATV throw us around from side to side, forward and back, as we hung onto the handlebars, like we were riding one of those mechanical bulls in a bar. For split seconds we would think we were about to come off, but every bump we survived made us feel more fearless. We needed to test how fast we could go over the dunes without taking a tumble, and the answer was, pretty darn fast. The wheels were so enormous on these things that it would have been tough to lose your balance.

The guide started to climb up the higher dunes toward the clifftops, so we followed him. He led us up onto a trail running alongside the beach, looking down on the white sands and the endless blue waters— an incredible sight. Julia knew Tommy would have gotten such a kick out of seeing her leading the way at the front of the pack. Ann felt like she was a kid again playing chicken on her bike with the neighborhood kids. Pattie experienced the guilty liberation of knowing she was breaking all the rules: "These machines cannot be good for the environment—think of what they do to the dunes. . . ." Meanwhile Claudia contemplated how much Bart would have loved the excitement of it all—the views, the speed, the feeling of sheer freedom. There was something about the rush of air against our faces and the roar of the engines that set our thoughts free.

Soon enough, we were winding our way down from the clifftops and back onto the dunes. Our guide signaled to us to stop. Then he told us to roam around on our own for the next hour. So we were off again. The couples headed in another direction and we headed inland. Julia cut in front of Ann. Pattie cut in front of Claudia. We zoomed around, weaving in and out of one another, daring one another to go faster and faster, shouting through our bandannas.

But then, all of a sudden, we saw something coming toward us and slowed down, turning off our engines so as not to disturb it.

Ahead of us was a brightly colored cloud, fluttering and shimmering in the sunlight, moving toward us. As it came closer, we could see that the cloud was made up of hundreds and hundreds of beautiful yellow butterflies. The butterflies kept moving, flickering around us, surrounding us, and the sight of them flew straight to our hearts. We'd spent two years looking and looking for our husbands. Over our shoulders, in the faces in crowds, in reflections in windows, out of the corner of one eye, in the shapes of the clouds. But The Boys were no longer in one place. They were free and they were here, coming to find us in the most unexpected places—like butterflies in a cloud appearing from nowhere, on a beach in Mexico, blown from land toward the sea.

WHEN WE CLIMBED off our ATVs an hour later, we took photos of one another. In those photos, we are happy. Our faces are black from the nose up, our eyes are relaxed, our smiles wide and easy, our bodies limp from hanging onto the bikes all morning. And in those photos you can see that time is not responsible for any healing that's taking place. A hundred years could pass and nothing could ever take the love we feel for our husbands from us, or the pain of losing them. What's healing us is this love of life that's blasting through us on the beaches of Mexico— the ocean views and the pumping engines and the wind in our hair and our best friends right behind us and hundreds and hundreds of butterflies and the smell of the spray and the pull of the surf and being there, alive, with all the hours in the day to experience it together. That's what's making us smile.

Julia

Back in the city Claudia and Pattie continued seeing John and Stanley. Ann had been going out on dates for a year now. Julia still considered herself the late bloomer of the group—she was convinced she wasn't ready to date. She just wasn't in a place where she felt comfortable with the idea of going on a date. Sometimes Julia wondered if she would ever be ready.

The WC kept reassuring her—"Julia, you are the only one that can truly make the decision as to whether dating is right for you or not. There's no rush."

Before the trip to Mexico, right at the tail end of summer, old friends of Tommy's had decided to play matchmaker, inviting Julia out to their beach house for the Labor Day weekend without telling her that a good friends of theirs, Matt, would also be there.

As Julia walked into their house that Friday, Matt was in the dining room. "Hmmm," thought Julia, guessing that possibly something was afoot. As her friends prepared dinner, Matt and Julia talked. She could remember thinking how interesting he was and how kind his eyes were. Here was someone with a nice personality and a great smile, who put her immediately at ease. They ate dinner, and ended up playing board games late into the evening, with Matt and Julia playing on the same team. At some point that evening, Julia looked up and realized she was having a lot of fun with someone who was not a friend and who was male. Matt and Julia ended up talking until three in the morning. On her way to bed, Julia had that heady, teenage feeling, like she'd just flirted with a guy for the first time.

The next day, Matt had to leave to go to a college football game with friends, but before he left, he very politely asked Julia if she would like to go out with him sometime. He let her know he was traveling for work over the next month but he would be back in mid-October. Would she like to have a drink with him when he returned to New York?

Julia thought, *Sure, why not have a drink with a friend of friends?* This couldn't be a date because she didn't date.

Was this a date? Did he just ask me out for a drink or did he ask me out? Surely he didn't just ask me out.

After all, Julia was still married to Tommy.

Am I still married? Is Matt asking me out as a favor to our mutual friends? Does he feel obligated? Does he feel sorry for me? Am I interesting enough that he actually wants to go out with me? What am I? Single?

No, Julia wasn't single; she was married.

Would I be disloyal to Tommy if I went out with someone? Am I over-thinking this? What am I doing?

"That would be great!" she told Matt, reassuring herself that he probably wouldn't call.

He definitely wasn't going to call. And if he did call, it wouldn't be for the next month.

It was okay. Julia had a month to prepare herself.

SOON AFTER THE WC returned from Cabo, Matt called and suggested he and Julia meet for a drink and then go to a Broadway musical. Julia agreed, reluctantly and willingly. Nothing is simple for a widow. She wanted to go and she didn't want to go. She was all over the place on this one.

The night before the date, Julia was having a really bad day. She left work in the afternoon because she was having really big "Tommy moments." That's what she called them—Tommy moments, those moments when she just missed him so much, when she felt overwhelmed with dealing with everything, when she didn't want to cope with trying to manage her life. She felt so depressed that she went home and went to bed. The next morning, Julia called in sick to work. She didn't get off the couch that day. She just sat and watched TV and cried.

Curled up on her couch, snuffling away, she called the WC and told us she was going to cancel the date. She just wanted to stay home. She didn't want to go out at all, let alone on a date. She kept hoping for a different answer, but we all told Julia the same thing: that she would feel worse if she stayed home, that she would feel better if she just got up, got dressed, and got out of the house for a few hours. Why not escape from reality for a while?

A combination of desperation and sheer determination got Julia up off the couch that evening and into a shower. She dressed and took a cab to the Theater District. She stood on the corner outside the restaurant. Should she go in? What was she doing here? A friend called to wish Julia good luck. Julia told her she didn't think she could go through with this, that she was going to leave. She felt sick with nerves. The friend persuaded her to stick it out, telling Julia she was going to have a great time.

"Yes, I know I'll probably have fun with Matt," Julia told her. "But it's the thought of going out with a guy that freaks me out."

She thought she'd finished with dating when she married Tommy.

Julia could see Matt coming toward her, smiling. No backing out now. Besides, nothing could be as hard as Julia was expecting this to be. Once inside they began to chat. Not hard. Easy. Matt was great; he was a friend of friends after all. They had some drinks and ordered appetizers, but the food was taking so long to arrive that they ended up getting it packed so they could take it with them to the theater. During the intermission they had their own "tailgate" party in the lobby, snacking on calamari and drinking beers. Julia had to admit she was actually having a good time. After the musical, Matt walked her home and kissed her on the cheek. He e-mailed her the next day. They continued to talk, and made plans to see each other again.

19 · *Transformations*

Claudia and Pattie

Pattie:

In the early days after Caz was killed, traveling had been difficult for me. I didn't like going beyond the confines of the familiar. Back then, both my homes brought me so much comfort; I had no desire to go beyond their boundaries. When I ventured outside of that zone, the world intruded, reminding me that everything changes, everyone moves on. The blanket of sadness weighed heavily on my shoulders. I didn't want to experience any of life's pleasures—travel included—when I wouldn't be able to share them with my husband.

When you travel, you deliberately disorient yourself. Before, I was so disoriented that travel was confusing for me. But over time, I began to feel differently. As I felt my sense of self returning to me, I began to actively want to travel again. I'd always been attracted to new cultures, languages, ways of living. This was part of the reason I was so strongly drawn to Caz—he was an expatriate. Just being around him expanded my horizons. Now I realized that I wanted to have that sense of reinvention and release that being in a foreign environment brings. By traveling, you seek to lose yourself, in the hope that you'll come upon a new version of yourself. I had become profoundly lost when Caz died, but in the past month or so, I was beginning to find my way again.

I wanted to truly begin traveling again, in that old spirit of freedom and adventure.

After I came back from Cabo, I had plans to visit Caz's mother, Kate. It was a great blessing to me that my relationship with Kate continued to deepen. My mother-in-law is an incredibly strong, beautiful, and determined woman. After the death of her son, she went through an unimaginably painful period, an experience that helped inspire her to fulfill her dream, as Caz had always encouraged her to do. She moved to the Dordogne in France, to a little house in the middle of the countryside, where she could tend her garden and master the French language.

That November, I flew to France. Caz's sister, Sarah, came in from London. The three of us reminisced for hours over family photographs, indulging our need to talk and share stories about Caz. We spent our days driving around visiting churches and villages, stopping at food markets, eating lunches in bustling cafés. One of our favorite activities was foraging at the local *brocantes*, tiny thrift shops filled with hidden treasures.

One day, we were combing the shelves at a *brocante* in a nearby town. On the racks, I noticed a beautiful short fur coat. Very Audrey Hepburn in *Breakfast at Tiffany's*. We oo-ed and aah-ed. I tried it on and it fit perfectly. It was glamorous yet practical, and definitely suited me. But it was unlike anything else in my wardrobe. This just wasn't the kind of coat I owned.

"You should get it!" Sarah and Kate said in unison.

"No, no, I can't!" I protested.

"Why not?" Kate and Sarah insisted. "It looks fantastic and the price is great."

"It's just not my style."

"But it suits you perfectly."

"Oh, what the heck," I conceded. "It's fun."

. . .

THE TRIP TO France had been a success. The difficulties came, not from being away, but from coming back. Landing at an airport and being unable to call him. That feeling of dark loneliness at the end of a long flight when I wanted to tell the person I loved the most in the world that I'd see him soon.

It was an unspoken rule in the Carrington household that whenever you went away, you brought home a present for the person left behind. Even when I went on a business trip, I had to bring back a "prezzie." Caz became the recipient of a beer mug from the Chicago airport and barbecue sauce from Kansas City (such is my glamorous work itinerary). These ridiculous items made him as happy as a child, proving once and for all it's the thought that counts.

Now every time my plane touched down in New York City, I would ache to call Caz and tell him, "Guess what I brought you this time?" If it weren't for Lola waiting for me, the return to the apartment would have been unbearable.

Coming back from France, I brought the little fur coat, my gift to both Caz and me.

A transformation was beginning. Soon afterwards I found myself leaving my apartment looking down at the three-quarter-length gloves my brother had given to me, three-inch heels on my boots courtesy of Claudia's discount, and the fur coat from France. I looked up and giggled.

"Caz, what's happening to me?"

I knew how much Caz would have appreciated the coat, which was not important for itself, but only for what it symbolized. The coat was frivolous, extroverted, extravagant. I was raised to be humble, to blend into the background, to be modest. In my family, it wasn't good to stand out, to be the beauty in the room. Leave that to someone else, my parents taught me. My brother, sisters, and I were not encouraged to win a game; we were instructed to help our team. My parents are incredible people: intelligent, warm, hardworking, wholesome. But when I met Caz, I was so impressed by how little he cared about "blending in" and "being humble." Here was someone who was fearless. He marched to his own drum. He loved to stand out in a crowd (how could he not?). His presence was always *felt*.

Now, every time I put on that coat, I think of Caz and how pleased he would be that I bought it for myself. Purchasing it went against the grain of modesty. I was getting my hair highlighted, my nails manicured, going for massages. They're little things, and I'm not suggesting they mean much in the grand scheme of things. But I know how much it would tickle Caz to see me looking after myself like this. He was always encouraging me to be less frugal, more indulgent. "Buy the cashmere scarf, not the wool one!" He wanted only the best for me. In Caz's absence, I was internalizing him, the things that he showed me. His confidence was becoming mine.

I couldn't give him a "prezzie" anymore when I returned from my travels, but I could do him the honor of letting his spirit animate my life.

Not that I didn't suffer from the occasional guilt pang—it's too entrenched in me. My parents' words will always flash through my mind—"There are people in Africa who are starving!" But now when I look at the little fur coat, I see Caz, I see his mother and sister encouraging me and cheering me on.

"Why not?" they say.

Claudia:

Over the summer, I'd already begun to introduce John to my family and closest friends. We were spending so much time together that I'd started to feel guilty about not having enough time for people who had helped me get through the past two years. It was scary, but I made the decision to share the news of my relationship with my wider circle of friends and colleagues. I knew I wasn't doing anything wrong, that John was going to be a permanent part of my life, and that people could accept it or not. But I had to give them the chance, no matter how much I feared being judged.

Of course there were some people who weren't easy. We were out to dinner one night when one of my friends told John he had "big shoes to fill."

"I'm not trying to fill anyone's shoes," John told him. "I'm just being myself."

But the underlying sentiment was hurtful and judgmental. John wasn't trying to fill Bart's shoes. John was a confident, independent man with big shoes of his own.

And then there were those people who were genuinely happy for me—the WC, of course; my own family. I was especially blessed because Bart's family immediately embraced John. He met Bart's brother, Mark, and they hit it off. We went out for dinner with Kathleen and Larry. Bart's mother, Pat, met John that fall at my nephew's christening.

Pat walked right up to us in church. "Hi, I'm Claudia's mother-in-law," she said to John. "It's truly a pleasure to meet you. It's not every day you get to meet your girlfriend's mother-in-law, is it?"

The Ruggieres wanted me to be happy—they knew that Bart would want that—and their support made a world of difference. Kathleen put it best when she said: "I'm happy for you. If this were the other way around, and you were the one who'd died, I would want this for Bart. I would want Bart to be happy, to fall in love, to be thinking about having a family."

Now I had to tell my work colleagues. Everyone at work had been overwhelmingly supportive since Bart was killed. These were people I saw every day, who had reached out to me and supported me in countless ways. They had taken the time to learn about Bart and grieved with me. As a result, I was worried about what they would think of John. As it turned out, I was pleasantly surprised by my colleagues' reactions. When I told them I was in love, they seemed genuinely happy for me.

My therapist, Cheryl, helped me enormously during this transition phase. I would talk to her about this and other issues, but by now I knew in my gut when decisions were right or wrong. Eventually Cheryl told me she didn't feel like I needed to be in regularly scheduled therapy any longer. If we stopped now and I went through a particularly difficult period, I would know I could pick up the phone and call her. It felt good to graduate from therapy and to know it would always be there if I felt I needed it.

Caz at the marathon

Pattie:

By now, everyone in the WC was aware of how important the New York City marathon was to me. It was an event that Caz and I looked forward to all year. My husband once said that he looked forward to marathon day more than Christmas, and that's saying a lot from a guy who loved gifts and surprises more than anyone I know.

The marathon was coming around again—the first weekend in November. This year, Julia, who lived closest to the route, suggested we have a party at her place so that the WC could experience the marathon together. I remember feeling touched that Julia wanted to do this for me, and of course, I agreed to go. But at the same time, I was hesitant. On marathon day, I wanted to be around people who had known Caz and who understood the day's significance.

I'D STARTED WATCHING the marathon long before I met Caz. In 1989, the year after I graduated and moved to the city, college friends of mine were sharing an apartment on the Upper East Side, and so we went and stood on the corner of their block, at First Avenue and Seventy-first Street, to watch the runners go by. It was a beautiful, bright early winter's day, and as the first runners started to pass, our excitement began to build. The determination and grace of those front runners were breathtaking—they were already at mile sixteen and they were still sprinting, whizzing by with looks of calm determination on their faces. It was impossible not to be impressed by their dedication and strength. But these were just the front runners.

As the hours passed, we became more and more involved in the race, as the participants toward the back of the pack came through. These runners were tall, short, heavy, skinny, old, young, male, female, physically able and physically disabled, blind, seeing, in wheelchairs, walking with sticks or with the help of low-rider bicycles. They were from every country on the planet, wearing their names and nations on their shirts. These people weren't running to compete; they were running to prove they could make it through twenty-six miles, no matter how long it took them. We shouted and cheered, swept up in the urge to encourage these people. As time passed, and the runners struggled more and more, our cheers and shouts kept increasing in passion and volume. We wanted to contribute to their success in any way we could, so we went to the grocery store and bought oranges, candy, Vaseline, Advil, and water. We yelled the names people had painted on their shirts, telling them not to give up, to make it through the next ten miles to the finish line. We were losing our voices from screaming: "You can do it, good for you!" A soon-to-be legendary line.

The police had to keep reminding us to stay behind the barriers. We laughed at how swept away we were becoming, welling up with emotion at the sight of so many people pushing themselves beyond their physical limitations.

It was an incredibly inspiring afternoon.

Then another mantra started among us. It catches everyone who goes to watch the race: "I'm doing this next year, I swear."

BUT THE NEXT year came and went and we were still battling the bulge that we'd acquired during our college days. We were in no way disciplined enough to prepare for such a grueling event. Instead, we turned out again to support the runners and brought our friends. Every year, our marathon "tailgates" became more elaborate.

Finally, in 1994, I ran the race. It was a fantastic experience. I confess, I hadn't followed a proper training regimen or changed my social habits, but on the other hand, I wasn't in it to win. I just wanted to have the experience of being part of the event. When I got to Seventy-first and First Avenue, my crew was there, so I stopped to bask in the attention. After finishing, I was so proud to have the aluminum blanket they wrap around you at the end that I proceeded to join my friends without going home to change. I kept that blanket on until midnight, when I finally called it a day.

My friend Sandy was hooked by the mantra next, and she decided to run the race in 1996.

This was the first year Caz joined us. He had never been to the marathon before and didn't know what to expect, although I had let him know how much he was going to love it.

That day, I remember, he had on a furry mustard-colored Patagonia jacket that matched his newly buzzed hair. Caz had recently shaved his head to raise money for autism, the only person in his office to volunteer for a sponsored head shaving. Typical Caz. My husband, always the comedian, had a fascination with his own head—he loved to put things on it, including hats, lampshades, and, most hysterically, a plunger. After the head-shaving incident, Caz and a friend decided it would be a great idea to bleach what was left of his hair à la Billy Idol. Unfortunately the mixing of the chemicals didn't go quite right. Instead of peroxide white, his hair came out burnt orange.

Caz's contribution to marathon day was a giant thermos of hot apple cider and rum. Right away, he fully entered into the spirit of the marathon crowd, carried away by the emotion of cheering for the runners along with the rest of us.

"You can do it! Good for you!"

He had a particular soft spot for the underdogs, the blind runners, the wheelchair racers, the runners with prostheses, the teams running for a loved one lost to cancer. He patted their backs, he would make them laugh, he told them they could do it; he shouted their names so loud they wouldn't dare not finish. If a runner was struggling, then he would run alongside that person, not stopping until he finally got a smile, even if it took a few blocks.

At the end of the day, he even repeated our mantra with a serious face. "I am going to do this next year, I swear. How much do you want to make a bet?"

Caz never ran the event, but he was always the noisiest and most colorful cheerleader in our group. In the following years, the marathon was a favorite date on our calendar—a day to anticipate. One year, a band appeared on our corner, and they returned every year after that. The policemen assigned to the corner would come back year after year, and we got to know them—they told us they would compete to be assigned to our corner. Every marathon day we would see the same familiar faces. We cheered for everyone, staying until the very last runners came through. We even painted signs to show our support for the street sweepers cleaning up after the race: "GO STREET SWEEPERS!"

WE CHOSE THE weekend of the marathon for Caz's memorial, partly because it was such an auspicious day for him, but also as a means of avoidance, so we wouldn't have to go without him. I wondered if the policemen, the band, and the others we met at the corner of Seventy-first Street and First Avenue questioned why we stopped going in 2001. Did they suspect that something was wrong? Would anyone have guessed that someone as lively as Caz had been killed?

By year three—although I wasn't sure I was ready to face going to the marathon without Caz—I could at least dip my toe in the water. I would be at Julia's, not at our regular corner, and I wouldn't be down at the barricades for the entire event.

But when I made it out to the sidelines, that same spirit of marathon days came surging back to me. I began to shout. I didn't stop. Every time I cheered on one of the runners, I knew I wasn't just cheering for them.

"You can do it. Good for you!"

At one point I ducked under the barricade and was in the street running alongside a struggling runner, shouting at him: "You can do it! Good for you!"

The WC cheered on the runners just as hard as I did. We were all familiar with the concept of the endurance test. Like a marathon, widowhood tests the depths of your resilience. What counts is your ability to remain strong under conditions that are enormously stressful and challenging. Then just when you figure you can't go any further, someone appears on the sidelines and gives you the boost you need to go the next mile, the next, and the mile after that. You keep going through your own will and determination to keep going, and with the support of others.

"I am going to do this next year, I swear," promised the WC. I looked at them and smiled.

21 · The Gift

Ward, Ann, and family

The holidays were coming. Although we agreed we would prefer to go to sleep from Thanksgiving until New Year's—"Wake me up on the second of January, please"—we knew that wasn't going to be possible. So we did our best to at least attempt to make new traditions to offset the sadness.

We attempted to rationalize things. Yes, the holidays were tough, but we knew from prior experience exactly how tough, so at least we could be prepared. At least we could see the holidays coming. Sometimes it felt like it was much harder to guard ourselves against the little things. Seeing a gift in a store we wanted to buy for him, going past a restaurant that he loved, getting a call from a telemarketer asking for him—the everyday work of missing your husband.

Christmas is a time for family, and we were all trying to figure out where our duties lay. No longer afforded the status of wives, it was like we had been demoted back to being the child again in our respective families. Julia was going off to Dallas, where her family was spending the holidays at her sister's house—even so, she didn't want to be there on Christmas morning, so she decided to wait and leave mid-afternoon so that she wouldn't have to wake up on the day and fake a smile. Pattie was dreading driving alone to her parents', no longer a married woman and banished back to her childhood single bed again. Claudia was spending her first Christmas with John. She would spend Christmas Eve with his family, Christmas Day with her family, and go to a special Christmas celebration with Bart's family the week before. Ann decided to spend Christmas in her own home, visiting friends instead of family. She wanted to have a chance to make new traditions for herself and the kids.

NOT SURPRISINGLY, OUR WC Christmas celebration was the highlight of the season. No pressure, no guilt, just fun. We arranged to meet at The Grill, at our table under a plaque commemorating Bart on the wall. Everyone was going to bring a gift, and choosing them became one of the unadulterated pleasures of this otherwise difficult season.

Claudia's present to us was a mixed CD made up of songs that were meaningful to us. She put a photo of the WC surfing on the cover. The title of the CD was: *It Would Be Wrong Not To . . .*

When Ann saw the cover of Claudia's CD cases with our surfing photo on it, she insisted we skip to her gift next, knowing she had used the same photo to decorate four red leather bookmarks. We could use them to put inside the book we'd already decided we wanted to write together, as a team.

Julia brought us silver necklaces with the word "courage" on them. She also gave each of us a "Mr. Wonderful" doll. Press his hand and he tells you what you want to hear. "Yes, dear, I would love to go shoe shopping with you." Or "Oh, your mother's staying another week. Great!"

Pattie brought us each a small oil painting she'd commissioned from her friend Sandy, of the American flag.

Ann saved the best for last, pulling out her final gift—black thong underwear for each of us, customized with the words "Be Wrong Not To" on the front and "WC" in red embroidery on the tiny triangle of fabric on the back. What better gift to make fun of our emerging selves? It would be wrong not to laugh at ourselves. It would be wrong not to wear a sexy thong, in the knowledge that your three friends were wearing them too. Silly, fun, laughable—the perfect gift for the WC.

Of course the whoops and howls of laughter from our table turned heads, but what was priceless was our waiters' expressions—three men who had taken care of us over the last couple of years. They didn't quite know how to react to four widows waving thongs in the air. Their discomfort, which quickly turned into smiles for us, made us appreciate the moment that much more.

And we got to spend that evening unabashedly reminiscing about Christmases past, the ones we had spent with The Boys. We were all asking ourselves the same question: What would we be doing if he were here this year?

THEN, THE DAY before Christmas, we went to visit Ground Zero together, making our way through the crowds of people racing by with their armloads of shopping bags. It was a surreal feeling of being suspended in time, while the rest of the world got caught up in the holiday rush.

We were going to visit the family memorial room, a tiny makeshift structure, like a classroom trailer, about twenty-five by eighteen feet, with windows overlooking the site. As we stepped inside, our stomachs sank, just like they always did down there. Every square inch of wall space in that room was plastered with photos, letters, remembrances, notes, flowers, "missing" signs, prayers, and mass cards. Thousands of faces, people from all backgrounds and nationalities, nearly all of them young, smiled out of photos taken at weddings, celebrations, vacations, family gatherings. None of them looked as if they could be dead—no one poses for a snapshot in order to have it pinned on a memorial wall someday.

Sitting at a table in the room was an older Indian man wrapping Christmas gifts. He began talking to us, showing us the presents he had brought for his son. He showed us his son's photograph—the boy was twenty-two and had only just graduated and started work. This man's whole life had been focused on raising and caring for his only child. And now what? He'd come into the city to bring his son Christmas gifts. He didn't have a body to bury, and this was the only place he felt he could come to be close to his son.

We could see the agony of the recently bereaved in every part of his being. His eyes were two dark hollows inside his face. This man was at the very depths of his despair.

We recognized that place. This man was at the bottom of the pit and needed someone to throw him a rope. We tried to talk to him, to console him, but how can you possibly console a grieving parent? We paid our respects, said our good-byes, and then left.

Julia was going to visit the cemetery before delivering gifts to Tommy's family and friends. Ann needed to get home. That year, Pattie was having an especially hard time, so Claudia went with her to the hotel across the street for a drink.

On this rare occasion, the cocktail and the company of a fellow widow didn't immediately help. The hotel was depressing; the people in it were depressing. At the bar were groups of businessmen who obviously couldn't wait to leave and get home. After all, who wanted to be in a Wall Street hotel on Christmas Eve?

Pattie was dealing with the holidays, with her ongoing relationship with Stanley, with going home alone to her parents', and with missing Caz. The only mercy was that Claudia and Pattie both knew it was okay for her to be utterly miserable about the situation. In fact, that complete misery was probably the only sane reaction to such a situation. Claudia didn't say what most people might be compelled to say. She didn't say that it would be all right, that it would pass, that Pattie still had things to look forward to in life. Instead, she told her that she agreed, that life was unfair, that it's harder than you ever thought it was going to be.

PATTIE TOLD CLAUDIA about the first Christmas Caz came home to visit her parents. She was a little nervous, as all daughters are taking a new boyfriend home for the holidays. How would her family's reserved New England style mesh with Caz's outspokenness and energy?

"That was the year Caz took part in the annual Christmas football game," remembered Pattie. "But he managed to mix up the rules of rugby and American football."

In his typical manner, Caz was one of the most enthusiastic participants in the game, dressed to the nines in a brightly colored rugby shirt, with a pair of reindeer antlers on his head. Between plays he would run around in circles, taking swigs from his beer. On the final play of the game, Pattie's father caught a pass and was running up the sideline toward the goal.

"I saw Caz lock his gaze on my father," Pattie said. "He moved in his direction. I realized trouble was at hand. The next thing I saw was my father flying into a hedge of rhododendrons. My dad wouldn't admit he was hurt at first, but the tackle resulted in a broken rib and broken nose for Christmas that year."

As Pattie's family headed off to church for the Christmas service, it was such an unseasonably mild December morning that Caz decided to turn on the seat warmers and put the top down on the convertible. It was his way of celebrating the gorgeous weather. Pattie was used to Caz's grand gestures, but her first reaction was to worry about what her parents were thinking, especially after the rugby debacle. Her second reaction was: "Who cares if Caz doesn't immediately win my parents over? I'm sold."

Now, years later, sitting here talking to Claudia, her whole world changed, Pattie couldn't believe this was her life.

"The fact is, I'd rather stay here in the horrible oppressive hotel than have to face Christmas without him," she told Claudia.

"Pattie, can't you just hear him saying it?" asked Claudia, before putting on her best English accent. "Love! Have you thought about how pathetic that sounds?"

Something about a conversation with someone who could make her laugh, and who understood, made things seem almost tolerable. Pattie needed someone to throw her a rope, and Claudia was there.

Ann:

Christmas morning I woke up in my own bed and in my own home. My first thought before opening my eyes was "It's Christmas morning." My second thought was "And Ward's not here." Even so, I was determined to make this a good day. Before I'd had time to properly wake up, Billy was climbing into my bed wanting to know if he could open his presents. I told him he had to wait for the others. Then I went and got Elizabeth and put her in bed with her brother. I turned on cartoons for them and I went to make coffee. TJ the typical teenager had to be woken up. I gave Billy this job, and once he'd accomplished it, everyone was allowed to go downstairs to see what Santa had brought.

THREE YEARS BEFORE—our last Christmas with Ward—we had just initiated a new tradition of hosting the annual family celebration in our home. Prior to this, we'd always gone to my parents' or his mother's. That year, we wanted to be the grown-ups and have our combined families over to celebrate at our home.

There were twenty-five people coming. On Christmas Day, between opening gifts and putting the finishing touches on the house, not to mention preparing for dinner, we were completely overwhelmed. At 3 pm, the time I'd told people to arrive, I was still standing in the kitchen in my PJs. Ward and I looked at each other and burst out laughing.

"Remind me why we insisted on hosting Christmas?" I asked him. It would have been so much easier to show up at someone else's house.

Ward reminded me that this was what we'd wanted. This was our home, and we were proud to be welcoming our families.

For dinner, the table extended out of the dining room, well into the living room. We'd prepared far too much food, but I was only relieved that it all came out well. It was a relaxed and happy afternoon, where everyone overindulged, so much so that no one could move by the end of the day. Ward and I fell into bed that night completely exhausted, but happy that everything had turned out so successfully.

I look back and feel thankful that we chose to initiate that holiday at our home. Yes, it was a lot of hard work—we laughed at each other when we both realized we were so busy trying to make it wonderful for everyone else that we barely had a moment to enjoy it ourselves. But it was our day, something we accomplished together.

The first Christmas without Ward, I was like a zombie. I did what I was told. There wasn't a decoration in the house. I packed up the kids and went upstate to be with my parents. The second year was not dissimilar. Holidays had become such a tough, sad time of the year.

. . .

THIS WAS NOW our third Christmas without Ward. We were spending Christmas Eve with Ward's family, and were going to be having Christmas Day festivities with friends in the evening. This gave me the morning and afternoon to be with my children—just TJ, Billy, Elizabeth, and me. I wanted to wake up in my own bed and have the children open their presents in our home. I wanted them to start having new memories of having Christmas as the family we were becoming.

It was a good decision. The house was decorated to the hilt, hundreds of Christmas cards strung along the banisters and walls, a wreath on the door. I bought the Christmas tree and lugged it home myself. We decorated it with little white lights, and ornaments that Ward and I had bought together in years past, each one of which we talked about as we put it on the tree. We hung up a stocking for Ward, and remembered the Christmases we'd spent with him. We were reassuring one another that we could talk about Ward and allow our memories of him to make us smile.

We were still a family: a mother, three kids, and two dogs.

As I fell into bed that night, exhausted again from the day, I thanked my husband for the gifts of family, celebration, home. I thanked him for his love. I thanked him for our memories.

Julia and
Tommy

Claudia
and Bart

Ward
and
Ann

Caz
and
Pattie

Julia:

My husband, Tommy, grew up Catholic, and although he wasn't what you would describe as a pious person, he had strong beliefs and a definite affection for his Catholic upbringing. He still enjoyed the ritual of going to church. Tommy loved to sing the hymns. I remember once we were in church and he was sitting next to a man who was singing really loudly. Of course, Tommy, being a natural competitor, started to sing even louder. I tried to ignore the fact that every member of the congregation was turning around to look at my husband belting out the hymns at the top of his lungs. By the end of the service, it was clear that Tommy had won the singing competition, but when it came time to give the sign of peace, my husband and his fellow competitor hugged like old friends.

Even when there weren't any singing competitions, I enjoyed church too. I'd started to attend Catholic mass when I was in college, feeling drawn to the atmosphere and rituals of the service. Even though

I'd grown up Southern Baptist, I felt comfortable in a Catholic setting. I found I tended to connect more directly with the priest's message there.

After our marriage, every so often, when Tommy and I were home on Sunday evenings, we would attend mass together at the Church of St. Vincent Ferrer in Manhattan. The church was near our apartment, and once you stepped inside, it was hushed and darkened, a real haven in the middle of the city. Each time we visited, as I waited for Tommy to return from taking communion, I would think to myself, "Someday, I'll get confirmed, then I can go up and take the sacrament." But as a newly married woman with a busy job and a full social life, it was easy to put things off, and becoming a Catholic wasn't a priority.

Now I had two very good reasons to get confirmed. The first was that it had been something I'd wanted to do for a long time, and this gave me a goal to achieve, something I knew was good for me. The second was that my husband was buried in a Catholic cemetery. Only Catholics could be buried there, and I knew I wanted to share the plot with Tommy. Separation in life was hard enough, as I pointed out to the WC. I decided to sign up for confirmation classes.

The first step was meeting with a priest so that he could "evaluate" me. I was pretty nervous about the meeting, mainly because if I wasn't accepted into the church, I knew I would be extremely disappointed. This was at a time when so many Catholics were leaving the church or at least questioning it on every level. Meanwhile, I was worried the church wouldn't let me in! Only looking back now can I see how far my self-esteem had sunk. But the minute I met the Father, I instinctively liked and trusted him. He was younger than I'd expected, with a gentle and welcoming manner. I think so much of feeling part of a religious community comes from your connection with your priest or rabbi or whomever. I told him I'd thought long and hard about confirmation. I told him that it was possible I wouldn't make it through the process of becoming confirmed, but that I wanted to learn about the Catholic religion all the same. I was searching for answers.

"Why don't you start on the classes and see how it goes?" he suggested.

The Father explained that as part of the initiation, I must attend a series of classes to prepare me for joining the Catholic faith. He made sure I knew that I was beginning a serious journey. How would my hopes and values stack up against what I might find in the classes? I wasn't sure, but I was ready for the next step.

IN THE MONTHS after Tommy's murder, there had been many times when I came close to abandoning my faith. I guess if anything is going to test someone's belief in God, it's the murder of thousands of innocent people in the name of religion. I have a friend who did give up on his faith after Tommy was killed. This friend had lost his sister in sudden circumstances a few years previously, and Tommy's death was one death too many for him. He could no longer believe that there was a divine force in the world. At times, I could understand his logic.

But even as I questioned my faith I didn't abandon it. Even in my lowest moments, I was too busy arguing with God to accuse Him of not existing. I had too many questions that I needed answered before giving up on Him. Why did you take Tommy? How could this happen? Why him? Why so many killed in the name of religion? I had been taught that when someone dies they go to a "better place," and although I knew that the idea of Tommy being in heaven was supposed to be a comfort to me, now I needed to know what was it like in this "better place." Where was heaven? What went on there?

There were no easy answers, and I felt I could take nothing for granted. But I had choices to make. I could lose touch with the sense of community and consolation I felt at church, or I could decide to put my beliefs to the test. Although my decision to get confirmed was initially prompted by wanting to be buried with my husband, now I decided I wanted to make it my mission to study religion and understand it better. Over the last few years, my goals had been to get up in the morning and make it through the day. Having such a meaningful new focus was a big step for me.

My class consisted of six "candidates." Every week, we would go through the readings from the Sunday before and discuss what they meant to us. In the class, I found myself discussing theology for the first time in a long while. It wasn't only about finding answers to my questions; it was about finding a setting where people felt comfortable talking about faith, doubt, meaning, devotion. Every class there was a new lesson, and each class seemed to take my mind away from what I'd lost and to put the focus onto what I had. I recognized that the advantage of getting a religious education at this point—rather than having it forced on me as a child—was that I could appreciate this learning process. I began to look forward to Monday evenings.

I had plenty of questions. Whatever the subject of the class, it seemed like I always managed to turn the conversation around to my overriding preoccupations. When somebody dies, what happens? What happens to his or her body? What happens if a person dies without last rites? Where is heaven? What's it like? Will I see my husband again? Will I know him? Will he know who I am?

There was a passage in Revelations that my teacher directed me to that helped to ease my fears that Tommy was suffering: "God will wipe away all tears from their eyes, there will be no more death and no more mourning or sadness or pain. The world of the past has gone." It did give me a degree of peace to think that Tommy wasn't in pain, that he was in a place without sadness.

What I learned in class encouraged me to spend less and less time asking "Why?" and instead to begin praying for hope, wisdom, and acceptance. The classes were helping me to shift focus, to stop fixating on Tommy's death and to appreciate what I'd gained from knowing him in life. On the day Tommy died, I knew, he was at peace with himself, his faith, his family, and with me. That's what I was working toward, that same sense of peace. It would be a long time before I would truly absorb what I had learned—I'm still absorbing it—but seeds had been planted.

IN SPRING OF 2004, after seven months of studying, I was finally ready to take the sacrament, a nice Southern Baptist girl about to be confirmed into the Catholic Church. Better late than never, I told myself. The service for my confirmation took place the Saturday night before Easter, and the WC insisted on throwing me a confirmation party afterward. Matt was going to be there. I bought a new dress for the occasion, a colorful, turquoise party dress. After so many years of watching others go up to take communion, I walked proudly toward the priest and received the host, even if I forgot to take the wine. Evidently,

I needed a little more practice. As my friends came up for communion, they passed where I was kneeling in the pew. As each one went by, smiling at me, giving me the thumbs-up, my heart felt fuller and fuller. It was my Jimmy Stewart at the end of *It's a Wonderful Life* moment. There's a Bible verse in Corinthians: "If I have all faith, so as to remove mountains, but do not have love, I am nothing." That day of my confirmation, surrounded by friends, I felt I had faith and I had love. I prayed to Tommy, thanking him for everything we'd had together. I felt truly lucky.

Having Matt there was great. Over the past few months, we'd been seeing more and more of each other. He would surprise me with secret dates—he would have me meet him somewhere in the city and have the day planned with lots of different activities. He would always bring me flowers and funny gifts from his travels. He was the kind of guy I wanted to have in my life. He never once made me feel guilty or was threatened by my past. He understood me and understood my situation. He knew how to comfort me when I was having a really bad day. Once, he sent me an e-mail that included a quote from Anne Bradstreet, "If we had no winter, the spring would not be so pleasant: if we did not sometimes taste of adversity, prosperity would not be so welcome." I loved his perspective on life. He would tell me, "The view always looks better from the high road." This was someone who was generous, confident, and mature. I knew I should embrace this relationship with Matt.

But even so, it was still hard for me to let myself go and fully enter this relationship. There was always part of me that felt that seeing Matt was a betrayal of my love for Tommy. I couldn't divide up my heart. Often I would feel like it was being torn in two.

Claudia:

When I first met John, my sister-in-law and I were still in the planning stages of renovating the apartment I'd shared with Bart. As the relationship progressed, the time came closer for the work to begin. It was Kathleen who suggested we scale back the project.

"Claudia, it's crazy to spend this kind of money on an apartment you're never going live in. You don't have to do this as a tribute to Bart."

Kathleen understood how serious John and I were. She had made me feel comfortable enough to talk to her about marriage and a family with John in the future. Her support had always been given gracefully and unconditionally. So we scrapped the plans for major work and went with what we had, finally replacing my buckled floors, and adding new living room furniture and kitchen cabinets.

When we were ready to start the work, I had to pack everything up and store it in the bedroom. This was an opportunity to sift through my things and to decide what I was going to keep and what I was going to give to Goodwill. There were still so many of Bart's belongings in the apartment, and I knew I wasn't going to be able to save all of them—I stayed focused on the little things that were important to me. For instance, I had to figure out what to do with the one remaining DoveBar in the freezer.

Bart had an incredible sweet tooth and always needed a treat after dinner. His favorite was dark chocolate with vanilla ice cream—my husband was a purist. There was still one DoveBar left in the box, but when the renovation work began, I knew I was going to have to unplug the freezer. I came up with a master plan. I decided to throw away the actual bar but keep the box and put it back in the freezer when the kitchen was complete.

One day a friend was over helping me get organized. I hadn't told her about the priceless value of the empty DoveBar box, and when she saw it put aside, naturally she threw it out.

Over the past two and a half years, that box had come to mean so many different things to me. In the beginning, the box made me cry because I missed Bart so much. Later, I would open the freezer door and feel furious because Bart was never going to eat ice cream again. But just recently, the box had started to make me smile. I could picture Bart eating the DoveBar, enjoying his dessert—I remembered how he used to tease me because he knew I wanted one but foolishly wouldn't allow myself to indulge. Now the loss of the box had reduced me to tears again. When the renovations on the apartment were finished, I would nervously go to the freezer, willing the box to be there. But as time went by, I began to understand that I didn't need the box anymore. Every time I opened the door, I thought about it and smiled anyway. The box itself didn't contain my memories of Bart. My memories were mine, and would always live in my heart. It's impossible to take something away as long as it's remembered.

Since clearing the way for the renovations, I was a little lighter in possessions. But knowing that Bart would always be with me in memory made moving forward possible.

Pattie:

In early May, I found myself in Italy. My travels had begun as a short business trip to London. Then, over dinner with an old friend who lives in England, I mentioned that I was thinking of going to Italy to celebrate Caz's birthday the following weekend. Immediately, my friend wanted to know why I didn't extend my stay and fly directly to Rome from London. After all, Caz's birthday was just a week away.

"Well, you have a point," I responded, "but I can't."

"Why?" she wanted to know.

"Well, there is a lot going on and I just shouldn't, and my coworker is leaving in two weeks and a new employee is joining our group. I have a new boss. I just can't."

"You have to!"

Caz's voice inside me joined in the chorus. "You must . . ."

However, changing course in midstream isn't something that comes naturally to me, and I continued to make excuses until, well, the idea began to seem enticing. By the end of the meal I started to see the wisdom. Maybe staying in England before going to Italy was actually an *important* thing for me to do. Although I was frankly terrified to go back to this place that I associated so deeply with Caz, the plan began to make sense.

For the past two and a half years I had almost completely devoted myself to my job. I'd stayed late, worked weekends, always put in the extra effort. Work had been my crutch. I depended on the familiarity of my job at a time when I felt intensely lost.

But I knew I didn't want to bury myself in work forever.

Since Caz's death I understood how beautiful, tenuous, and brief our lives are. I was constantly aware that I only had a defined period of time on this earth and that I had to make the most of it.

The next morning, I sent out the e-mail to the WC announcing my trip:

Okay ladies, I did it! I am proud of myself and a little scared. I came over to London for business at the end of last week and decided to stay. I am about to write an e-mail to my boss to say that I will work out of our offices here for the next two days and then I am going to take the balance of the week off and go to Italy. Am I crazy? I am sorry I cannot make Wednesday but I think I need to take this chance.
Love you all. Pray for me!

From: Gerbasi, Claudia
OK I am sooooo excited for you. The biggest regrets in life are the chances we never take. This sounds like a perfect plan. Pattie—I am so excited and proud of you, our little fancy pants!!!
LUMI

From: Collins, Julia
F-A-N-C-Y P-A-N-T-S!!! Yahoo! So glad you made the decisions you made . . . go for it! I'm thinking I'm in the wrong business . . . I'm in Wisconsin, for work, freezing my ass off and you're going to ROME!!! Something's really wrong—hee hee! You're doing the right thing and the 3 of us will toast you on Wed night!!! xoxxo loving you and meaning it!!!!!

From: Haynes, Ann
That's our girl! Pattie way to go!!! Make the most of your time—no matter what, you have proved to yourself that you can do this. He's up there cheering you on—enjoy the wine, the food and finding you. LUMI.

Yes, I heard myself saying, it would be wrong *not* to take advantage of being in Europe. Why should I fly back to New York first?

The next day I e-mailed work and told them about my plans to work from London. My boss's response was:

Don't worry about New York this week. I think you have us pretty well trained at this point and we will manage fine. Best to the Queen and Tony Blair!

So I booked my trip to Rome with a few days at a coastal hotel in Tuscany beforehand. Three days later, after working via e-mail from my friend's basement in London, I boarded my plane for Rome.

ON THE PLANE out, I pictured Italy as I had left it the last time I was there—blue skies and silvery olive groves, verdant green hillsides and sun-baked hilltop villages. When I got off the plane in Rome, it was pouring rain. The rain continued throughout my train ride to my Tuscan hotel. I spent the next three days sleeping and reading in my room or watching the pounding of the rain on the waves outside the window. It didn't matter—I even began to find the rain soothing. I had long lunches with delicious food and wine, and tried to use this time for contemplation, always struggling with the ongoing conundrum of the obvious absence, that someone who was once here with me could no longer be here with me now.

After a few days, I took the train back to Rome. In this breathtaking city, I walked from sight to sight—the Spanish Steps, the Colosseum, the Forum, the Pantheon, Trastevere, the Piazza Navona. I walked over to St. Peter's Square—the Piazza San Pietro—and stood at the top of the steps, with the basilica behind me, its massive architecture looming down on me. I leaned my back against one of the giant columns supporting the facade, allowing it to take my weight. The last time I'd stood here, I was with Caz. Or was I dreaming? Had I really been married?

This is where Caz had proposed.

The proposal was a surprise that Caz had planned with enormous care. He'd even gone so far as to call my boss, conspiring with her to get me to a meeting in Chicago for the night, thereby allowing him time to pack my bag before our departure for Italy.

It was just like Caz to plan such a complex and devious surprise. After my night in Chicago—where my meeting mysteriously didn't materialize—I got on my flight to La Guardia Airport in New York. As I exited, I saw Caz waiting in the greeting area, with a big smile on his face.

"Just thought I'd meet you from your trip," he said and grinned.

"Why?" I asked. "You've never done that before." He was definitely up to something.

Caz handed me a gift wrapped in leopard print paper. He was jumping up and down with excitement. I opened it up, looking at him with a certain amount of suspicion.

Wow, a Gucci bag. Great, Caz had just returned from England the weekend before and hadn't given me anything from duty-free. It was an interesting way of presenting me with my prezzie, but then Caz was always looking for ways to surprise me.

"Unzip the bag!" Caz instructed, arms flapping around with excitement.

Inside was a book wrapped in the same paper—it was a guide to Rome. Caz knew Rome was my favorite city, and I assumed the choice of the book was somehow related to the Italian designer Gucci.

"What? What's going on?" I asked Caz.

"Open the book!" he told me.

Inside the book was a thin present wrapped in the same paper: tickets to Rome.

"Great! We really need a vacation." I hugged and kissed him and thanked him for being so thoughtful.

"No!" Caz exclaimed. "Look at the tickets!"

I looked again. Yes, they were to Rome. Wait a minute. What's the date today?

We were going to Rome *today*. In *two* hours.

We climbed in a car and Caz told the driver to take us to JFK Airport. Meanwhile, I explained to Caz that I couldn't go to Italy in two hours, that I needed to pack.

"Did it," said Caz. "Your bag's in the back."

"I have to tell my brother, my parents."

"*Did.*"

"I've got to tell my boss."

"*Did.*"

Little did I know that everyone in the world knew about this trip, apart from me.

Ten hours later, when we arrived at our hotel in Rome, there were flowers and champagne in the room addressed to Mr. and Mrs. Carrington. Interesting, I thought.

Meanwhile, Caz had a mission and a map. The plan was to go for a long walk, heading in the direction of Vatican City, stopping for lunch along the way. This sounded good to me. I'm never happier than when strolling around a European city, especially Rome. Caz and I stopped for wine, to look in the occasional shop, to pose for a picture, and to read from the guidebook. We bought cones of gelato—double scoops, of course, so that we could try four flavors.

By the time we reached the Trevi Fountain, the sun was beginning to set and there was a chill in the air. Caz put his sports jacket around my shoulders. But when I went to put my hand in the jacket to pull out a coin to throw in the fountain, he lunged at me and gave me a coin from his trouser pocket. Why was my boyfriend behaving so strangely? Why didn't he want me to look in his jacket pocket? Why did we have to go to Vatican City right away?

Side by side, we each threw a coin, over our left shoulders, and made a wish. Mine was to our health and happiness. I don't know what Caz wished for.

We walked up the long, wide boulevard that leads to Vatican City. At the doors of the Sistine Chapel, to Caz's dismay, we were told that it was already closed for the day. In the beautiful cool, clear air of the Italian evening, we headed over to St. Peter's Square. Rows of chairs were lined up in front of the steps to the basilica in preparation for Easter services later that week. As we stood in the middle of the otherwise desolate piazza, Caz got down on one knee.

"Love, I want you to be by my side for the rest of my life. I want you as my partner because I love and cherish you."

I started to giggle. Caz was a joker; I spent most of my time laughing when I was with him.

But Caz wasn't smiling anymore. He was serious.

"You make me a better person," he said.

I agreed. The feeling was mutual.

"But why are you on your knee?" I asked him, still giggling.

"Pattie, will you be my bride forever? Will you take this ring as a symbol of our engagement?"

Tears rolled down my face as I jumped into his arms, his embrace.

"Aren't you happy?" he asked me.

I was laughing, crying; I couldn't speak. Of course, he already knew the answer was yes.

That evening, we ate dinner at Il Convivio, a restaurant on the Piazza Navona. We were walking on clouds. I remember looking at Caz and thinking, "This is really happening. This is the guy I will have a family with and grow old with. This is him. This is us." And at the same time, our relationship felt new, as if we were out on our first date. There was a new level of excitement that was affecting both of us.

The next day Caz decided we'd done enough walking and that we should rent a Vespa to get us around town. It was our way of fully taking part in the life of a city where every native rides a scooter. When in Rome . . . I held on for dear life, with Caz at the helm, racing around the city, taking our lives in our hands at every junction.

NOW, FOUR YEARS later, I was no longer whizzing around Rome, but slowly and sadly retracing our steps, trying to relive the experiences I'd shared with Caz. This trip had begun in the spirit of adventure, but now it felt almost foolish. I knew I was trying to fulfill an impossible desire. I couldn't recover the past. Being here didn't bring Caz back. I didn't want to have a gelato alone; it wasn't the same. I couldn't fully participate in this experience. I was once removed.

After I left the Piazza San Pietro, I walked toward the Colosseum. Everywhere I went, I saw couples on Vespas, on their way to who knows where, the sounds of their engines like swarms of mosquitoes. Exhausted from my day of walking, I sat down on a bench. The Colosseum was ahead of me, the ruins all around me. I sat and watched the cars and scooters circle the ancient structure.

I told myself I had to find a way to get back into the flow. Life was racing along without me, while I stood on the sidelines.

"Things change," I told myself. "That's a fact of life. It happens to you; it happens to everyone eventually. But you can't allow your life to slip by. You have to keep moving, just like those Vespas."

Imagine if Caz hadn't arranged the Italy trip. (He'd wanted to propose in the Sistine Chapel; he said he wanted to go to the Head Office.) Imagine if we hadn't ever come here. Imagine if we hadn't rented the scooter. Imagine if we hadn't eaten that gelato and stood at the Trevi Fountain at sunset. My life was richer for my time with Caz. It was poorer without him. But I didn't want my memories to stop *with* him.

That evening, I set off from my hotel to Il Convivio for dinner. When I arrived, I discovered that the restaurant was fully booked. It hadn't occurred to me to make a reservation for just one person. When I stepped back out into the Piazza Navona, long blue shadows stretched from one side of the square to the other. I cut a path through the groups of tourists and locals, disappointed in myself for not making a dinner reservation.

But then it struck me. Maybe I wasn't meant to have dinner at Il Convivio. Maybe I was meant to try something new. Maybe I was supposed to create a new memory for myself. That evening, I ate dinner alone, in a new restaurant, absorbing the sights, smells, and sounds of my last night in Italy.

Almost immediately after my return, I broke off my relationship with Stanley. I explained to him that I knew we didn't have a future together, and I didn't feel that I could in good conscience continue to be with him. Stanley had given me so much. He'd proved to me that it was possible for me to be with someone, and to love again. But there wasn't room for him in my heart, or for anyone else. I trusted that I would be ready one day, just not yet.

Ann:

That spring, my whole company was undergoing a massive reorganization. There were going to be extensive layoffs and relocations. Almost everyone in the New York office was going to be affected. I knew that relocating to a different city wasn't an option. I couldn't uproot my children, and besides, my support system was here.

Also on the table was a very nice severance package. Maybe I was ready for this change. What's more, I had a great idea of what I might do next. I wanted to use my skills and be able to be with my family more. My new business idea was pretty obvious given my skills and my history: I wanted to provide financial counseling to women who had been widowed or divorced, to help them to become better informed and more confident about their finances and, by extension, more in control of their lives. Over the years in my job, I'd often met with women who were afraid of dealing with money. Many of them had been raised to believe that someone would always come along to the rescue when it came to money matters. Many of them were simply so afraid of working with money that they put their head in the sand. I knew how hard it could be. When a woman is left alone for whatever reason, because she is widowed or divorced, in addition to dealing with her loss, she also has to get in control of her finances, a task she may have shared with or left to her husband. She has to make important decisions all by herself. It had been so tough for me to put my family's affairs in order in the aftermath of Ward's death—and I had twenty years' experience in financial services!

Even so, to put my business idea into action meant leaving my sensible job for a somewhat uncertain future. In the immediate aftermath of Ward's death, I'd really needed the consistency of work to help me maintain an even keel—going into a familiar office where I was responsible for helping my clients allowed me to escape my own problems. But now, two and a half years later, my priorities had begun to shift and I was ready to work on those problems. Still, just the thought of no longer working at the place where I had been an employee for twenty years was pretty scary.

Instinctively, I felt that Ward would approve. I kept Ward's upbeat attitude uppermost in my mind. When we found out I was pregnant with twins, Ward left a job he loved, working as a photo editor at a major sports magazine, in order to take a job in finance, where there was more opportunity for professional advancement and financial gain. Ward didn't have a background in finance. When he was starting out, he knew little about commodities and nothing about brokering. Not only did he learn to do his job, he learned to do it well. His clients became his allies—Ward had that friendly, easy confidence that drew people in and made them want to do business with him. His natural abilities became the key to his success. For him the nudge to switch careers came in the shape of the twins, but he found skills that he may not otherwise have realized he possessed, and ended up in a job that he loved.

When I'd been wrestling with a decision in the past, Ward liked to remind me of his grandfather's favorite saying: "Life is not a dress rehearsal." Ward lived that way. From the day I met him, I sensed that "live large and live for the moment" spirit and admired him for it. Ward was always looking on the bright side; he had such a positive attitude. Now I was beginning to take on those qualities. I was the one who didn't want to risk wasting any opportunity to experience as much as I could from life.

I recognized how fortunate I was to be able to make these choices about my work and to feel empowered by them. I knew that if I left my job, we weren't going to have to move out of our family home, that I would be able to pay for Elizabeth's care and for TJ and Billy to go to college. My severance package would tide me over as I transitioned into this new phase of my life.

And if I failed, what was the worst that could happen? I had learned so much these past two and a half years, and come out stronger for it. What if I didn't like working alone or failed at my own business? Even if the worst happened, I knew I would have already gained so much in the process, *especially* from failing. If I didn't try, I would have to live with the regret of never knowing what I might have achieved, or how it might have changed me.

I began to look forward to lending my time and knowledge to others. Maybe I *was* the right person to help make the process a little easier for someone else. Suddenly, my life had begun to feel incredibly rich and potentially very fulfilling to me, and I didn't want to waste my days on things that didn't contribute to that feeling.

I also felt that Ward would continue take care of the kids and me somehow. From the day I met him, he always had that attitude of "It will work out." I let myself be led by his inner belief. I felt him in heaven watching over us, and I became calm because of it. I had to believe it was going to be okay because he was there looking out for us.

In a cab on the way to dinner one night, I asked the WC, "What do I do? Do I take the severance? I feel this might be a great opportunity for me, but am I being completely crazy?"

Unanimously they yelled at me: "Go for it!" No hesitation, no doubt, full support.

Tommy and Julia

Julia:

In May my birthday was coming around again and I decided that, this year, I wanted a quiet evening with the WC to celebrate. The venue was my suggestion also: Felidia, an Italian restaurant on the Upper East Side.

The WC's first reaction was "Julia, are you sure?" Not because they had some other place in mind, but because they knew the significance of Felidia.

This was the restaurant where I should have gone for dinner with Tommy and his good friend and colleague Tim Byrne on Tuesday evening, September 11, 2001.

Back then, I thought that being able to meet my husband and his friend for dinner came with a lifetime guarantee. Neither of the men I was supposed to be meeting that evening survived the attacks. Now, two and a half years later, I was only just getting up the courage to go to Felidia.

The evening of my birthday I'd arranged to meet the WC early and decided to walk over to the restaurant, needing the time to think as I walked. Outside the restaurant, I took a deep breath before I walked in. Claudia and Ann were at the bar, greeting me with the words "Happy Birthday."

As we ordered a drink, I looked around. What had I expected to find here?

I'd never been to this place before, but I'd built it up in my mind to the point that walking in, I'd almost expected the heavens to open up, revealing Tommy and Tim dressed as angels and singing hallelujah. . . .

Felidia was just a restaurant, a very nice, elegant restaurant, but a restaurant all the same: pale yellow walls, crisp white linen on every table, vases filled with sunflowers. It was the kind of place you might choose for a special occasion like your wife's birthday. It was just Tommy's style to arrange for dinner somewhere like Felidia on a regular Tuesday evening. Thank you, Tommy.

PATTIE ARRIVED SOON afterward, and we went upstairs to our table in the corner, overlooking the floor below.

The conversation went back and forth; questions and answers about work, and the weekend. Everyone wanted to ask Julia how she was feeling, but we waited, aware that she might not even know the answer to the question just yet.

Before we ordered our food, we raised the subject:

"Julia, how are you?"

"Are you okay here, or shall we go someplace else?"

"No," Julia replied. "I'm fine. I'm with you guys. It means a lot for me to be here with you."

We toasted Tommy, Tim Byrne, and The Boys.

We knew we were no substitute for how things might have been, but we were determined to make the best of what was.

JULIA WANTED TO tell us her news.

"I talked to a woman at work today," she announced. "A friend of hers recently adopted her third child from China. She's asked this friend for the name and number of the adoption agency and she's given me her e-mail so I can discuss the process with her."

"Julia, this is huge."

"Listen, I don't know if I'm ready or not. At this stage, I don't even know if I'd be eligible. I just know I'm really looking forward to talking to this woman."

"You'd be a phenomenal mother."

"Well, who knows what will happen," Julia pointed out. "But if I do decide to adopt, then my child is going to have the three best godmothers."

PATTIE DIDN'T TELL the others, but the reason she'd been late for dinner was that John had called her as she was leaving the office. He wanted to get her advice on an engagement ring for Claudia. Should he go for a single stone or three in a row? Pattie and John got so carried away with the excitement of the ring, they'd practically planned the engagement party, wedding, and honeymoon before the end of the ten-minute call.

Pattie arrived at the restaurant buoyed up by the good news and wondering how she was going to hide her perma-grin from the others.

"So, how are things with you?" she asked Claudia, in her best deadpan.

"You know, it's funny you should ask that," Claudia replied, "because I'm feeling pretty good. I think John's going to propose soon."

Pattie stifled a shriek. "What?" Wait a minute, Pattie thought to herself, how does *she* know?

"Oh my God! That's great news," everyone said.

Then Pattie asked: "But what makes you think so?"

"Well," Claudia replied, wondering why Pattie looked so shocked, "it's almost a year since we first met on my birthday, and, you know, we had a conversation a while back about how it seemed right to wait a year to get engaged out of respect. And he's been acting a little strangely lately, like he's excited about something but trying to hide it from me."

"Don't get your hopes up," said Pattie, trying to throw Claudia off the track. "Maybe it's just a surprise party."

. . .

AS SHE LOOKED around the table that evening at Felidia, Ann felt like the odd one out. Claudia was about to get engaged to John. Pattie had purposefully chosen to end her relationship with Stanley, and Julia was seeing Matt. When Ann looked at her own situation, she felt far from optimistic. She was alone and also feeling very unsettled by her relations with the opposite sex over the past year.

Of the four of us, Ann was the one who had really gotten out there and dated. Maybe it was something to do with living in a small town with so many people looking out for her, but Ann had found meeting people easy. But with each man, she would get to that one- or two-month mark and realize that she didn't want to be with him any longer. There was always something that didn't work out. It was either the wrong guy or, for whatever reason, the wrong time. Thankfully, Ann had been smart enough and strong enough not to stay with someone who wasn't right for her.

For the past month or so, Ann had been dating someone. She'd guessed from the beginning that the relationship might not have a future, but he was a nice guy and she thought maybe if she gave it a chance, there could be that possibility. Eventually, it was obvious that she would only hurt his feelings in the long run by continuing. So she'd broken it off.

This most recent breakup had left Ann feeling worried. What if the failure of this latest relationship was a bad sign?

She began to confide in the rest of us. "I keep blaming it on the guy or the timing. But maybe it's not that. Maybe it's me . . . ," she told us.

We reassured her. This was a familiar fear. After everything we'd been through, we all worried about the damage that had been done to our ability to love. It was such a risky thing to allow ourselves to open up again. With love came the immediate possibility of loss and pain.

"But I'm just getting so tired of living in the same cycle of seeing someone and then breaking it off before it gets serious," Ann said. "I don't think it's doing me any good. I think I need to be on my own for a while. But I just keep thinking about how my life was with Ward, and it was just so much more fulfilling."

Ann began to cry. Our friend Ann is one of the strongest people we've ever met. It had always been easy for the rest of us to lean on her.

She's someone who can always envision the brighter picture, making us believe that things would get better in the future. But now we listened as she told us that she had come to the conclusion there might never be another true love for her.

The rest of us knew that it was unthinkable that someone like Ann could never fall in love again. But we're always respectful of what another widow is feeling. The WC would never say, "Of course you'll meet someone." We've learned not to automatically expect anything from life. We've learned that life isn't always easy or predictable or fair.

So instead we talked about how lucky we were to have known The Boys. In a sense, we'd been set free from constantly searching for romantic fulfillment because we'd already experienced it in our lifetimes. Maybe it was ungrateful to pray for more than the enormous amount we'd already been given. In the meantime, it was still important to be open to finding love again.

"Maybe I'll just give up dating altogether," Ann said, mustering a smile.

"Hey, don't do that." Julia grinned at Ann. "A girl's gotta eat!"

Ann and Family

Ann:

Up until now, when I went out on a date, I'd always been hopeful. I'm a naturally hopeful person. I honestly believed it was possible to meet the right man again. With every date I went on, I would think to myself, maybe this time around I'll be in the right frame of mind to be able to allow someone back in my life.

I kept accepting dates because I craved a relationship. If a man fell for me, gave me special attention, made me a priority in his life, it made me feel good. It was an ego boost—it reinforced that I was still desirable. Without Ward's love and support, and after going through such a traumatic period, I didn't mind admitting I needed my self-esteem built up.

That spring, however, I realized I wanted to be on my own for a while. I wanted to be certain I would be able to live a full and happy life without a partner. More than that, I needed to make sure that even if I did find love and lost it again, I would still be okay. I think every widow or divorcee or brokenhearted person who hesitates to become romantically involved again fears being hurt and fears losing that loved one. When you become a widow—perhaps especially as the result of a sudden death—the stakes are particularly high. Even if we all met amazing men like John, men that we wanted to be with forever, how long might forever last? What if the worst happened? Would it be possible to live through this twice in a lifetime? For a widow, there's a real terror of exposing yourself to that degree of pain again. You instinctively close yourself up, as a natural and necessary defense mechanism.

After Julia's birthday, I went through a period where I deliberately didn't date. This was good—I was feeling independent and much closer to a degree of contentment with being single. I began to think about the qualities I wanted in a partner, rather than just hoping and praying that one day someone would want me, a widowed mother of three. I knew that I needed to be with someone who had a positive attitude, who appreciated life, and whom I could trust completely. If I didn't find those qualities, then I knew I would rather be alone. I wasn't going to settle, and that knowledge felt empowering to me.

The stronger I became, especially from spending time alone, the more I was certain that I would always do the best that I could to live a fulfilled life. I knew that whatever came my way, I would be able to be strong, because I had survived so much already.

THEN, IN EARLY summer, against my better judgment, I went out on another date. When this man asked me out, I explained right from the start that I wasn't ready for a relationship. But his persistence gave me that "good feeling" about myself, so I accepted a dinner date, telling myself that I had been up front about not wanting a relationship. Julia's words "A girl's gotta eat!" were definitely ringing in my head.

It was a very pleasant evening. We had a few laughs and a nice meal, but I knew that was as far as it would go.

After dinner was over, the evening took a sudden and different course. As we left the restaurant, I happened to check my cell phone. Eight messages. Eight! My first thought was "Oh my God, what's wrong?" Thankfully, all the messages were from the same person, my friend Karen, who sounded like she'd had a few too many drinks and urgently wanted me to meet her at a nearby restaurant. I made my excuses to my date and headed over.

Karen was waiting for me. I asked how long she had been here. "Too long and without enough food" was the obvious answer. Karen told me she wanted me to meet someone.

Before I knew it, Karen was dragging a man over in my direction.

"Kevin, this is Ann. His wife just passed away," she announced. "Her funeral was today."

As I later found out, Karen had been sitting at the bar next to a group of people that she didn't know. Karen likes to know everyone in Rye, and so she was curious to find out who this group was and what they were doing here. She introduced herself to the woman sitting on the bar stool next to her. Karen learned that the group had come from the funeral of a friend who had fought a lifelong battle with cystic fibrosis, a disease that had eventually destroyed her lungs. She had received a life-saving double transplant two years ago, but tragically her body had rejected the new lungs. Karen was introduced to Kevin, the husband of the woman who'd died. When she saw how much Kevin was suffering, Karen decided to call me and see if I could make it over to offer some words of consolation. She wanted to help this man find someone he could talk to who'd lost a spouse as well.

After Karen introduced us, I offered him my condolences and told him I had some idea of the pain he must be in. The sight of Kevin—so completely exhausted and emotionally drained—inevitably brought back memories of the evening after Ward's memorial service. I could remember exactly how that felt. Kevin was wearing sorrow in every muscle of his face. I knew that as much as he didn't want to be in a bar with his friends and family that night, he also knew it was probably the best place for him. More than anything, he looked like he needed his wife to hold him and get him through this. The person he wanted most wasn't around.

Kevin and I spoke for a few minutes before one of his friends came over to rescue him.

"Please take care of yourself," I told him. "Your wife would want that, and you will honor her by doing that."

I never imagined I would see Kevin again. I left having been reminded of how hard and how unfair it is to lose your spouse.

. . .

A FEW WEEKS later, I was at a fund-raiser with some friends, one of whom was Karen. While we were there, a man came up to us and said, "Hey, I remember you." I assumed he was speaking to another friend of mine as I couldn't place him. The friend started talking to him, and Karen and I carried on our own conversation.

It was only when our friend mentioned that she'd been talking to someone who'd just lost his wife that I realized who this was. It was Kevin, the man I'd met the week before. I felt badly that I hadn't recognized him, and I decided to go up to him and say hello. I just wanted to let him know that if he ever needed help, someone to talk to, he could call me.

When I next spotted Kevin across the room, I went over and we started chatting. But it was the end of the evening—the bar staff was already beginning to clean up around us. Between Kevin's friends and mine, there were about ten of us who didn't want the night to end just yet, so we arranged to meet at a nearby bar to continue the evening.

At the bar, Kevin came and sat beside me, and we continued our conversation. The group was in a fairly festive mood. One of Kevin's friends—to his wife's embarrassment—decided to entertain us all by making a tie out of toilet paper and hiking his pants up to his chest. There were a lot of laughs. Meanwhile, Kevin and I were absorbed in talking about our spouses, trading stories, expressing how much we wished they were here with us now.

Kevin told me about his wife Lucia. He had known she might become sick when he met her, and that their time together might be short. But they always had that hope that the power of their love would change the odds in their favor. Despite everything, they were grateful for the love that they shared. I told Kevin about Ward, and how hard it was to live without him, but that despite the pain I would never sacrifice our time together. It had made me the person I was.

Kevin and I were sitting close to each other. I remember I was wearing a halter top—it was a warm summer's evening—and all of a sudden I felt Kevin's hand on my bare back. I was startled. Did he realize how that made me feel? Was his hand there intentionally or by accident? Was he interested in me in that way? How could he be? Kevin kept talking, and without saying it in so many words, he was letting me know that this was okay.

Before long, we looked around and realized that the others in the group were leaving to go home. It was only Kevin and me who wanted to stay. And Karen. The bar was closing. The three of us piled into Karen's car, and after realizing that most places in Rye close at midnight on a Monday evening, we decided to go to my house to continue.

I put on music. We sat around my kitchen table. Soon afterward, Karen announced she was going.

It was just the two of us. We continued our conversation. That night, Kevin and I talked until dawn. We couldn't stop. Our need to speak to each other superseded the need to sleep, or to do anything else.

We talked, of course, about Ward and Lucia. We spoke about the kinds of people they were, how much we loved them, the void they had left in our lives. Although Ward and Lucia had died in such different circumstances, there was no doubt that Kevin and I could and would help each other. Before Kevin left, I gave him my business card, with my cell phone number added to it. A few hours later at work, I got my first of many daily e-mails from him. I sensed from the beginning that this exchange was special, and I saved even that first e-mail.

In the following days, Kevin and I e-mailed back and forth several times a day. We spoke on the phone. In a short time, we had forged an important bond, one that was almost instantaneous, as if we'd known each other for years.

A WEEK LATER, I was out having dinner with some girlfriends in town. That's when I saw him walk in through the back door.

I felt my stomach flip-flop. I couldn't even look at him, I was so nervous. Fortunately my friend told him to come and sit down with us. Kevin and I had e-mailed several times that day, but we hadn't discussed our evening plans. And yet here we were, meeting by chance again. I was so jumpy I could barely look at him. I literally had to get up and walk around while I figured things out. "Why am I so uptight about running into him again? Why is this so unnerving?"

Soon it was time for the group to meet our friend Karen. My invitation to Kevin, in my anxious state, was "You can come if you want to." Not surprisingly, Kevin declined. However, he did walk with us, the other women rushing ahead, leaving the two of us to walk and talk by ourselves. Now that we were alone, my nervousness vanished and I was comfortable again. We got to the next restaurant much too quickly, and stood outside, not wanting to leave each other. My friend Karen saw us, rushed outside, and ran across the sidewalk. Karen isn't subtle; she grabbed Kevin by the arm and dragged him inside.

A few hours later, Kevin and I ended up back at my house again. We talked and talked. Kevin and I were on the same page, in the same place about so many things. We both felt incredibly lucky to have had such strong and loving marriages, to have found our soul mates on earth. We recognized how fleeting life can be, and we both wanted to move forward with our lives in the spirit that knowledge gave us.

We talked about how this could be happening so soon after Lucia's death. Kevin told me about Lucia, how she was the least selfish and jealous person he'd ever met. Even when she was very ill, toward the end, her last concern was for him. We talked about how strongly connected we felt after just meeting a few weeks ago. We laughed about the coincidence of our chance meetings—we'd never laid eyes on each other before, and now we had run into each other three times. Kevin described how he could envision Lucia and Ward getting together in heaven, plotting our meetings, until we finally did something about it. I told Kevin that this definitely sounded like something Ward would have wanted to have a hand in.

Once again we talked until the sun came up.

WHEN I MET the WC at The Grill, I told them about what was happening. I couldn't believe that so much had changed since Julia's birthday dinner at Felidia when I was crying because I was convinced I would never meet anyone. Now this amazing person had come along. But at the same time, I also felt that this relationship with Kevin might not last.

"It's so soon after his wife's death," I told the WC. "I keep thinking that at some point he's going to realize that he can't be involved with anyone just yet. I think I might be his TG."

Even if I was Kevin's "transitional girl," I told my friends, I was going to risk the rejection. I was helping him and he was helping me. I wanted this to continue, even if that meant allowing myself to be hurt in the long term.

That night, Claudia asked me how it felt with the shoe on the other foot. After all these months of being the widow on the date, now *I* was the one dating someone whose spouse had died.

"So how does it feel?" Claudia wanted to know.

"You know what?" I replied. "In so many ways, it's like being with you guys."

25 · Lady Liberty

John and Claudia

The WC knew something was up when John called to tell us to meet at the restaurant Apizz at 7 pm one night in June, just before Claudia's birthday.

John picked Claudia up from work at 6 pm in a limo. Wait a minute, Claudia thought. What's going on here? But she told herself to stay calm, not to get ahead of herself. She got into the limo, and gave John a big kiss as he popped open a bottle of champagne. Hmmm. Champagne? The car took them down the east side of Manhattan, but whenever Claudia asked where they were going, John made some kind of vague comment about traffic. Then the car pulled into the Thirty-fourth Street heliport. John grabbed Claudia by the hand and told her to follow him.

They climbed in, and the helicopter lifted them up into the air and out across the Hudson River, heading south. The glowing city was just visible under an early summer haze. John was so calm that Claudia wondered if it was a hoax. It would be just like him to do something completely over the top for no reason at all and then to propose on the fire escape the following week. Claudia attempted to remain composed.

The helicopter soared toward the Statue of Liberty. Although John and Claudia had talked about visiting Lady Liberty since their first date, they'd never gotten around to it. Until now. John started fidgeting with his six seat belts. After managing to free himself, he got down on one knee on the floor of the helicopter with a ring box in his hand.

He had to shout above the noise of the helicopter blades spinning above them.

"Claudia, you've made me one of the happiest men in the world! Now make me the happiest! Will you marry me?"

Claudia was hugging him and crying and saying, "Yes, yes, I love you, I love you."

After a quick fly-by over Yankee Stadium, they landed. Claudia felt like she was still floating miles above the ground. They got back in the limo and headed downtown, where the driver pulled up in front of Apizz, the restaurant where they'd met one year ago.

John opened the door for Claudia so she could walk into the restaurant first. That's when Claudia saw their closest family and friends smiling and shouting, "Surprise!" "Happy Birthday!" and "Congratulations!" The best part was that everyone was wearing a green sponge Statue of Liberty visor, as instructed by John.

Claudia didn't know if she was more surprised to see them or to realize that John had orchestrated the most perfect, romantic, creative proposal ever.

What followed was such an absurdly happy night, everyone toasting, kissing, hugging, and talking. We ordered family style and had amazing antipasto, pizza from the brick oven, pasta and meatballs, followed by dessert. John had remembered his promise of a gag gift for Claudia's birthday the year before and placed stacks of Goya beans on the table.

Halfway through the evening, the WC snuck away for a quick smoke outside.

"Can you believe how crazy my life is?" Claudia asked.

One year ago, on that rainy night of her last birthday, when she'd been too sad to want to celebrate, she could never have dreamed that she was about to find her life partner, someone she could love with her whole heart. And yet here she was. John had arrived in her life. It was impossible *not* to feel guilty sometimes for loving him so completely. And at the same time, her love for Bart, and the agony of living without him, had made this new love possible. This was a path she never could have chosen for herself, but she realized it had made her heart capable of loving and cherishing more because she understood how essential, how precious it is to love and to be loved in return.

Part III

◆

September 2003 to May 2004

To laugh often and much;
to win the respect of intelligent people and the affection
of children;
to earn the appreciation of honest critics and endure the
betrayal of false friends;
to appreciate beauty; to find the best in others;
to leave the world a bit better, whether by a healthy child,
a garden patch, or a redeemed social condition;
to know that even one life has breathed easier because
you have lived.
This is to have succeeded.

— ATTRIBUTED TO RALPH WALDO EMERSON

26 · The Third Anniversary

Bart

Ward

Caz

Tommy

On Sunday, September 4, 2004, we opened our morning newspapers. On the front cover was a picture of a child lying on the ground, wounded and bleeding. The terrorist attack on a school in Beslan, Russia. Hundreds of mothers and fathers had taken their children to school that morning, never considering that someone would want to terrorize and murder their sons and daughters. All those lives ruined in an instant halfway around the world.

The things we used to take for granted: going to work in the morning, going to school, coming home safely. Before, when terrible things happened, although we had empathy for those affected, we were able to close the newspaper and go on with our day. But now we were vulnerable to horror. We phoned one another, not needing to explain why we were calling.

It didn't get any easier. This year at the anniversary ceremony, the victims' parents were reading the names. No one should ever have to outlive his or her child.

We stood and listened. Again, we made our way down into the pit. As we paid our respects and laid our flowers, we looked up to see a train rumbling into view from the west end of the site. The new PATH station had been completed, and the tracks skirted the perimeter. As the train passed, we could see the faces of the passengers staring down at us. We weren't so naïve as to think that nothing would ever change down here. But even so, none of us were prepared for the sight of those people, the everyday progression of a train into the station that morning.

AFTER THE CEREMONY, we went to The Grill, to toast The Boys, to drown our tears. Midway through the afternoon, Ann's phone rang. It was Kevin. She went outside so she could hear him better away from the noisy restaurant.

Kevin was in Atlanta on business, but even so, Ann had spoken to him several times that day. Every time she called, or he called her, she experienced that same comforting reassurance she always had from the sound of his voice. Ann knew he wasn't going to be home waiting for her at the end of this day—Kevin had meetings and had to take clients to dinner in the evening—and so hearing his voice was going to have to be enough. She kept telling herself, "This is business, his career; you can't ask him to stay in New York for you."

"You okay?" said Kevin.

"Uh-huh," Ann mumbled.

"Are you at The Grill? What are your plans?"

Ann told him she was going to stay a little longer and then head home.

"Can I come and get you?"

"What do you mean, can you come and get me? You're in Atlanta."

"I'm at La Guardia. I postponed the dinner. I want to be there for you. I want to help."

Ann couldn't respond—she was crying too hard. Kevin had understood her grief, recognized his need to support her, and he knew that his presence would help her.

There were so many reasons that Ann loved Kevin. She admired his will to make the best he could of his life, his positive attitude, his sense of humor, his inner strength, his integrity, and his courage. She loved talking with him. She could share everything with Kevin—every feeling, every hurt, every happiness—without fear of being judged or misunderstood. It was a given between Kevin and Ann that they both loved their spouses deeply. This knowledge didn't cause the slightest bit of jealousy. Quite the opposite. They wanted to get to know each other's spouse, to talk about Ward and Lucia, to know everything there was to know about them. Ward and Lucia were a part of their lives and always would be. The love they felt for their spouses formed a bond between Ann and Kevin from the very beginning. In a very real sense, their losses had brought them together.

27 · The List

Ann, Pattie, Claudia, and Julia with Italian sommelier

On September 13, after an eight-hour flight, dazed from the third anniversary, the night flight, and the jet lag, we disembarked from our plane in Sardinia. We'd planned this trip many months in advance so that, in true WC tradition, we had something to look forward to after the anniversary. This time, inspired by Pattie's visit to Italy earlier in the year, we were venturing farther than we'd gone on our previous trips.

Waiting at the carousel in the airport, watching the last straggling suitcases coming around and around, we realized that Pattie's luggage was missing. The airport staff told us not to worry, that her luggage would be delivered to the hotel the following evening.

"Not exactly a problem . . . ," Pattie pointed out, swinging her carry-on bag over her shoulder.

No, comparatively speaking, losing your luggage truly wasn't a big deal.

"Oh my God, if this had happened before, I would have had a cow if my luggage was lost! Not anymore," Claudia agreed.

"Hey, at least this way I get to borrow your clothes," Pattie noted.

Julia:

For the past few months, I'd been holding the date of September 12 in my mind. This was the day when things could start getting better for me. We were going to Italy. We were all looking forward to the trip—a few days in the sunshine in Sardinia, then a couple of days sightseeing and dining in Milan, the perfect way to recover from the ordeal of the anniversary. But now that September 12 was actually here, this new beginning wasn't a beginning at all. I'd woken up the morning of our flight feeling worse than ever, like there was a thousand-pound boulder pressing down on my chest.

A few weeks prior, I'd finally finished the arduous process of settling for the Victims Compensation Fund. All the paperwork, the lawyers, the discussions—I'd found all of this very hard. The fund had raised so many questions without any obvious answers. Should families of high-salary decedents receive more money than families of low-salary decedents, and if so, how much more? Should families of people who died on September 11 be treated differently from families of people who died during other attacks, such as the Oklahoma City bombing? If another similar attack happens, should Congress enact a similar fund? So many questions, so few answers. It was extremely difficult to be going through the grieving process and at the same time have to understand the complexities and legalities of the fund.

I'd assumed that finalizing the settlement would bring me some degree of resolution, but instead it left me feeling depleted and empty. It didn't bring me any closer to closure or relief. It only added to the misery; it didn't take it away. The simple fact is, it didn't bring Tommy back. It was just one more confirmation that he was gone. And then the anniversary came around again like a knockout punch.

As we sat in the bus that was taking us to our hotel, I was barely registering the foreign landscape outside the window. I listened to the others talk about how excited they were to be in Sardinia. Pattie was talking about her love of travel. Claudia was remembering previous trips to Europe. Ann joined in—she had been planning a trip to Italy with Ward that spring for her fortieth birthday. I felt as if I had nothing to contribute. It flashed through my mind that everyone else in the group was much more worldly and experienced than me, that the three of them seemed to be so much further along.

We arrived at the hotel. Overhead, the sky was gray, threatening rain. Our rooms had views over the harbor, with mountains in the distance. I tried not to think about how much Tommy would have loved to inspect all the boats in the marina, but how could I not? I told myself that it was a privilege to be here. It was up to me to see the beauty in my surroundings, to embrace this new experience. Smile through my tears. Be the life of the party. Appreciate what I did have and not ask for more. Don't feel bad for living. Don't feel guilty for being here. Tommy would want me to be happy.

Over dinner that evening, I made some jokes, told some stories, tried to be "myself." That night, we made friends with the waiters and introduced ourselves to the handsome sommelier, who suggested some great wines.

The next morning, I woke up again still on the edge of tears, the boulder pressing on my chest heavier than ever. It was early, six o'clock in the morning in Italy, the middle of the night in New York. I went for breakfast alone while the others slept.

I sat looking out over the boats across the marina, thinking about Tommy and how he was always happiest out on the water. Things would never be the same, and it was so hard for me to accept that. If I was stronger, I might be happier, I told myself. It was up to me to stop feeling this way, to get a grip on my misery and to enjoy this vacation. I might never have this opportunity to spend time here again.

That morning, I knew I wasn't going to be able to appreciate being here in Sardinia. Actually, I hated being anywhere without Tommy. Instead of cherishing my life, all I knew was that I wanted my pain to end. Maybe I could just stay here in Italy and never go back to New York. Disappear. Run away. Fall off the end of the earth. Anything so as not to have to deal with this anymore.

When the others got up, we decided to spend the rest of the day relaxing and recuperating. The cloud cover had cleared and the sun came through. We sat by the saltwater pool, swam laps, and lounged. Later in the day, we worked out in the gym. We played tennis, alternating partners. I decided to take a tennis lesson. At least I could pretend that I was doing okay. Good to go! G2G! Hoping if I kept faking it, I'd start believing it.

I kept looking at the others and wondering why I couldn't be more like them. The anniversary had been incredibly draining for them too, but they were still making the most of this trip. How did I fit into this group? I feared that if I couldn't find the positive in my situation after three years, then maybe the WC wasn't the haven I'd thought it was. It was only a matter of time before the others were going to stop wanting me around. After all, who wants to spent time with someone who's depressed, sad, and anxious all the time?

I hoped they hadn't noticed. I didn't want to ruin the trip for everyone else. So I kept pretending to be having a good time even though I was constantly on the verge of tears.

WE ALL SENSED that something was going on with Julia. She was on edge. She drifted in and out of conversations. She was quieter than usual. This wasn't like her.

During dinner, Claudia asked the question.

"Julia, what's wrong?"

The restaurant was packed with other hotel guests. The last thing Julia wanted was to cause a scene in the middle of a crowded restaurant.

"I don't want to talk about me," she implored. "Not now."

We backed down, feeling that it wouldn't be right to push the issue. We respected Julia's decision not to talk if it was the wrong time and place.

After Ann and Julia got back to their room, Ann waited for Julia to get into bed, switched out the lights, and then asked her again: "Julia, are you okay?"

Ann and Julia were sleeping in twin beds pushed next to each other. Ann could hear Julia begin to cry.

"I can't keep going, I can't do this anymore, I'm sorry." Julia kept crying and she kept apologizing. "I'm so sorry, I'm such a mess. I shouldn't be here. Please don't tell Pattie or Claudia."

Ann told Julia that we knew that she was suffering. It was only natural to miss Tommy. The anniversary was only just behind us. The settling of the compensation fund had been an emotionally draining experience. We were all experiencing the fallout.

"Of course you feel this way," Ann told her.

Julia kept crying: "I'm not good enough. I shouldn't be here. Why would you guys want to hang out with me? I don't belong with you."

"Julia, what are you talking about?"

Ann realized that it was one thing for Julia to be unhappy about her circumstances, but that it was another thing for her to be unhappy about herself.

"You're an amazing person. This is a tough time."

Julia kept crying and apologizing.

Ann kept saying, "Julia, we're going to get through this together. It's the four of us; we're in this together."

But nothing she said seemed to reach Julia.

Meanwhile Pattie and Claudia were awake trying to figure out how they could help our friend.

THE NEXT MORNING, Ann woke up and saw that Julia had gone for breakfast early again. This gave Ann an opportunity to speak to Pattie and Claudia. Ann was worried. Nothing she said to Julia seemed to be making a difference.

That day, we all watched Julia for signs of improvement, but she had closed herself off. After lunch, she disappeared back to her room, and the rest of us went to find her there.

When we walked in, she was in a ball on her bed crying.

"Julia, please tell us what we can do to help you. . . ."

"There's nothing," Julia sobbed. "I shouldn't be here. I shouldn't be around you anymore."

"What do you mean? We're always going to be together," we protested.

But Julia kept telling us to stay away.

"You're all so great and smart and talented. I'm just ruining things for everyone. . . ."

Julia had managed to convince herself that the three of us were moving on, and that she was dragging us down.

"Julia! You can't get rid of us that easily. We're always going to be here for you. That's the deal."

"You can feel anything you want, but never, ever feel that you're alone."

"Please reach out to us when you need it. . . ."

We told Julia we were going to work this out and get her whatever help she needed.

"I'm sorry, I'm sorry," she kept saying.

"Don't apologize!" we told her.

Julia had sunk so low, she'd actually thought we were judging her. She didn't even have the confidence to tell us about her difficulties, because she thought she might be rejected.

THE NEXT DAY we were booked to fly back to Milan before returning to New York. Now that Julia had opened up, we felt that she was starting to turn the corner, and we wanted to seize the moment while we were all together. Right there in the middle of the airport departure lounge, sitting on the floor by the food counter, the WC staged an intervention.

"Julia, we're always going to be here for you. We love you and that's unconditional."

"You have to stop worrying about what everyone else thinks—even what *we* think. You have to start thinking about yourself and what *you* need."

"What you're going through is extremely tough and very personal to *you*. It's totally different for each of us. We're all going at different paces."

The WC told Julia that we were going to help her to come up with a plan. We told her that we knew that making changes would be difficult and emotionally draining, but that it was going to be worth it.

We got out a piece of paper and a pen and had Julia make a list of her priorities for the coming year.

Julia's September 2004 To Do List

1. Take charge of my life.
2. Call Claudia's therapist as soon as I get back.
3. Reprioritize at work.
4. Don't worry so much about pleasing everyone else; worry more about doing the right thing for myself.
5. Remember what Tommy said: "There are energy takers and there are energy givers. Make sure you surround yourself with the givers not the takers."
6. Don't feel guilty for living.
7. Start treating myself more often: massages, facials, the little things that cheer me up.
8. Above all, be easier on myself.

It wasn't a case of telling Julia what to write. It was a case of getting her to listen to herself for long enough to come to her own conclusions. Something about seeing her goals in black-and-white helped to bring Julia out of her shell. It wasn't that things got any easier after that. The hard realities of Julia's life hadn't changed. But she felt a new determination to make a different picture out of the same pieces of the puzzle.

Julia and Claudia

Julia:

When I returned from Italy, I got to work on my "to do" list.

First, I made an appointment with Claudia's therapist, Cheryl.

I knew I had to get some professional help. In Italy, the WC had helped me to see I couldn't continue to do this on my own, even with their support. However hard I tried to move on with my life, something was holding me back.

It wasn't that I hadn't tried therapy before. In the first few months after Tommy's death, everyone kept telling me that I needed to seek professional help, and at the time, I was willing to try anything. I got the number of a woman therapist through my office. She would sit in a chair facing me, taking notes, listening coolly while I talked. Her technique was to let me speak while she gently guided me from subject to subject. She would never advise me, she never answered my questions or made suggestions. She only ever seemed to say: "Uh-huh."

One day I confronted her. I wanted to know why she never asked me how I was, or told me what she thought about my situation.

"Julia," she told me. "I'm not your friend, I'm your therapist."

I'd never had therapy before, so I didn't have anything to measure this experience against. I only knew that I was spending an hour a week talking to a stranger when the only person I wanted to talk to was my husband. I would walk into those sessions as if I were going into a seminar or a college class where I should learn how to better deal with my grief. But I came away feeling none the wiser. After several months, I decided to quit. I knew why I was sad—I missed Tommy and I wanted him back—and I didn't understand what I could gain from talking to this person. My first experience with therapy wasn't that positive, but frankly, even if this woman had been the best therapist in the world, I doubt I would have gotten much from the sessions.

My first appointment with Cheryl took place in October, after we returned from Italy. In the waiting room, a tall, attractive woman came toward me, smiling. "You must be Julia," she said.

We went into her tiny consulting room and she gestured for me to sit down in a comfortable love seat opposite her. There were pictures of seascapes on the walls, a candle on a side table, and soft lamplight.

"Let me get to know you," said Cheryl.

I told her how much I'd been struggling since Tommy's death. I told her about everything that was on my mind, my feelings of guilt about living now that Tommy was gone, how much I wanted him back. When I said something, Cheryl would react: "Really?" "Wow!" "You're kidding!"

She would interact. With every response, she made me feel like I wanted to tell her more. She asked me about Tommy. What was he like? What did he do? What did we do together? What kind of marriage did we have? Cheryl appreciated how central Tommy was to my life. She got it.

She asked me about my lifestyle. She wanted to know what I did to relax, if I had any breathing exercises that I used. She asked me if I'd thought about yoga. She talked about drinking enough water throughout the day, and reminded me that alcohol is a depressant and to be careful that I wasn't using it as a crutch.

At the end of the session, as we said good-bye, Cheryl turned and said to me: "It's going to be okay. You're going to be okay."

I called Claudia as soon as I got home: "I love her!"

IN THE COMING weeks, Cheryl and I talked about how my experience of widowhood wasn't going to be the same as Claudia's, Ann's, or Pattie's, or anyone else's for that matter. I'd been comparing myself so much to the other three, thinking I had to live up to some kind of standard for widowhood. But my experience of being a widow was something entirely personal to me. I had to allow myself the time and space to change, to readjust, to acclimatize myself to a reality that I found so very hard to deal with. The WC loved me and they would never judge me—they would give me the space I needed to do this.

"Julia," Cheryl told me, "one thing we're going to have to work on is helping you begin to accept that Tommy's not here."

"What do you mean?" I asked her. "I know he's not here. That's the problem!"

"I know," Cheryl replied, "but you're still living your life as if he's gone away and he'll come back and *then* you'll feel better."

Of course, on a rational level I knew this wasn't the case. I knew Tommy was gone. But in my heart, I still believed that getting my old life back was my only chance at happiness. I'd given up on any other version of my life but the old one. I was scared to move on or take the next step in my life, because then I would be leaving Tommy behind. I would feel so badly about enjoying myself when his life was cut so short. I worried that moving forward would mean that I no longer loved him.

"This isn't going to be easy, Julia," Cheryl warned me. "When you truly let go of the idea that Tommy is gone, you're going to grieve for that loss."

I talked to Cheryl about my relationship with Matt. On the one hand, I knew he was a great person and I wanted to be around him. On the other hand, I still couldn't figure out how it made sense to be with another man when I was still in love with Tommy. Cheryl asked me questions that really made me take a hard look at myself, and try to figure out what was right for me, as well as what I thought was right for the relationship.

Eventually, I came to the conclusion that it was only fair to either commit to Matt or end the relationship. Matt had helped me so much. He had been so patient with me. But I was depending on him to distract me from the reality of my life. I was beginning to realize that I needed to be on my own. I had to truly go through this grieving process, and I didn't think I could do this with Matt at my side.

Matt and I agreed that I needed to step away and work on myself before I continued with this relationship, or any other relationship for that matter. We told each other it was for the best.

Claudia:

When we first started discussing what kind of wedding we wanted, John told me, "If you want to elope, that's fine with me." He understood that I had already done the big wedding thing and might not be comfortable doing it again.

I thought about it and realized that I didn't want to elope. John comes from a big family—of his seven brothers and sisters, he was going to be the last to get married. He has a large circle of friends, many of whom we both shared by now. Everyone was so excited for him that he'd finally met "the one." I wanted him to be able to experience the euphoria of sharing that day with the people most important to us. So we decided on a destination wedding, the kind where you get to spend more than just a day with your guests. We wanted it to be unique and to reflect our personalities. The Bahamas are only a three-hour flight from New York; the wedding would be easy to get to, and that way everyone could make a mini-vacation of it. We would get married at the end of April.

Even so, I was going to be a low-maintenance bride, mainly because I had to be. I was incredibly busy. I was promoted in December of that year. John and I were apartment hunting. I was working on this book. The added benefit of getting married a thousand miles away from home was that I could do everything on-line. John and I agreed that all that mattered in the end was that we got to share our marriage bond with our families and closest friends. Everything else was superfluous.

I didn't even think to ask the WC to be my bridesmaids. It was a given.

One evening in a cab heading to The Grill, Pattie asked, "So are we in the wedding?"

My response was: "Wait a minute. Didn't I ask you already?"

Marcella would be my maid of honor and the WC would be my bridesmaids. I couldn't imagine standing at the altar with anyone else.

"Wait a minute. Aren't we too old to be bridesmaids?" Ann asked.

"We could be barmaids," Julia chimed in.

And so the WC agreed to be my "bridesmaids." I reassured them of two things: I didn't care what they wore, and more importantly, I wasn't going to make them walk down the aisle. If the groomsmen could appear magically at the front of the church at the beginning of the service, why couldn't they? I knew what it meant for a widow to make that walk. When I'd walked with my mother behind my father's coffin, she'd turned to me and said, "The last time I walked down the aisle I was a bride." All these years later, I still remember how sad that made me.

One evening that winter, on my way to meet the WC, I was talking to my mother on the phone.

"What are you up to?" she asked.

"I'm meeting the widows," I told her.

"Claaw-dia," my mother told me. "You know, after you're married you're not going to be one of the widows anymore."

"Wanna bet?" was my reply. But my mother got me thinking. After I got married, could I really call myself a widow anymore?

I'd spent three years hating being a widow and wanting to be a wife. Now I was about to become a wife and I wanted to stay a widow.

Being a widow had become a part of my identity. I was finally in a place where I liked who I was, and being a widow was a part of that.

When I told the WC about my dilemma, they laughed.

"Of course you're a widow!" said Pattie.

"You'll be a married widow," said Ann.

It was settled. When people asked who was in my wedding party, I would respond, "My sister and the widows." Needless to say, this answer caused a few sideways glances. . . .

Julia, Pattie, Ann, and Claudia

Julia:

My therapist had been right. The process of talking this through, of coming to these realizations about my life, was extremely difficult and painful. After a few months of therapy, I still wasn't sleeping well. When I did fall asleep, I would wake up in the middle of the night feeling panicked. I couldn't switch my thoughts off. During the day, I started to have problems swallowing and breathing. At first I thought maybe it had something to do with my vocal cord disorder. I went to see my doctor. He checked me out and found nothing wrong with me. He wondered if perhaps I was allergic to something.

Later that winter, I decided to take part in the "Tower to Tunnel Race," a 5K race through the Brooklyn-Battery Tunnel to honor one of the many firefighters who was killed in the World Trade Center attacks. By the time I got halfway through the tunnel, I was having problems breathing and swallowing. I had to be helped to the finish line. This wasn't like me. I'm in pretty good shape—a 5K run is something

I had done many times before without any problems. The paramedics checked my vitals; nothing was wrong.

I talked to my therapist about what had happened during the race.

"Julia," she said. "It sounds to me like you're having anxiety attacks."

It was at this point that Cheryl suggested that it might be necessary for me to go on some kind of medication.

"I'm not someone who usually suggests that my patients take medication," she explained, "but in your case, I feel that this is going to be a big help for you."

This didn't sound good. I protested. There was no way I was going on medication. It just wasn't my style. I wanted to do this on my own. As we talked it through, I explained to Cheryl that, for me, medication seemed like I was giving in. I've always been a very "anti-drug" person. It was too embarrassing to think that I wasn't going to be able to get better naturally, with Cheryl's help and with my WC.

But with her usual gentleness, Cheryl explained her thinking to me. She believed I needed this extra assistance.

"Sometimes it's the case that when something very traumatic happens to someone, no matter how hard they try, they can't get back to their previous level of capability," Cheryl explained. "When Tommy was killed, the shock was so intense that your body's chemistry was thrown off balance. I think you need help getting your equilibrium back."

Cheryl explained that I didn't need to worry; a professional would monitor me; they would evaluate me very carefully and find the right medication.

"The medication is going to help take the edge off your anxiety and sadness and make it possible for you to function a little better while you're going through this process," Cheryl insisted.

Was I actually medically imbalanced, or was I simply going through a tough grieving process? I'd been convinced that antidepressants weren't for me—and they're not for everyone—but at this stage, I was ready to do whatever I needed to do to feel better. By now I trusted Cheryl implicitly, so I decided to at least try what she was suggesting. Whatever was going to happen with medication was probably preferable to what I was experiencing right now, and if the medication didn't do me any good or if it made things worse, then I could just stop taking it.

I made an appointment with a doctor in Midtown.

Dr. Mahelsky met with me for a few hours and decided to start me on the correct dose of antidepressants. I would start taking them in the new year. Maybe the medication would help me; maybe it wouldn't. But I was willing to take a chance, and hopefully move into a new phase of my life.

I started out on half the dosage, in order to prepare my body for the change to my system. The first month, I was miserable. I have a small frame and I rarely take any type of medication, so I experienced every symptom in the book: dry mouth, nausea, diarrhea, weight loss, night sweats.

I called Dr. Mahelsky and Cheryl to tell them that I couldn't keep taking the medication, that I felt terrible. Both the doctor and Cheryl assured me this was normal, that I was okay and that I should stick with it. I knew I had to believe them and that I was going to have to see this through.

With Dr. Mahelsky's supervision and Cheryl's support, we found the correct dosage and the symptoms began to subside. I began to understand why it's so important for a good physician to continually observe you while you're undergoing treatment like this—the dosage needs to be supervised, and the doctor needs to meet with you regularly to do that. Having a good therapist you feel comfortable with and can meet with during the process is also absolutely vital.

I actually began to feel better.

Cheryl had explained to me that the drugs wouldn't make my pain go away, but that they would take the edge off my unhappiness and make it possible for me to function a little easier. She was right. I was still grieving for Tommy, but I wasn't having anxiety attacks anymore. I was sad, but it wasn't an unmanageable sadness. This was something that I didn't fear and that I could cope with.

In the meantime, Cheryl was encouraging me to become more honest about my feelings. She was helping me to understand how much I'd been hiding behind my smile, my personality. I'm a naturally talkative, upbeat person. I like to tell jokes and to get the attention of the room. It had been easier for me to put on my brave face, to keep playing to the crowd, than to explain to others how I was really feeling. I always felt that I had to overcompensate for my sadness—I never wanted to be the person bringing everyone down. And at the same time, I would feel as if I was betraying Tommy and his memory by smiling, by behaving as if I was having a good time. I'd been outgoing without feeling confident. I was celebrating while in pain. I was appearing to be happy while feeling guilty for being alive.

My fear was that by letting go of mourning for Tommy, I would be letting go of Tommy. Cheryl kept reassuring me.

"Julia," said Cheryl. "You need to find a place for Tommy, somewhere special, where you won't worry that you're going to lose him."

Cheryl helped me to understand that Tommy was always going to be with me, no matter what. His legacy, his one-liners, his humor, his generosity and love of life—those would continue through me. At first, it was a question of just discussing these things with Cheryl. Gradually I started to believe them. She was right. No one could take Tommy away from me, if I chose to carry him with me in my heart.

I spent less and less of my time trying to figure out how my life would be if Tommy were here. I knew I had to start looking at what was going on today, not daydreaming about some parallel universe where Tommy and I could be together. I needed to start figuring out if there was any way I could reclaim my future. I started thinking about my options for becoming a mother. I wanted to start my own family. Maybe it wasn't going to happen for me in the traditional sense, but then nothing was "traditional" for me anymore.

I thought about my September "to do" list.

"Don't worry so much about trying to please everyone else; think about doing the right thing for myself."

Through my friend at work, I got the number of an adoption agency and gave them a call. They told me it could take a while to get an appointment, but they'd let me know.

Claudia:

After a few months of searching, John and I found our ideal apartment, a loft downtown. We loved the neighborhood, and the place was large enough for when it came time to start a family. We were moving in the week between Christmas and New Year's. There was this sense of the year beginning with such excitement.

I was moving forward, but keeping a secure hold on my past. I had already decided to keep my tiny apartment on Fifty-fourth Street, and I counted my blessings that I was able to make the decision based on what was best for me and not because of financial constraints. I wanted it to be a family apartment—a place where people could stay when they were in town, somewhere that our nieces and nephews would be able to live if they wanted to spend time in New York after college. But this wasn't only going to be a shrine. It was a place that felt warm and comfortable and lived in. It had already become a kind of clubhouse for the WC, somewhere we met for weekly meetings while writing this book.

Packing was minimal because I was leaving my furniture uptown. It was just a case of sifting through everything and figuring out what I wanted to take with me. One day, while I was going through my closets, I came across boxes containing the dozens of Christmas ornaments that Bart and I had picked out together. Each ornament brought back a memory of where we'd been when we'd bought it.

I smiled remembering the year that Bart ordered a Christmas tree from L.L. Bean. "You're crazy!" I told him. "Who gets their Christmas tree delivered?" Bart went ahead and ordered a "large" tree. It arrived. The tree was too small. Another call. Not happy with the tree. An extra large tree and next day delivery, please. We had two trees that year. One enormous one inside our six-hundred-square-foot apartment and another smaller one out on the terrace. Bart adored the holidays. We would have a dinner party almost every weekend in December, with my husband cooking up a storm. No cutting corners. We would drive into Brooklyn to get the supplies—the bread store for fresh bread, the butcher for the meat, the Italian market for homemade pasta and fresh mozzarella, champagne for the refrigerator.

Sifting through the ornaments, I decided to keep the ones that meant the most to me, and to give everyone in our family a "Bart ornament" for Christmas. I wanted our eight nieces and nephews to have a special ornament that they could hang up every year and think about Uncle Bart. Our siblings—who knew how over the top Bart was when it came to Christmas—would each have a piece of that spirit to hold onto.

I found an old silver Bergdorf Goodman box that was filled with the ornaments Bart had made as a child: dried pasta swirls glued together, an empty spool of thread painted red, Popsicle sticks in the shape of a cross. I decided I wanted to give these to Bart's parents. I knew it would be heartbreaking for them to see these treasures again, but I also knew that it would mean the world to them.

I've always tried to share what I have of Bart with his family. Initially, I wanted to keep everything to myself, as if that would mean that I was holding onto Bart. But quickly I realized that nothing could bring him back. I knew that by sharing these things with his family I was acknowledging their grief and hopefully giving them some kind of comfort. I gave our nephew David Bart's trademark red vest he wore every year during the holidays. I gave Bart's older brother Frank his high school ring. I gave everyone in the family one of the credit cards that were recovered from Ground Zero.

I would have a chance to deliver the ornaments on December 19 when we celebrated the "Ruggiere Christmas" at Bart's brother's apartment. Mark and his girlfriend Krysten were hosting. John was invited. I knew how hard it must be for Bart's family seeing us together, but that didn't stop them from taking the high road and making sure my fiancé was included in our family gathering.

It was our fourth Christmas without Bart. Traditionally we had gotten together at his mom's or sister's in the suburbs, and now we were in Mark's compact Manhattan apartment. Everything felt strange and different. At one point, there was a lull in the conversation, and I looked over at Kathleen, and I could see how much she was missing Bart. He had the ability to transform the simplest get-together into a full-blown celebration. He would be telling stories, keeping everyone eating and drinking and laughing. To someone looking in, it would have seemed like a perfectly nice celebration, and it was. But Kathleen knew it was different.

John was wonderful, chatting easily with everyone and playing with the girls. At one point I looked over at Bart's mom, and she was watching John. He was helping her granddaughter dress her new baby doll. I knew by now that Pat was genuinely happy that I had found love again with John. But at the same time, how many mothers can look at their daughter-in-law's fiancé and not think: "Why not my son? Why isn't he here?"

When it came time to exchange presents, I gave the girls their gifts first. This allowed the adults time to prepare. I explained that Uncle Bart loved Christmas and this was something special for each one of them from me and him. They loved the ornaments—not quite as much as the Game Boys I also gave them—but hopefully when they're older, they'll fully appreciate the meaning of the gift. When I handed Pat her box, with its cheerful holiday wrapping and big red bow, I suggested she might be more comfortable opening hers in private. I let her know what was in the box. She gave me a look that conveyed everything about her gratitude and sorrow.

When we got home, John told me he wanted some of Bart's ornaments on our tree. Before, when we'd first spoken about this, John suggested that it might be a good idea to have a fresh start, to have new ornaments that we'd bought together. But after seeing the significance for Bart's family and for me, John knew it would be a beautiful tribute.

Ann:

On the morning of Christmas Eve I was up early. I'd roasted two turkeys the day before that I was donating to the church's program. It was a frigid winter's day and I bundled Billy into his warmest clothes and into the back of the car.

"Mom, why do I have to go?"

"You know why. Because we're lucky to have food to eat, and it's good to help others."

In the car on the way to drop off the turkeys, I told him how the WC had "adopted" a family through Julia's church—a widow and her two sons who were going through difficult times. I told Billy that the presents I'd bought for that family were some of the most important things I'd bought that Christmas.

"It's up to us to help other families who need a little help," I told my son.

After dropping off the food, Billy and I headed into the city. We were going to Ground Zero, where we were meeting the WC.

Billy was four when his father died. Now he was seven, and I worried that as he grew older, he would lose his memories of his father. I wanted him to understand what had happened, to make sure that he didn't forget, especially during the holidays. It was important that he always feel comfortable talking about Ward and the events that surrounded his death. When the mother of one of Billy's classmates passed away recently, I took Billy to the wake with me. We talked about how this happens to other parents too, that this was part of life.

I was constantly amazed by Billy's resilience and matter-of-factness regarding what had happened to his family. When your father dies and you're four years old, it's almost as if you have a better chance of adapting to your situation.

Before the end of the school semester, for example, I had been testing my son on his spelling. The word "widow" had been on the list.

"What does that word mean, Billy?" I asked him.

"It's an old lady," he told me.

"It is?" I challenged him.

He adamantly defended his definition.

I smiled as I told him that a widow was a woman whose husband had died, and therefore, since Daddy had died, I was a widow too. Daringly, I then asked him if I was an "old lady," as he loves to announce in every public place exactly how old I am. To my delight, he admitted that I wasn't an old lady.

The fact that my son—who lives the reality every day that his mother is a widow—chose the stereotypical definition of the word makes sense in a wonderful way. Everything around us—fairy tales, books, cartoons, TV, movies—depicts widows as wrinkled old ladies, wallowing their lonely days away, just waiting to join their husbands in the Great Beyond. Thank goodness he didn't equate me with that definition. Thank goodness he saw me as a regular mom. Thank goodness he sees his own life as "normal," despite everything.

That Christmas Eve morning, Billy had asked to wear his roller sneakers and I okayed it, even though they weren't exactly in keeping with the gravity of the visit. As we walked up to the doorway where we were meeting the WC, Billy literally rolled toward them along the sidewalk. Usually, we'd approach the gates to the family viewing site in trepidation—it never gets any easier to take in the enormity of the site—but now we were following Billy on his skates, gliding ahead of us. It was impossible to feel as heavy-hearted as usual with that child leading the way.

I watched as the girls chatted with Billy, asking him about school, getting him to talk about his friends, about what Santa was going to bring him this year. No one wanted to get visibly upset, to make Billy feel uncomfortable about being here or talking about Ward.

In the family room, I started to pick out faces that I recognized from the thousands of photos pinned on the wall—I'd come here enough times before to feel like I knew some of these people, even though I'd never met them. I started pointing them out to Billy. This was important. I didn't want him to remember only the event—in fact, my instinct as a mother was always to protect him from it—I also wanted him to remember the people.

"Mom! Look."

Billy had found a photo of Ward I'd left here the year before. It was Ward's mass card.

A few minutes later, we heard Claudia say: "Oh my God, the note I wrote to Bart two years ago is still here."

It was like finding two needles in a haystack. We were actually overjoyed to find these tokens. We stayed awhile longer, picking out different names and faces and showing them to Billy.

That little boy on his roller sneakers helped us more than he knew. We all felt it in that room that morning: Billy's presence had made our trip to Ground Zero not quite so sad this year.

I SPENT THE rest of the day getting ready for Christmas—making food, setting the dining room table, wrapping gifts I hadn't yet wrapped.

Often, there's an assumption that the holidays are a time of unremitting celebration, but for families coping with loss, November and December can be the most arduous months of the year.

I was very aware that this was Kevin's first Christmas without his wife. I knew from experience how hard the holiday period was going to be for him, how much he was going to miss Lucia. The holidays brought up so many issues for a widower—and for his widow girl-friend. Whose family do you spend the day with? Your own? Your in-laws'? Each other's family? Each other's in-laws'? Kevin and I didn't want to add to anyone's pain by being insensitive to our relatives' feelings and selfish for our own needs. So we decided to spend Thanksgiving with our separate families and our respective in-laws and then Christmas together. I always want to be a part of Ward's family. Kevin feels the same way about Lucia's parents and siblings.

For Christmas Day, we'd invited friends to celebrate with us. Julia had decided not to go back to her parents'. She was bringing her newly married friends Peter and Michelle. Kevin had invited his friend Chris and his new girlfriend.

We started to refer to this gathering as the "misfits" Christmas—this was a group of people who, for one reason or another, had purposely decided to celebrate with friends.

We started dinner by toasting to Christmas, and toasting to the ones who weren't with us today. We toasted to Ward and Lucia. We toasted to Tommy. We toasted to Michelle's former fiancé who had died years ago in a rafting accident. We toasted to Caz and to Bart, and other family members who were no longer with us. After the toasts, I set the rule that everyone had to say a few words about what they were grateful for, what their resolutions were for next year. This was a group of people who didn't really know one another, and it was a good way of breaking the ice. As it turned out, everyone around that table had experienced some kind of loss or was going through a period of transition. The evening began to gather momentum, everyone laughing and toasting, taking the time to think about what they were thankful for and their hopes for the year ahead.

I'd changed so much. Here I was hosting Christmas for a room filled with people who didn't know one another very well but were having a great time. I'd created this event, something that in the past I would have left to Ward. Over the years since his death, my personality had changed and blossomed to become more like his. He was such a magnetic personality. Compared to him, I'd always been the quieter one in social situations. I'd never been the first person to walk across a room and make a new friend, or initiate a conversation with someone I didn't know. Now I didn't think twice about inviting a disparate group of people into my home. That Christmas I sensed it more than ever: just as much as Ward lives on through our children—their wit, their charm, their friendliness, that twinkle in Billy's eye—his spirit lives on in me too.

Pattie:

I ended the year with a new optimism. In December I'd broken my wrist in a snowboarding accident but I didn't let it curtail my newfound spirit. It was true that I had to cancel the flying lessons I'd previously booked, but even so, I forged ahead. I was starting to learn Spanish; I was making arrangements to travel more. Although my accident had re-minded me that I couldn't always control which way I was heading—and it wasn't like I needed reminding of that—I sensed that I was at a cross-roads. It was up to me to determine the route going forward.

One winter Saturday, I was sitting in my apartment talking to my brother, Fran. We'd just received the news that a publisher was going to publish the Widows Club book. Work on the chapters was beginning, and Fran wanted to know how things were progressing.

"Great," I told him. "How about that? Your sister is going to be a published author."

I told Fran that I had something on my mind. How I was going to go back to my mundane job at the bank after completing something as meaningful as writing a book?

"Can I really show up at my desk again after I get back from my book tour?" I wanted to know.

We laughed at the idea that I had suddenly been transformed from someone who works at a bank to a person who might give book read-ings. Wouldn't Caz have loved that.

The more we talked about it, the more I realized that I felt like my time at the bank might be coming to an end. These past three years, ab-sorbing Caz's death had been all the change I could handle. But now there was a growing sense in me that I didn't want to be working at this job for the rest of my life.

"I just keep thinking about what I'm going to do next," I told Fran. "Shouldn't I start thinking now about making a change when the book gets published in 2006? Should I go traveling? Live in another country?"

"No, don't run away," Fran insisted. "You have a lot of good things going on right now. And anyway, you can't put Lola in your backpack."

"Then what about school?" I asked Fran. "What about studying again?"

My brother knew that I had always harbored a desire to do graduate work so that I would be able to teach.

"Maybe now's the time to actually make it happen," I suggested.

Fran's response was "Dr. Patricia Carrington, published author and Ph.D. It has a certain ring to it. . . ."

We talked it through. Going back to school would mean leaving my job, something that seemed like a huge risk, especially for someone like me. I've always been a reliable and steady person when it comes to my career, creeping up the gradual incline one promotion at a time. What's more, I come from a family where you just don't leave a good job. I knew how my parents would react if I ventured to have this conversation. They would be worried. They would want to dissuade me.

But I was curious; I was looking for something different.

What's more, it was possible for me to take this risk. Leaving my job to study never would have been an option before for many reasons—Caz and I were planning for the future, for a family. But now I was on my own. I strongly believed that the financial compensation I'd received after Caz's death was a gift from my husband and should be used extremely carefully. It was a responsibility, this money, and if I was going to use these funds for myself, I had to do something worthwhile that would enable me to give back in the long run.

That evening, I searched the Internet, eventually finding an interdisciplinary master of arts program at a local graduate school. I scrolled through the various components of the course. I would be able to study the arts—always my passion—how they influence our lives and how they've changed the course of history, politics, religion, and culture.

I sat back in my chair and contemplated the future. Ahead of me was a wide, clean, blank canvas. I wasn't on that traditional track of marriage, kids, and family anymore. There were no guarantees. Sometimes, the blank canvas seemed scary because I didn't know what the picture was going to be. But sometimes that blank canvas felt liberating, creative, undefined. It occurred to me that some people might even be envious of my situation, so I should appreciate it. Many people are trapped in their jobs, their marriages, their circumstances. I was wide open to a million possibilities and opportunities.

What if I couldn't get into school? What if I got in and couldn't succeed there? I hadn't been a student in more than fifteen years, and to be honest, even when I was at college, I wasn't the most gifted of scholars. But I was a hard worker. I knew that much, and I had resilience. If I really set my mind to it, this goal wouldn't be able to elude me.

Claudia's words came back to me: "If we can survive this and survive this well, we can do anything."

I downloaded the graduate school application forms.

Bart

Caz and Lola

Tommy

Ward

Claudia:

In February, John and I were booked for a one-day Pre-Cana, the marriage counseling session that every couple is required to have before getting married in a Catholic church. Even though I might take issue with some of the church's positions—on homosexuality, on divorce, on birth control—I knew that when I needed it, my faith continued to sustain me. Like me, John was raised Catholic, and we'd decided we wanted to have a spiritual union.

I wasn't necessarily excited about a second round of Pre-Cana, but I was happy to share the experience with John. I remembered being surprised by how much Bart and I had gotten from our Pre-Cana classes five years earlier. John and I were scheduled for a one-day session on Saturday, February 12, and that evening our friends were throwing us a Valentine's dinner party to celebrate our engagement.

I got up on Friday morning the day before and went to visit a customer in New Jersey, then rushed back into the city to get my hair colored. I dropped the car off in the parking garage under my old apartment and ran up to use the bathroom. While I was there, I popped into the bedroom to check my messages. Even though I don't live in this apartment anymore, I still get an occasional message, although it is mostly a solicitor or a friend wanting to hear Bart's voice on the machine.

The message light was flashing and I hit play. As I sorted through a large stack of mail, I heard a male voice saying with hesitation:

"Ummm, yes, this message is for Claudia Ruggiere. Can she please call me at the New York Medical Examiner's Office on this number. Umm, thank you very much."

I froze. The only time I'd heard from the Medical Examiner's Office was when they'd identified Bart. What did this message mean? There must have been some kind of mixup. It had to be a mistake.

I played the message again, and then again. First to let it sink in that this was real, but also in order to be able to write down the number. I picked up the phone and sat at the kitchen table flipping through a Pottery Barn catalog. Everything had to be normal because I was looking at a Pottery Barn catalog.

"Hello, Medical Examiner's Office."

"I'm returning your call. . . ." These words never got any easier to say: "My husband Bart was killed at the World Trade Center."

The cheerful-sounding voice went momentarily silent.

"Oh." Pause. "What was your husband's full name?"

"Bart J. Ruggiere."

"Can you spell that, please?"

I did. Another pause.

"Can you please hold on?"

She came back on the line after a minute and informed me that the Medical Examiner's Office had reached the end of their DNA identification process and they were notifying me that there were additional remains of my husband that had been identified.

I stared down at the Pottery Barn page.

Knowing I couldn't bear the weight of the answer, I asked the question "What have they found?" like I was asking what color the towels on page 32 came in. I never thought that she would tell me. I thought I would have to go down to the office to find out. I wasn't prepared for the answer. I still can't acknowledge it.

She answered.

I couldn't speak.

"I'm sorry," I said and hung up.

I called John. From the sound of my sobs, he knew something was terribly wrong. I got the words out. John wanted to leave work and come to me, but I had plans late afternoon to meet the WC to work on our book. I knew it would be comforting to be with these women, and John understood. I promised him I would come home early. My next two calls were to my sister and Pattie. Marcella would call my family. Pattie would call the WC.

I cracked open a bottle of Scotch and, trembling, poured myself a glass. Within minutes Pattie was at my apartment.

"What the hell is happening?" Pattie's face was all concern. "How could he be identified again?"

I was beginning to figure out what must have happened. When Bart was identified the first time, I vaguely remembered being handed a form to fill out. There were three boxes. I had to select one.

If there were additional remains, the form asked, did I:

1. Want to be notified every time Bart was identified?
2. Have a final notification at the end of the identification process?
3. Have no notification and the remains would be included in a memorial downtown?

The third option wasn't an option—it would be too disrespectful to Bart. And I knew I couldn't endure the raw pain and emotional roller-coaster ride associated with the first option. I must have chosen option two. I had requested that I only be identified again at the end of the process.

The Medical Examiner's Office had reached the end of the process.

Pattie hadn't heard anything. What about Ann? Would either of them get anything? Or would they never have any remains? Would it be better if they did or they didn't? Was there any such thing as better?

Bart had been identified twice. Caz and Ward not at all. Tommy the week of the eleventh. With or without remains, it was all unimaginable.

"How am I right back here again?" I asked Pattie. "How have three and a half years gone by?"

There was this feeling of complete disbelief. How was it possible for this to be happening three years later?

"This is unbelievable."

Now I had to get up the courage to call Bart's family. I drained my drink to steady my nerves.

I phoned Bart's father first. I hadn't scripted the words I was going to say; I couldn't process the information, much less imagine saying it out loud. That through the wonders of modern medicine, three and a half years later, DNA had been used to identify his beloved son, *again.*

As soon as Frank Sr. answered, I went numb. I couldn't believe that I was having to break this news to him. I wanted to comfort him, but soon I was crying so hard that he ended up comforting me, speaking gently into the phone with genuine concern.

"You don't need this now," Frank told me. "You're getting married soon."

We spoke as long as we could.

I didn't want to call Bart's mother at work, so I called his sister next. She answered right away, telling me that she was in her car on the way to pick her daughter up from school. I knew I was about to shatter the normalcy that had taken her three and a half years to rebuild. Immediately Kathleen burst into tears and had to hang up, the only rational response. By the time I got hold of Bart's mom and his brothers, Kathleen had already spoken to them. Mark had dropped everything and was already on his way to my apartment. It was his first thought to come and comfort me.

Mark, Julia, and Ann arrived within minutes of one another.

"How is this happening?" everyone wanted to know.

I told them I felt like Bart had died on three different days. The day of his death and each day of his two identifications.

We kept asking questions. Without any answers, all we could do was keep asking.

"How did this happen? What's going on?"

. . .

MY FIRST REACTION was that I couldn't go to Pre-Cana the next day. I didn't even know if I would be able to wake up in the morning. I was in no mood for any kind of spiritual guidance right now. If there was a God, then how could He allow this to happen to Bart?

But the next morning I did wake up. John and I did go to Pre-Cana. John understood how hard all of this was for me, and his compassion confirmed my determination to go. I could appreciate how difficult it was for him to see his soon-to-be wife so upset on a day when we should have been excited. Our Pre-Cana became a time for reflection. It made us focus on our blessings, and gave me the forum to appreciate John, my family, the WC, and everything that we did have. I came home and went to the engagement party. I rallied; I wanted to do it for John. I wanted to do it for us.

On Sunday I shut down. I didn't get out of bed for the entire day.

I was not myself at work in the coming week. When I met with my boss one day, he happened to comment that I seemed a little out of sorts. I confided in him. I told him about the identification, about calling Bart's family, and about the emotional toll it had taken.

My boss wanted to know why I'd told Bart's family. Wouldn't it have been kinder to spare them the news? The only answer I could give was that it never even occurred to me not to. We had survived these past three years together as a family. The situation we'd been forced into was completely unnatural, but at the same time we were a family with real bonds, trying to maintain Bart's spirit of love and generosity, even in the most unconscionable of circumstances.

Ann:

Three and a half years after my husband's death, I finally completed the process of getting a headstone for Ward's plot. The announcement that the examiner's office had put the identification process on hold indefinitely made me confront the fact that we would probably never have any remains to bury. Although I couldn't have predicted how I was going to feel, the news that the identification process was over brought with it a sense of relief. I wouldn't have to live in fear anymore of getting the call or of hearing the knock on the door.

I'd always wanted to get some remains. I knew from my widow

friends that it wouldn't change things. I'd seen the acute pain and con-fusion that two identifications had caused Claudia. Thanks to Julia, I knew that having a body to bury hadn't brought her any sense of accep-tance. Like me, Pattie had nothing of her husband—she was relieved too that the identification was over. She'd never wanted to get that knock on the door.

For two years I had an empty plot that I would visit when I needed to pay my respects and say hello to Ward. Often I would go past the cemetery on my morning run, clocking my time there to see if I was going faster or slower. I'd say, "Hi, honey!" and keep running. The plot was just a vacant patch of land. Next to his gravesite were three other headstones of victims of September 11, husbands of widows I knew from Rye and a son of mutual friends. I'd always wanted a permanent marker there, a beautiful memorial with Ward's name on it, but what I hadn't realized was just how long and difficult the process of getting it made was going to be. The headstone had to be perfect. I spent months researching different shapes and sizes. I looked at every style of etching, every shade of granite. I'd wander around local cemeteries taking pho-tos of headstones that I liked. I wonder what the occasional mourner thought of me, striding around the plots with my camera.

Then there was the dilemma of the spacing on the headstone. The plot was big enough for three caskets. If the bodies were cremated, this plot was sized for nine urns. I knew that Elizabeth would probably be buried there. Billy and TJ might decide to be buried with their wives and families. And what about me? I could no longer be sure that I wanted to be buried next to Ward someday.

After avoiding and agonizing over the decision, I finally knew ex-actly what I wanted, and ordered it in the summer of 2003. A simple black stone with Ward's name and his date of birth and date of death engraved, and enough room for at least four names below. The months passed. There were problems with the quarry, problems with the ship-per. Every time I called there was always another excuse for the delays.

Finally, in March of 2005, the headstone was ready. I went to the monument showroom to see it and was directed out into the backyard. The headstone was covered in a dark tarpaulin. When the salesman pulled off the covering, I became physically nauseated. They had inscribed the wrong year of birth on the stone. It said 1952 and Ward was born in 1965. I went to the owner of the place in tears.

"This has to be perfect," I told him. "It has to be. This is the last thing I can do for my husband."

When the headstone was finally ready, its dates correct, I went to see it installed. There it was, a plain black stone, with simple engraving, the way I'd wanted it. Even so, seeing that stone was profoundly disappointing. What had I been expecting? It was just a piece of granite. It didn't change anything. Over the months and months of preparing for this, I'd built the stone up in my mind, and now the final result couldn't even begin to match up. It was nothing more than letters carved into granite.

One more task of putting Ward to rest had been finalized, but it didn't give me any sense that anything was over. My loss was a scar on my heart that I hoped would continue to fade but that I knew could never wholly go away.

Pattie:

In the new year, after many months of deliberation, renovations on my Brooklyn apartment began.

This place had been Caz's home since 1989, seven years before I arrived in his life. The apartment had a definite air of elegant English bachelorhood to it. The furnishings were very masculine, beautiful dark wooden dressers and sideboards; long, white, woolen drapes. Everything reflected the taste of a young Brit who had just arrived in the big city and started to earn money. All these years later, there were still Caz's accumulated possessions everywhere, cluttering the shelves and packed into closets—hundreds of old VCR tapes, a huge TV that I never watched, remote controls, video games, various gadgets the function of which I wasn't even sure.

Even admitting that the apartment needed freshening up was a big step for me. Since the beginning, I'd sworn that I would never change anything. I wanted to preserve the smallest details, from the placement of the furniture to the dozens of ties hanging in his rack in the closet. His toothbrush in the holder, the books by his bedside, the chair in the corner—they had been put there by Caz, and I had no intention of ever rearranging them. Heaven protect any person who tried to shift something by as much as an inch. In the bedroom, I'd even kept the time on our alarm clock set for six, the same as it was the morning of September 11. It wasn't just the alarm that I wanted to stand still—my plan was to stop time altogether.

But as hard as I'd fought to keep everything frozen in the past, I was losing the battle. Inevitably, things changed. I changed. I acquired things. A vase here, a book there. A friend had persuaded me to throw out Caz's medicine bottle on the bedside table, saying, "Pattie, if he comes back, he's not going to be sick!" Time had done its work. The floors of the apartment were scuffed; the walls needed painting; the curtains had turned gray at the edges. Everything about this place was three years older. I was older too. I was a woman in my thirties who had outgrown Caz's twenty-something taste.

It was time for an upgrade. Not only was I beginning to consider changing the time on the alarm clock, I even thought about trading it in for a new model.

Any changes I made would have to be a mix. I wanted to incorporate the elements that would always remind me of Caz with an increased sense of my own style. I wanted to add a little more sophistication—re-covering certain chairs, adding some new pieces of furniture and lamps, refinishing the floors—but I needed to keep those things I couldn't part with. In the bedroom, our bed and dressers stayed, but I got new window treatments. Instead of having Caz's possessions cluttered in every corner of the apartment, I was going to pare them down and put them into a shelf unit in a single corner. I no longer wanted the apartment to be frozen in time. I wanted it to come and meet me in the present.

The first step was to sift through a decade's worth of accumulated objects. Gritting my teeth, I began in the bathroom. Out went his oatmeal scrub and electric toothbrush, razor and medicines. I kept his cologne and body lotion. After a momentary panic where I realized that I wanted to keep the scrub and the toothbrush, I called in Sandy for help and moral support. In the kitchen, I admitted defeat and placed in the trash the last box of eggs that Caz had bought before he died—they were hollow; their contents had long since evaporated. Next we attacked his closet. His dozens of T-shirts, boxers, and socks would have to go. I kept just a few of each to stand in for all the rest, mixing them in with my underwear. I saved all his ties and cuff links. I had the hardest time throwing away anything that had his handwriting on it, and so all his old files had to stay.

Even so, by the end, there were eleven huge black plastic bags out on the sidewalk.

The possessions that remained needed to be packed away so that the floors could be sanded and refinished. There were some heart-wrenching moments. When the decorators shifted the table from Caz's side of the bed, they put his pile of books on the floor, three books that he'd been reading: *The New New Thing, Kitchen Confidential,* and *A Walk in the Woods.* They hadn't been touched in three and a half years.

The New New Thing had a flip cover tucked in to mark his place. *Kitchen Confidential* had his business card slotted between the pages. *A Walk in the Woods* was spread-eagled. I turned to the page he'd been reading in *The New New Thing,* a book about a Silicon Valley tycoon. Un- til now, Caz had been the last person to touch the book. His thumbs had been here, resting against the margins. His eyes had read the same words that I was reading now. How could the book be here but not Caz? I pulled myself back from the edge. "Keep going; don't stop," I told myself.

THREE WEEKS LATER, the floors were finished. I walked through the door in time to witness the new box spring being delivered. The place was empty of furniture and possessions. The floors were shiny; the walls and woodwork were newly painted. But as I watched the de- liveryman haul the box spring into the bedroom, I felt my heart sink. This was meant to be a new beginning, but instead I felt the changes like a crushing blow. Although I never lost sight of the importance of doing this, doing it without Caz hurt more than I'd predicted. When the deliveryman left, I broke into tears.

In the coming days I had the task of unpacking boxes and putting everything back. Replacing books into the bookshelves, I came across our travel guides, receipts, tickets, and maps pressed between the pages, the remnants of all the trips we'd taken together. I found the business card of the restaurant where my mother first met Caz. I hadn't looked at it in ten years. The memories flooded back. I paged through books that one or both of us had read, some with comments written in the margins. I found the last book Caz had finished, *The Color of Water,* a beautiful memoir by a son about his indomitable mother. After reading it, he'd sworn he was going to write a book about his Nanna. He'd loved *The Color of Water* so much he'd FedExed a copy to his mother in England. Kate had received it after his death.

I remembered how we would sit next to each other reading our books in bed. Caz and I would always read before sleeping, Lola on the chaise on the other side of the room. My husband would turn to me to tell me what he was reading about, although I was trying to read as well.

He had read every biography of Winston Churchill.

"Love, did you know that Winston Churchill was terrible at mathematics and had to try three times before he passed his Maths A Level. Just like me!"

Sometimes he would read sentences out loud to me, as if he was reading a bedtime story.

"Love, I gave that book to you," I would say. "I've read that one."

But Caz wanted us to be together, to share everything. He was not someone who was separate—he always added the encompassing gesture.

Julia:

That spring, I got the call to say I'd been granted an interview with an adoption organization to discuss the possibility of becoming a mother. I knew I wanted to move on to that next stage in my life where I wasn't only thinking about my own situation, where there was another human being in my life who needed me and whom I needed. But even though my treatment was going well and I felt better than I had in years, of course, I questioned whether this was happening too soon. Maybe I wasn't ready for such a big step.

My therapist and the WC agreed that I should at least go to the meeting to find out more, as adoption was bound to be a lengthy process.

The WC called me the morning of the meeting: "Good luck. You're going to do great. We're thinking of you!"

I met with a social worker, and she talked me through the adoption process. We discussed my various options. I told her I was interested in adopting from China—I had a very good friend of Chinese origin who could help me acclimatize the child and keep a connection with the child's native country. We talked about the process of assembling the documents required by the state, the federal government, and the Chinese authorities. We discussed the sex of the child. Both girls and boys are available for adoption, but it would be easier to adopt a girl from China, where thousands of female babies are abandoned every year. The social worker showed me pictures of some of the children who had been recently adopted. Looking at them, I felt my heart quicken— but I pulled myself back from getting too excited until I knew this was even a possibility.

"How much harder is it for a single parent to adopt?" I asked.

The social worker told me that due to a Chinese policy that applies to all U.S. adoption agencies, only 8 percent of the total number of completed applications in any year could be from single parents, and that the single parent quota had already been reached for this year. However, this didn't mean that I couldn't adopt; it just meant things might take a bit longer than they would otherwise. I should fill out the necessary paperwork, as it was possible that a single parent applicant might drop out for whatever reason and I could step in and take his or her place.

"Who knows?" the social worker advised me. "Toward the end of the year, you might get your application in and have your baby by the following year."

I left the meeting feeling philosophical. I knew I had a lot to offer a child and that a child would have a lot to offer me. If I managed to adopt, then so be it. If it didn't happen, then other options would come along; I was certain of it. Adoption might take a few years, but that was okay—I still had some learning to do in the meantime, and I had been through so much already that I knew I would be able to persevere during a lengthy and complicated process like this one. The main thing was to keep putting my best foot forward.

On the way home, I put my earphones in and switched on my iPod. Just recently, I'd started taking my iPod with me wherever I went. I took it with me on the subway, on business trips, to the gym, walking around the city. I was rediscovering my CD collection, getting into all kinds of music, everything from rap to country.

It had been three years since I'd last been able to appreciate listening to music. After Tommy was killed, all I wanted to do when I got home was to crawl into bed and watch hours of brainless TV. It didn't occur to me to switch on the stereo. Music had too many happy associations to bring me any comfort. Now when I came home, I popped the iPod into the speakers and kept listening. I began to actually enjoy being in our apartment alone. Sometimes I'd catch myself in the living room mirror. I was dancing.

One day in the elevator of my apartment building, "Shining Star" by Earth, Wind & Fire came on my iPod. I love that song. As there was no one else in the elevator, I started singing at the top of my lungs. I was so lost in the music that I didn't notice when the elevator stopped and a man who lives in my building got into it. When I opened my eyes, he was dancing along with me.

We danced all the way to the lobby.

John and Claudia

Ann, Julia, Claudia, Marcella, and Pattie

Claudia:

The morning of my wedding, Pattie and I met for a yoga class. This felt like the perfect way to start my wedding day—I'd already come to love the balance of strength and tranquility that practicing yoga brought me. After class, I headed back to my room for a soothing bubble bath. Wrapped up in a hotel robe, I went to sit out on the terrace, looking out over the palm trees, white sands, and turquoise waters of the Bahamas.

The sound of the waves landing on the shore, the warmth of the day, and the ocean breezes—all this gave me a sense of overwhelming peace. I talked to Bart and my father, and thanked them for helping me become the woman John had fallen in love with. I spoke to John's mother and told her I was sorry I hadn't gotten to meet her, and thanked her for doing such an amazing job raising her son. Next I told The Boys that the WC was sending them lots of hugs and kisses and were looking for some in return.

Since we arrived here two days ago, I'd been wedding-jitter free. All I cared about was sharing my life with John and having a spiritual ceremony in front of God and our closest friends and family. Everything else would just have to fall into place.

I went to get my hair done—a tight, low knot at the base of my neck. Around lunchtime, the WC came over to my room to get ready. Ann, Julia, and Pattie came bearing their bridesmaid dresses, three pink-and-white chiffon gowns printed with roses and hibiscus flowers. My brother-in-law Larry—president of the American arm of the German fashion house Escada—had helped arrange for the girls to get these fabulous gowns. They were light, bright, and easy, perfect for a tropical wedding.

My own dress was in a garment bag waiting. I had chosen it during a lunch hour. I knew what I didn't want: the typical dress that had a full skirt and was strapless. I fell in love with a silk-satin ivory sheath which had a net halter top and a low-cut back. It was sophisticated and glamorous in a 1930s Hollywood sort of way. Initially, I worried that it wasn't exactly traditional, but Kathleen's words of advice encouraged me: "Claudia, it's your second wedding. Don't be afraid to look a little sexy."

I realized that it's not every day that your brother- and sister-in-law help you to pick out your wedding attire and bridesmaids' dresses, but then Bart's family, who were coming to the wedding, had proved that they were far from your average in-laws.

Over champagne sips, the WC zipped, adjusted, laughed, and toasted. I'd opted to do my own makeup. I usually don't wear any, and was afraid that the island ladies might get carried away—I wanted to look like myself. Rummaging through the little supplies that I had, I realized that I was lacking even the basics.

I turned to Pattie and asked, "Is it okay to use mascara that's approximately five years old on my wedding day?"

"You're asking me?" was Pattie's reply. "But my guess would be no—"

Luckily, Ann and Julia jumped in, ready to help.

My mother and sister arrived with my nephew and niece, who were going to be my ring bearer and flower girl. As we snapped pictures and toasted, the phone rang and it was the best man. He and the groomsmen were on their way to the church with John and they didn't have the rings. The best man had assumed John had them and John had assumed the best man had them. I thought they were in the safe in our bedroom, but when I went to look I couldn't find them. Even this didn't shake me—if necessary John and I would have gotten married with the rings from the top of a Diet Coke can. Luckily, the actual rings were quickly discovered hiding under the little rug in the safe.

I remained composed until the moment I was about to walk into the chapel. John and I had fallen in love with the church's intimate old world charm, its whitewashed stone walls and red wooden doors, the surrounding palms and pink bougainvilleas. I had gotten permission from the monsignor that my bridesmaids could enter through the side door at the front of the church, as the groomsmen often do. Ann, Julia, and Pattie had already gone to take their places. Marcella and I were standing outside alone. I reached out for my sister's arm. Now that I was here, I was overcome and there were tears in my eyes. Until now, I hadn't let myself believe that this moment would arrive.

Marcella walked in first, and then I moved into the back of the doorway. I had decided to walk down the aisle alone. Even from that distance, I could see John's enormous smile and bright blue eyes. I stayed focused on this man I couldn't wait to share my life with. The church was filled with family and friends. Everyone turned to look at me as I made my entrance. It was as if their love and happiness was a tangible being walking beside me in place of my father.

When I reached John, he kissed me and grabbed my hand and never let it go. I felt like I had come home. Listening to the powerful and soothing voice of the island monsignor, I wanted to preserve every word. We had spent so much time discussing the readings, and as John's sister read the Song of Songs, I listened carefully for the significance:

> *Set me a seal on your heart*
> *As a seal on your arm*
> *Deep waters cannot quench love*
> *Nor floods sweep it away.*

When Marcella's husband, JC, stood up to read the prayer of the faithful, I braced myself. He was going to read Bart's name, along with those of The Boys. I knew it would be hard for him and many other people in the church. But there had never been any doubt for John and me that they should be part of the ceremony.

The monsignor began his homily. He told us that in marriage, our two separate lives became one. He reached for two candles on the altar and brought the flames together to demonstrate. He told us that marriage was like a good cup of coffee. Once you add cream, there is no way to separate the two. Then the monsignor held our heads close together and told us to remember Jesus' words—"Love one another as I have loved you."

When it came time to exchange our vows, the monsignor asked John if he took Claudia Ann, and then stumbled over which of my last names to use. John graciously interceded.

"I, John Francis Donovan, take Claudia Ann Gerbasi Ruggiere to be my wife."

When it was my turn to speak I found my voice was stronger than I'd expected. I wanted every person in that church to hear me say my vows of love and fidelity to John.

"I will love you and honor you all the days of my life."

Before the ceremony ended, we went up to the altar to sign the registrar's book. I heard the soloist begin to sing in deep, slow bass: "This little light of mine, I'm gonna let it shine."

After I finished signing the book, I looked up. The soloist's voice had built in power and volume, and by now the entire congregation was clapping and swaying and singing along in true gospel fashion. As we walked to the front of the altar to declare ourselves married, the priest asked John to introduce his wife to the congregation. John introduced me as Claudia Ann Gerbasi Ruggiere. I laughed and corrected him, proudly announcing myself as: "Claudia Ann Gerbasi Ruggiere Donovan," and loving what each piece of my long and complicated name signified.

Julia:

Before, when someone was getting married, all I could think about was: "I had that! That used to be my life!" If I went to a wedding and there was a cute couple on the dance floor, I couldn't stop myself from thinking: "Ugh, if Tommy were here we would have been much better dancers than them." I hated being on the dance floor without him. I didn't want to dance alone. When I went to weddings, I'd either find a friend to dance with or I'd stand on the sidelines, watching.

But at Claudia and John's wedding, I didn't feel cheated, I felt joyful. What could be better than a fellow widow finding happiness again? It gave all of us hope. At the reception, John gave the most incredible toast. First he remembered absent friends and family, including his mother and Claudia's father. Next he toasted The Boys—Bart, Ward, Tommy, and Caz. Then, after a very funny preamble, John ended by saying:

"Claudia is the best person I know and makes me a better person. Please everyone raise a glass to the love of my life."

I can honestly say that John's tribute to The Boys, his celebration of his new bride, and the whole experience of being at that wedding helped change my life. His words allowed something to shift in me. For the first time, I let myself believe that a widow could love again and that her new husband would accept her loss and love her more because of it. John and Claudia were proof that this miracle was possible.

For the first time in a long while, I got out on that dance floor and truly enjoyed myself. I was singing along, leaping around, cracking my usual jokes. I was loving it *and* meaning it. I didn't have a date and I didn't care, I wasn't going to let that stop me from celebrating. That night, I danced until my feet hurt. There wasn't a minute where there wasn't a widow in a pink-and-white dress leaping up and down on the dance floor, and that widow was usually me.

THE FOLLOWING DAY—still with a big smile on my face from the celebration—I was flying to the tiny island in the Bahamas where Tommy and I had gotten married five years ago. This time around I was taking three of my friends—Ariane, Peter, and Jennifer—to the beach at Green Turtle Cay where Tommy and I exchanged our vows. We would cruise over to the spot where the wedding had taken place, just like Tommy and I had done.

It was a cloudless spring day just warm enough to make you feel grateful for cooling sea breezes. When I stepped off the boat onto the white sands of Green Turtle Cay, I drank in the sight of this beach with its palm trees and little cabanas, allowing the memories to come flooding. It was so important for me to share this place with friends. Tommy and I didn't have a video of our wedding, just a few photos. Now I wanted to describe the whole event so that others could picture the scene. I wouldn't have to be the only one who knew what had happened here that day.

I had an idea, and the others went right along with my plan. I was going to act out my wedding and get the others to film it. My friend Ariane took hold of the video camera.

I played both the parts, as well as the Bahamian commissioner, switching positions back and forth, while the others applauded my performance.

"Do you, Julia . . . ?"

"I do."

"Do you, Thomas . . . ?"

"I do."

The reenactment was no substitute for the real thing—we were giggling so hard I barely got through to the end of the ceremony—but even so, it was the only wedding video I had, and I was loving every minute of it.

Heading back to the marina that day, I sat on the deck of the boat and let my eyes drift across the afternoon sunlight dancing on the translucent blue waters. The boat roared into motion, and a rush of sea air blew my hair from my face. Suddenly, I started to cry, but not because I was sad. I was crying because I loved that Tommy and I chose to get married here. This place was perfect. Our wedding had been incredibly special to us. I didn't have to dread coming to a place where Tommy and I had been happy. I knew now I could move forward, and my memories of Tommy and my love for him would come right along with me.

In that moment, I looked up to the skies and thanked my husband. I asked him for a sign that he approved of the new way I was seeing the world.

A little while later, Ariane yelled over the noise of the engines: "Look!"

I turned around to see what she had found. The name of the boat—

The Bottom Line—was painted on a life preserver. But there was a strap covering the letters B-O-T. The letters that remained spelled T-O-M.

Ann:

When I returned from Claudia's wedding, I made an important decision. I decided to scale back on my many commitments. The process of getting Ward's headstone—something that had been on my "to do" list for three and a half years—was completed. It had brought a chapter in my life to a close. Now I was entering a new phase.

At the beginning of the year, I'd packed up my office and closed the door on the company where I'd worked for the past twenty years. For the first time in my adult life, I was waking up in the morning without having to race out of bed to shower and put on a suit. I was at home most days, with the freedom to choose my own schedule. Instead of leaving my baby-sitter to get the children ready for school, I could talk with them while they ate breakfast. I could wave good-bye to them as they climbed onto the school bus. I was there when they came home in the afternoon.

Ever since graduating college I'd worked full-time. The only substantial "time off" I'd taken was immediately following the birth of my children (when I didn't even have time to shower, let alone think) and the four months I wasn't at work after Ward's death (at which point I wasn't mentally fit to contribute to an office setting, or any other setting for that matter). For the past three and a half years, I'd been commuting, holding down my job, managing the household without Ward, handling the family finances, settling his estate, keeping up a busy social life, all the while being a single mom to our children. Looking back, it seemed incredible that I was able to accomplish as much as I did while going through such an intense period of grief. But keeping busy had been a necessity—if I didn't have a long list of tasks to keep me occupied, I feared for my sanity.

Now, with all this newfound time on my hands while the children were at school, I had a hundred ideas for how I would use my day. I blitzed my home office, reorganizing so that I would be able to handle all the tasks I'd set myself: being more involved in my kids' school and activities, serving on two nonprofit boards, trying to start up my business, and writing this book. I made a long list of goals: catch up on photo albums, frame new photos, install the computer software I'd owned for over a year—all those little things that busy people want to get done but usually put at the bottom of the list. I made all the routine dentist and doctor appointments for the family that I would usually put off unless they were urgent. I joined the local YMCA. I took squash clinics and signed up for golf lessons.

But after returning from Claudia's wedding, I printed up my weekly schedule, took one look at it, and decided to throw it away. In the coming weeks, I resigned from one of the nonprofit boards. I decided to put off starting my company, at least for now. I made a conscious decision to stop making so many demands on myself.

Once, I'd thought that life could be figured out, that the day could be put into boxes and that the future could be arranged. I'm a financial planner. My whole professional life has been geared toward eliminating surprises, making sure life stays on an even keel. But what had happened to our family had proved, once and for all, that there's very little that's predictable, for better or for worse, even for the world's most ultra-organized planner. Now I wanted to give myself the chance to experience life, rather than always portioning it out according to tasks, lists, and schedules.

Besides, the children were going to keep me pretty busy and satisfied by anyone's standards—and they definitely responded well to my devoting more time to them. I was becoming more regularly involved at Billy and Elizabeth's schools, things that I could never have done while I was working. TJ rapidly began expecting me to drive him to his practices, and I loved being able to watch his football, hockey, and lacrosse games. I couldn't believe how quickly my days flew past. I was never bored. I started to relish my newly minimized schedule. When I caught myself worrying about not being productive enough, I would remind myself that our time here is precious, and that I should treasure it, not wish it away. The children weren't going to live with me forever. Soon TJ would be going away to college. Billy seemed to get taller every day. I had to grab this time to be with them while it lasted.

My "to do" list had been whittled down until there were only two entries: my children and Kevin. Now instead of fearing time alone to think, I sought it. In the aftermath of leaving my job, I'd realized that what I thought was right for me—starting my own company—wasn't truly what was right for me, at least for the time being. I was making time to savor, to sit in the morning with a cup of coffee, reading my e-mails, in the calm that the children left behind. It was a pleasure to discover this new side of myself, a side I never knew existed.

I knew that my relationship with Kevin was helping to make this slowing down possible. A part of me was at peace. I had someone to share evenings and weekends with, whom I could call several times a day to talk about whatever was on my mind or nothing at all. I knew I had a partner to share my future with, someone I could depend on and trust. My relationship with Kevin was making me more content, more joyous. I was in love. I would look in the mirror and see a face that was glowing, no longer pale and strained.

What pleases me more than anything is how well my boys have responded to having this new man around the house. Billy loves Kevin and jumps up and down when he arrives at our door. TJ is old enough now to understand that Kevin makes me happy and my son has found a new male role model. There had been a time when I thought my family would never be whole again. Now I know that although my family will never be the same, it can still be a wonderful family.

One day this spring, while I was standing in the kitchen making dinner, I overheard Kevin and Billy talking. Kevin was working on my computer, scanning in photographs of Lucia for a video that was going to be shown at a fund-raiser to honor her and the foundation she'd started for transplant patients and their families.

Billy knows about Lucia because her photograph is framed on the side table in my bedroom along with photos of The Boys. My son stood behind Kevin facing the computer. These were photos that he'd never seen before, and he was obviously intrigued.

"Is that your wife?" he wanted to know.

"Yes," Kevin told him.

"What's she doing in that picture?" he asked, pointing.

Kevin explained.

"What's she doing there? And there?"

There was a pause, and then Billy asked Kevin the following question:

"Do you love my mom as much as you loved your wife?"

I stood in the kitchen, listening.

"Billy," said Kevin, "I love both your mom and Lucia very, very much. Love is an amazing thing. It doesn't end when somebody dies. I'll always have that love in my heart for Lucia—just like you do for your dad. And the best part of love is that it can grow and you can love more than one person, just like your mom loves you and TJ and Elizabeth. She loves you all, and she loves your dad, and she loves me, because loves grows. Which is why I love her too."

Pattie:

Out at the beach, I began to take my first trips of the season to the garden center to get plants for the backyard. I bought white daisies and budding geraniums, bright blue lobelias. I started sprucing up the beds, mowing the lawn, making repairs. Soon I would begin hosting weekends again. My life here was continuing, always bittersweet, always a modified version of what it had been.

One day in the spring, I was mowing the lawn, putting my weight behind the machine to push it up the high banks of grass beside the pool. The ring of trees that surround the property were showing their new green growth, and there was the rustling of birds in the branches. Instead of appreciating the coming of the new season, all I could think about was the hole in the bottom of the driveway that needed filling. There were dangerous electrical wires exposed on the outside of the house that were going to have to be fixed. The garden gate was hanging off its hinges. I realized that as much as I loved this place, it could be a burden to me. The house was really too big for me to keep up alone. Yet here I was, and I had reached a point when I was actually afraid of another summer here. It wasn't just the maintenance that worried me—I feared the weight of the memories brought on by the change in season.

When I next looked up at the house, I suddenly saw it in a new light.

The house was just a shell.

If you took the house away, the memories of my times here would remain with me.

I didn't want to dread coming here. I wanted my memories of this place to be special to me, to make me smile. If I stayed here, it was possible that I would always be comparing my new experiences to the ones I'd had with Caz. I wouldn't be giving my new experiences a chance to flourish.

Maybe I could sell this place and move somewhere new. Maybe that was possible. Keeping the house had never been part of Caz's plan. We'd decided to put it on the market the same fall that he died. He'd always seen this place as a stepping stone to the next place. If I decided to sell now, what couldn't I leave behind? The only things I was certain I couldn't part with were a few plants, and those I could dig up and take with me.

FOR OVER A year, I'd been eyeing an empty house for sale in a perfect location only three blocks from the ocean. It was smaller than my current home. It looked like a house a child might draw: neat square windows, sprightly roof, and freshly painted front door. It sat in the middle of a manageable triangle of a plot. Not the best place for a family, but perfect for a single person like me, a little English cottage by the sea.

The house stood at the intersection of five roads, and one of them was called "Crossroads."

I was at a crossroads in my life. The universe was trying to tell me something.

The next morning, I drove over to the house and tried all the doors. The last one was open, so I let myself in. The place was completely renovated. It was compact, but with enough room for guests. Everything was painted white—white molding, white wainscoting, white tiles. As I walked around, I imagined my life in each room. I pictured myself arriving here on Friday nights, parking my car for the weekend. I would get a Vespa, just like the ones I'd seen in Italy. I would spend the weekend whizzing around, and relaxing in my new garden.

I heard Caz say: "Go south, south of the highway. Live a little!"

When I told my friend Kia about my new plans, she pointed out to me that if Caz were in my shoes, he would have already bought the house, built a widow's walk, and supplemented his income by taking pictures of the fancy neighbors for *The National Enquirer*!

"Either that or he would have gone over to borrow butter from the neighbor and asked if they had an available daughter . . . ," I added.

After dwelling on the matter of the house for the next week, I knew it felt right—healthy—to put in an offer. I bid low. The owners didn't even want to counter.

Bugger! as Caz would have said.

Patience, I thought to myself. All good things come to those who wait. I'll increase my offer after Labor Day. In the meantime, I stalked the new house every weekend, decorating it in my mind, seeing it in different lights at different times of the day. I began cleaning up the beach house to get it ready to put on the market. The real estate agent called to find out when she could come to show the house.

My reaction was one of overwhelming pain. I called Kia in tears.

"Why am I doing this? Why am I having to do this alone? I hate this. I hate my life."

Rationally, I knew that the house was only symbolic of my memories, and yet it was the most concrete manifestation of them that I had. I still wasn't ready to go through with this. While in my heart I knew that selling the house was the smart decision, the conundrum remained the same, of how to move forward while taking the past with me.

I was in limbo. I'd sent off my graduate school applications but was waiting to hear back. I didn't know what was happening with the house, with my love life, my job. I didn't know if I would ever have a family. In a sense, my life had come full circle. I was the girl who lived alone in New York, uncertain if she would have a life partner or a family, but determined to make the best of her days, to travel, learn, and to experience the world. In some ways, I was the girl I'd been when I first met Caz.

And yet, at the same time, I could never be that girl again, with her uncomplicated optimism and expectations of life. I was not even forty, and I had experienced great love and great loss at a very young age. Caz had blown into my life for five short years, but he had changed me irrevocably.

I know it isn't my destiny to live alone in that house by the sea forever. I know, more than ever, that I want to share my life again. I want to have that special person to turn to. I want to have someone to read lines from books with before falling asleep in each other's arms. This is what the experience of losing my soul mate has taught me, that love—the entwining of one life with another—is a gift and a joy that makes life richer, colors brighter, hearts bigger, existence better. Someday, I know I want to have that again.

Epilogue

✦

A proper attitude to death, if we can find it, is the
source of life.

— P. J. KAVANAGH

To The Boys: May 2005

Pattie, Claudia, Julia, and Ann

The day after Claudia returned from her honeymoon, we met at her apartment for our weekly meeting to work on our book. We were looking forward to seeing one another, excited to share wedding stories and hear about Claudia's honeymoon.

"So," we wanted to know, "how does it feel to be a married widow?"

"You know," Claudia told us, "I really didn't expect I'd feel any different after the wedding. But I do. I don't know exactly why. But my bond with John feels even stronger now."

Claudia was tan and relaxed from her trip. We could see in her eyes how happy she was and we shared in that joy. It was contagious. We talked about how much everyone had enjoyed the wedding, what a great day it had been, who'd been there and who we'd spent time with, our favorite moments on and off the dance floor.

"Well, tell her your news!" Ann nudged Julia.

"Tell me what?" Claudia demanded.

"Well, while you were away, I met someone . . . ," Julia announced.

"Who?" Claudia wanted to know.

Come to think of it, Julia had had a huge smile on her face ever since she'd arrived at the meeting.

"He's a friend of Kevin's," Julia explained.

"And guess where she met him . . . ," Ann interjected. "At my son's first communion."

Julia had been at Billy's first communion party the Saturday after she returned from the wedding. Kevin's good friend, Chris, who had been one of the guests at the misfits Christmas dinner the year before, was visiting from Boston—it turned out that since Julia had seen him last, Chris had become newly single. That evening, they had so much fun hanging out with each other. The connection was immediate and unexpected. The next day, Chris met Julia in the city for a walk around SoHo, sharing stories, getting to know each other. The day after that, he called her and told her that he'd canceled a client dinner and asked if they could meet. Things had progressed from there. Neither of them had been looking for a relationship, but even so, they felt strongly drawn to each other.

We couldn't remember when we'd heard Julia sound this excited.

"It's amazing how something like this can happen when you're least expecting it," Julia said. "If you told me even a month ago that I'd be feeling like this, I never would have believed you."

But Julia was in such a good place right now. She told Claudia about her trip after the wedding, about the sign on the boat, about how much better she'd been since then.

"The wedding was a big turning point for me," Julia explained. "I feel like I can finally appreciate the life I have, not the life I've lost. It's like I'm starting over. I've found a place for Tommy in my heart, and it's given me the peace I need to move forward."

For Julia, there wasn't one particular day that she woke up and decided that her grief was behind her, or that she realized she was able to go on. It was just that she found she could remember Tommy with happiness and thankfulness for the time they had together.

For the first time in a long time, her heart felt open.

Before sitting down to work, we toasted to The Boys, like we always did.

EVENTUALLY, WE GOT to work, reading through a new chapter, piecing together our experiences, sharing stories of our husbands and the many things they taught us. By writing all this down, we've been able to see in black and white just how far we've come and how much we've helped one another. In the time since we first met, all four of us have learned and grown more than we ever thought possible. It's as if we've been through a second adolescence together, a period of rapid change and emotional turmoil where friendship and love have been the key factors. Together, we've reached a point where we can look at our lives and know how truly blessed we are. We make sure to treasure every good thing that happens to us, because in life, nothing is certain.

Even so, three years after that first meeting in a bar on Park Avenue, and four years after the deaths of our husbands, we're still acknowledging the distance left to travel. This is extremely hard. The longing doesn't go away. There will always be loss written into our hearts. But we *have* come a great distance—the pain is finally beginning to cool. It lives on a deeper level now, like strata in rock, not visible on the surface, but always there, keeping us grounded, giving us the stability to stand taller.

We keep taking inspiration from all the people we meet and read about who have survived terrible losses in their lives—whether it's losing a parent, or healing from a divorce, or having a miscarriage, or struggling with illness. Although we've had to go through such difficult experiences before many of our friends, we know that everyone has tough times, and when our friends need us, we'll be there reaching out to them.

For us, friendship has been our North Star, guiding us to a place where we could see that losing everything brings pain, but it also brings a vital new perspective. Although we never could have chosen this path, loss has given us the opportunity to become more empathetic, more complex, more attuned. There's this fearlessness and passion we share, something to do with suffering so deeply. Now we see life—the demands of it, the fragility of it, the beauty of it—with all its possibilities. Maybe it's the intensity of having survived, but there's significance and meaning in the smallest of details: the kind gesture of a stranger, the new growth of the leaves in springtime, the smile on the face of a child.

This is what The Boys have taught us. We know there will be challenges in the future. But however many difficulties come our way, we'll always be there to remind one another: Keep your heart open. There can be hope after grief. Surround yourself with love. Immerse yourself in the many things that make life, not just bearable, but worth it. Don't close doors. In fact—do the opposite—keep flinging them open. Cherish the love you receive. Remember, the heart's capacity for love is unending. Make the decision to live. *It would be wrong not to.*